D0992812

Mold Making
for Ceramics

Donald E. Frith

Mold Making for Ceramics

Chilton Book Company   Radnor, Pennsylvania

A & C Black   London

Copyright © 1985 by Donald E. Frith

All rights reserved. No portion of this publication may be reproduced or transmitted in any form or by any means,
electronic or mechanical, including photocopy, recording, or any information storage and retrieval system,
without permission in writing from the publisher, except by a reviewer who may quote brief passages in a
critical article or review to be printed in a magazine or newspaper, or electronically transmitted on radio or television.

Published by

krause publications

700 E. State Street • Iola, WI 54990-0001
Telephone: 715/445-2214

www.krause.com

Please call or write for our free catalog. Our toll-free number to place an order
or obtain a free catalog is 800-258-0929 or please use our regular
business telephone 715-445-2214 for editorial comment and further information.

First published in Great Britain 1992
A & C Black (Publishers) Limited
35 Bedford Row, London WC1R 4JH
ISBN 0-7136-5148-2
A CIP catalogue record for this book is available from the British Library

Library of Congress Cataloging in Publication Data
Frith, Donald E.
Mold making for ceramics
Includes bibliographical references and index
1. Ceramics — Equipment and supplies. 2. Molding
(chemical technology) I. Title.
TP809.5.F75   1985   666'.442   84-21470
ISBN: 0-87341-692-9

Manufactured in the United States of America

To John Billmyer, Arthur Pulos, and Charles M. Harder,
each of whom played an important part in my life

*True spontaneity is the result of freedom
and freedom is possible only through knowledge.*

Tao

Contents

The goal of this book is to demonstrate the art of producing pottery forms from molds. At base, it is a "how-to-do-it" book, intended to enable eager and searching ceramists to successfully use molds in the fulfillment of their most inventive ideas or in the creation of beautifully designed products for the market. Beyond that, it is my hope that this book conveys the high level of craftsmanship and artistry involved in mold making. Beauty lies not only in the finished work, but also in the molds themselves and the techniques of their creation. I have made no attempt to express a philosophical viewpoint, assuming one could have one, other than that mold making is indeed an art, and that there is great pleasure and reward to be gained from making molds that exhibit beautiful craftsmanship and that serve to produce high-quality products.

The book consists of three parts, covering the following topics: (1) beginnings (historical review, tools and equipment, and working with plaster), (2) making and using press molds for plastic clay, and (3) making and using molds for slip casting liquid clay. In addition, it contains a review of the work of over 20 contemporary artists, showing in full color a wide variety of mold-made ceramics. In the preparation of the "how-to-do-it" chapters, over 500 photographs were taken. Each step, each process, was carefully photographed to assure that every detail would be pictured and explained. It was standard to shoot 50 photographs in order to get 15 that illustrated in a sequential manner exactly what is going on.

It takes much more than photographs and words to produce a book like this, and no one can undertake such a project without help. First to be thanked is my wife, Barbara Toepfer Frith, for the typing, correcting, and retyping of the manuscript.

For the most part, all the museums contacted gladly furnished photographs of pieces I was interested in for the book. In particular, I would like to thank Ross Taggert, curator of the Nelson-Atkins Gallery, Kansas City, Missouri, Ken Ferguson, and photographer Gary Sutton, who provided the beautiful close-ups of the 18th-century English press-molded dishes; Christopher Donnan, anthropologist at the University of California at Los Angeles, who

Preface

made possible the Chimu mold photographs; and Lawrence Dawson, anthropologist at the University of California, Berkeley, who furnished the panpipe mold photographs. I also want to acknowledge Lynn Turner of Berkeley, California, and Richard Notkin of Myrtle Point, Oregon, who not only sent me some very fine photographs of their work, but also sent me some sound information about mold making. Mary Rush Shaw, Alexandria, Virginia, supplied me with information on various rubber products and suppliers.

Part I: Beginnings

A Chimu stirrup handled bottle, 1100–1500
A.D., made in a two-piece, fired clay press
mold. Private collection; photograph courtesy
of the Museum of Cultural History, University
of California at Los Angeles.

Man's earliest endeavors to form clay objects often involved the use of molds. A mold is a form or object used to shape a plastic or fluid substance. Broadly speaking, then, the finger was undoubtedly the first press mold. The fingers of the ancient potter not only shaped the vessel or figure from clay, but often these same fingers were used to impart a repeated pattern of prints on the rim or foot of the vessel or figure. The fingerprint pattern thus became a press-molded decoration on the pot.

The paddle and anvil method was one of the first systems developed by potters to shape vessels from clay using implements rather than fingers. This system is still the basis of vessel making in many clay-working societies today. The manner in which the paddle and anvil are used permits both implements to be characterized as press molds. Often the paddle surface is decorated with wrapped cord or with a series of carved grooves or other patterns, and the decorative pattern is transferred to the clay when the paddle strikes it. In this case, the paddle truly acts as a press mold.

There are also many examples of ancient sherds with basket weaving imprinted on the surface of the fired clay.[1] Pressing clay into the inside surface of a woven basket produces a clay vessel bearing the pattern of the weaving on its outside surface. In making this type of pottery, the basket serves as a press mold.

From these few examples, we can see that clay can either be pressed into a "mold" or the "mold" can be pressed into the clay. (The act of pouring liquid clay into a mold is not being considered at this point in this historical review because the casting process did not come into general use until very recent times. However, the Peruvian panpipes are a unique exception to this rule, and they are discussed later in this chapter.)

Pressing or molding is one of the most ancient techniques of pottery making. Bernard Racham, in his excellent introduction to the subject of "Pottery and Porcelain" in the *Encyclopedia Britannica* (1951), states:

From this pure clay, vessels were shaped by scooping out, or cutting a solid lump or ball, by building up piece by piece or by squeezing cakes of clay onto some natural

CHAPTER

Historical Review

object or prepared mould or form. The potter's wheel, though very ancient, was a comparatively late invention, arrived at independently by many races of men.[2]

The development of methods of forming clay by pressing and squeezing clay with the fingers or using a paddle is completely natural. Anyone who has ever begun to work a ball of plastic clay with their fingers in some spontaneous way will soon press this exceedingly pliable material against something or press something into the mass of clay. The real miracle is that the clay, when hardened, retains the exact features of whatever is pressed into it. An especially important example of this "miracle of clay" is the

Fig. 1.1 Two identical molds of fired clay, indicating that they were taken from one master mold. Unearthed in the Gaza Strip in 1982, they probably date back to 1300 B.C. Photograph by Sisse Brimberg; © 1982 National Geographic Society

cuneiform tablets of ancient Assyria. The Assyrians "printed" records on clay tablets using a stylus with a triangular-shaped end. Their practice of writing on clay slabs and then preserving the slabs by firing them in a kiln has enabled scholars to learn many details of the Assyrian way of life. The stylus is indeed a type of press mold, and the imprinted clay tablets are in excellent condition even after some 3500 years.

HISTORICAL EXAMPLES OF THE USE OF MOLDS

The Ancient Mediterranean

In 1982, Israeli archaeologist Trude Dothan uncovered the two molds pictured in Figure 1.1 in a dig near Deir el-Balah in the Gaza Strip.[3] The molds are thought to date from 1300 B.C. The most interesting

Fig. 1.2 A red-figured Greek rython, clearly showing the seam mark of the two-piece mold that was used to make the head. Courtesy of The Metropolitan Museum of Art, New York, Rogers Fund, 1906 (06.1021.203)

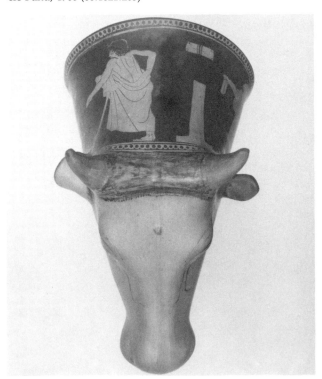

Fig. 1.3 Greek rython with ram's head. Courtesy of the Museum of Fine Arts, Boston, Perkins Collection, Purchase of E.P. Warren

feature of these molds is that they are identical, indicating that both molds were taken from one "mother mold." A careful look at the edges of the two molds reveals signs of the once-presence of the other halves of the molds. The two-piece mold would have produced a small figurine bottle with a front and back, a little standing goddess made by pressing clay into each half of the mold and then pressing the halves together. That the molds were evidently made from a "mother mold" or "case mold" indicates, in all probability, that many such figurine bottles were made and that the system of using a piece mold was well known some three thousand years ago.

There is no doubt that early Mediterranean civilizations knew how to use molds. The use of molds

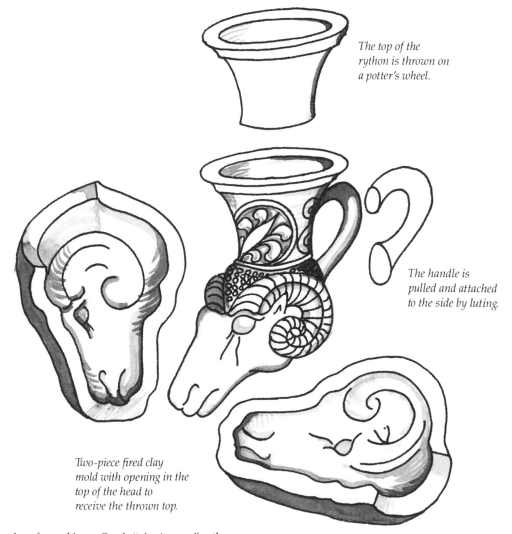

The top of the rython is thrown on a potter's wheel.

The handle is pulled and attached to the side by luting.

Two-piece fired clay mold with opening in the top of the head to receive the thrown top.

Fig. 1.4 Procedure for making a Greek "plastic ware" rython.

to aid in the production of clay and metal objects was well understood by many civilizations more than three thousand years before the Golden Age of Greece.

The potters of 5th-century-B.C. Greece were excellent mold makers as well as technical masters on the wheel. The Greek method of making molds was undoubtedly identical to the method employed by potters of other cultures. The object to be molded was covered with a layer of plastic clay; if a two-part mold was necessary, the clay that covered the object was cut to permit its removal from the object. The two pieces of the mold were then fired to a temperature high enough to harden the clay and yet permit the clay to retain porosity. Often the outside of the molds had grooves to permit the two pieces to be tied together securely with a rope.

The ancient Greek potters used molds to produce objects that could not be produced by the throwing process. According to Gisela Richter:

The Greek potter did not use moulding as a labor-saving device. He employed it only where the work demanded it, as in Athenian plastic ware [Richter uses the word "plastic" to describe objects that could not normally be formed on a potters wheel, such as a drinking vessel in the shape of a ram's head] . . . That the Athenian plastic vases were pressed into moulds rather than poured can be seen from the fact that the insides of these vases are rough and show finger-marks. . . . The joints of the two parts are clearly visible on many examples. . . .[4]

Greek rythons offer striking examples of such press-molded figures. Figure 1.3 shows a rython with a press-molded ram's head. In Figure 1.2, the seams of the two-piece mold are clearly in evidence. In making rythons such as these, the potter used a two-piece bisque mold to form the figure. Then he assembled the thrown top, pulled handle, and molded figure (see Figure 1.4). Although the exact details of the assembly method are not known, it is possible that the thrown top was attached to the head while the head was still in the mold.

Chinese Molds

From the earliest times Chinese potters used molds to form and decorate clay and metal objects. Indeed, the use of molds in Chinese ceramics and metal work is closely related. For example, there is much evidence of the use of fired clay molds to cast bronze vessels and sculptures.[5] The question inevitably arises as to which came first, the bronze vessels or the molded clay vessels? It is tempting to think that clay came first. A clay master mold is obviously ideal for use in the production of either clay or metal objects; moreover, the bronze vessels sometimes show a roundness typical of that produced on a wheel. Whichever came first, however, it is clear that the Chinese used molds to meet their reproduction needs, both in clay and in metal.

Fig. 1.5 A die-stamped hollow tile from a Han Dynasty tomb. Courtesy of The Cleveland Museum of Art, Cleveland, Gift of Mr. and Mrs. Ralph King

Fig. 1.6 In this detail of the Han Dynasty tile, the design and size of the repeating units can be clearly seen. Courtesy of The Cleveland Museum of Art, Gift of Mr. and Mrs. Ralph King

Fig. 1.7 Song Dynasty roof tile ending molds. Shown are the mold, bisque-fired piece, and glazed piece. Courtesy of Alm-qvist & Wiksell International, Stockholm

An example of excellent mold work by potters of the Han Dynasty (206 B.C.–221 A.D.) is the hollow tile pictured in Figures 1.5 and 1.6. The tile is decorated with repeated stampings of various geometrically patterned and figured dies. "Die" is the correct word for a mold that is pressed into soft clay. In this case, the die itself was probably made of fired clay. The size of the repeating unit for the figures can be

Fig. 1.8 Northern Song Dynasty fired clay mold, top view. Molds of this type were used in making celadon bowls with relief designs. Courtesy of the Philadelphia Museum of Art, Gift of Mr. and Mrs. Howard H. Lewis

Fig. 1.9 Northern Song Dynasty fired clay mold, side view. Note that the underside of the mold is similar in form to the top surface. The thrown character of the back of such pieces suggests that the mold was placed on a potters wheel and turned rapidly while a sheet of clay was pressed into it; then a foot was either thrown or trimmed. Courtesy of the Philadelphia Museum of Art, Gift of Mr. and Mrs. Howard H. Lewis

clearly seen in the detail (Figure 1.6). The lower design of two flying dragons employs a well-thought-out pattern that flows from one pressing to the next.

The potters of the Song* Dynasty (960–1280 A.D.) used fired clay molds to reproduce many kinds of ceramic items. (Nils Palmgren devotes an entire section of his book *Sung Sherds*[6] to the use of molds by Song potters.) The molds shown in Figure 1.7 were used to decorate the ends of roof tiles, and were made by pressing clay into a form. Since the dimensions of the roof tile were standard, it is possible that the images were made for this purpose alone.

Some of the most beautiful of all Chinese ceramic pieces are the "carved" bowls of the Song Dynasty. There is every indication, however, that the Chinese potters used molds to create the carvings or the pattern for carving. In this process, the pattern is established by pressing the clay against the mold, and then the design is carved using the pressing as a guide. The final product looks like a carved piece. Molds such as the one shown in Figures 1.8 and 1.9, which were used to make celadon bowls with relief designs, would lend themselves to this practice of pressing and carving. The molds themselves were made either by pressing clay over a carved relief bowl or, in some cases perhaps, by direct carving. Careful

Song is the official Pinyin romanization of the Chinese term. It was spelled *Sung* in the 19th-century Wade-Giles system of romanization.

observation of the pictured mold indicates it was made from a carved bowl and not carved directly. Even more important here, this particular mold would lend itself to being turned on a potters wheel while the clay was being pressed or "thrown" onto it (see Figure 1.9).

Figures 1.10–1.12 show two views of a Southern Song Dynasty Ting Ware mold and a reproduction piece made from the mold. Two interesting aspects of the design on the mold become apparent upon close inspection. First, the mold design was carved directly in the clay; second, there is a subtle eight-sided rim on the mold. The careful, lightly carved design, combined with an even more delicately designed rim, produces a very beautiful finished product. The bottom view of the Ting Ware mold (Figure 1.11) shows that this mold differs considerably from the Northern Sung mold shown in Figure 1.9. The bottom has a concave area that would permit placing the mold on the head of a potters wheel with the edge of the mold extending over the edge of the wheel head. This makes it very easy to put the mold in place and then remove it after a sheet of clay has been pressed over it.

Roman Pottery

By the time Rome had established herself as the dominant power in the Mediterranean, the potters of Rome were masters of all the ceramic technology that the Greeks, Etruscans, and other cultures had to offer. Fired clay molds were used to produce vessels, figures, coffins, lamps, and anything else that would lend itself to the molding process.

Fig. 1.10 Top view of a Southern Song 12th–13th century fired clay mold. This mold produced Ting Ware, which is generally a white-glazed ware with a delicate, raised pattern. Courtesy of the Freer Gallery of Art, Smithsonian Institution, Washington, D.C.

Fig. 1.11 Bottom view of the Ting Ware mold. The concave area fits the head of a potters wheel, with the edge of the mold extending beyond the edge of the wheel head. Courtesy of the Freer Gallery of Art, Smithsonian Institution, Washington, D.C.

Fig. 1.12 Modern bowl made in the Ting Ware mold and glazed in the manner of Ting Ware. The delicate eight-sectioned rim can be made out, but it is difficult to read positive and negative forms on the surface of the bowl. Courtesy of the Freer Gallery of Art, Smithsonian Institution, Washington, D.C.

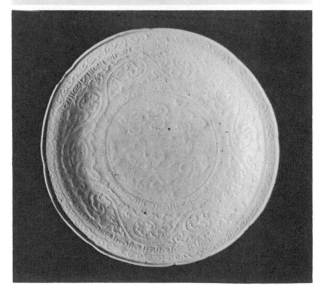

The techniques of the Roman ceramists were rarely innovative. Jennie Young expresses this succinctly in her book, *The Ceramic Art*:

When we turn to Rome, little investigation is required to satisfy us that there is no such thing as an independent Roman ceramic art. Whatever Rome possessed was acquired from without not developed from within.[7]

Nevertheless, Roman pottery makers were masters at adopting and adapting the techniques of the ceramist's art. As stated in Cox's classic work, *Pottery and Porcelain*:

During Roman times, along with the wares of bad taste, good sensible use was made of metal forms thoughtfully adapted to pottery as a medium, as we can see in the examples from Arezzo or Arretium in Etruria and which are variously called "Arretine ware," "Samian ware," or "terra sigillata."[8]

Forgetting the usual criticism that most authors voice about Roman art generally, and necessarily disregarding the terra sigillata technique, which was learned from the Greeks, we can still credit the Romans with two technical achievements in the use of molds, both exemplified in Arretine ware. The first is the molding of incredibly delicate and complex subjects. The second is the practice of rotating the mold on a potters wheel while pressing or "throwing" the clay into it.

Roman potters capitalized on the technique of impressing very delicate and intricate metal or clay positive reliefs (see Figures 1.13 and 1.14) into the inside surface of a moist clay mold that had the shape of a very thick bowl. Then they pressed a roulette with a positive pattern on it to create bands of negative decorative borders. The result was a thick, bowl-shaped mold decorated with repeating linear patterns and a series of figures in the space between

Fig. 1.13 A Nereid riding a sea horse. This carefully detailed clay stamp was made from a metal negative mold. Such stamps were used to make molds for Arretine ware. Courtesy of The Metropolitan Museum of Art, New York, Purchased through funds from various donors, 1926 (26.81.3)

Fig. 1.14 Another example of a fired clay stamp used in making molds for Arretine relief ware. Courtesy of The Metropolitan Museum of Art, New York, Rogers Fund, 1920 (20.227)

Fig. 1.15 A bisque mold for a large Arretine bowl. The mold is designed to fit on the head of a potters wheel so that the mold could be turned while pressing clay against the inside surface. Courtesy of the Museum of Fine Arts, Boston, Pierce Fund

Fig. 1.16 A pressed bowl made from the mold shown in Figure 1.15. The designs are in strong relief, yet they are not deep enough to prohibit the withdrawal of the pressed bowl after drying. Courtesy of the Museum of Fine Arts, Boston, Pierce Fund

Fig. 1.17 Mold for Arretine ware. The continuous patterns formed by a roulette wheel can easily be seen. The figures are in high relief, and it may have been necessary to fire the pressed piece and the mold together in order to achieve enough shrinkage in the pressed piece to enable its removal from the mold. Courtesy of The Metropolitan Museum of Art, New York, Rogers Fund, 1923 (23.1008)

The bowl is made by pressing clay into the spinning mold.

The clay mold is stamped with positive reliefs to create a negative design.

The fired clay mold is put on a wheel and turned while the pressing is done.

Fig. 1.18 The procedure for making a Roman Arretine bowl.

the repeating patterns. (See Figures 1.15 through 1.17.) The mold was then fired in a kiln to a bisque state. The mold, being round, could be put on a potters wheel and rotated as the potter pressed the clay against the inner walls of the mold (Figure 1.18).

To augment the above description of the manner in which Arretine ware was produced, the following quote from Rosenthal is offered:

In Italy, France and Germany, moulds and kilns for producing Samian ware (which is also called terra sigillata) have been found.

The decoration in relief on these Samian bowls was produced in the following manner. Stamps, either of bronze or fired clay, were modelled with the designs in relief and were used to impress a pattern on the interior

of a mould of soft clay. This mould was then fired to the required hardness and was ready for use. Next the clay paste, from which the Samian bowl was to be made, was pressed into the mould by hand, thus taking its outside shape in every detail, from the inside of the mould.

While still in the mould, and while still in a soft state, the interior of the vessel was shaped and smoothed by being turned on a lathe. Both the mould and the bowl were then placed in the kiln and baked. Note a very interesting point here! The mould had already been fired and would not shrink, whereas the bowl would. This makes it possible to use the mould in two capacities, firstly as a mould purely and simply (we use plaster of Paris moulds nowadays) and then as a "sagger" or container during the firing process. . . .

It can be seen from this short description that the art of mass production had already reached a high state of perfection in those far-away Roman days.[9]

Perhaps the use of the mold as a sagger for the pressed bowl could be debated, not because the technique is an unlikely one, but because the brilliant red color of many Arretine pieces indicates a highly oxidizing flame or fire. if the mold were used as a sagger, the close proximity of the bowl to the mold would cause the iron to reduce and turn black, producing a black pot. (Museums around the world seem to have black as well as red Arretine bowls.)

The reason for an extended presentation on Roman Arretine bowls lies not with their color or the method of firing. The main point of interest is that the mold was turned while the plastic clay was pressed against the inner walls. By rotating the mold on a wheel, it would be possible for the potter, instead of pressing a slab of clay into the mold, to actually put a ball of plastic clay into the mold and proceed to "throw" the clay against the mold's sides. Throwing

the clay in a spinning mold was in all probability not an invention of the Roman potters; however, it does present an opportunity to consider this important technique in an historical setting.

Middle and South America

There is ample evidence that the civilizations of Middle and South America were accomplished in many areas of technology, including mold-made ceramics. In fact, by the time of the predominance of the Mochica civilization in northern Peru around 100 A.D., much of the pottery produced was made using molds. The Mochica civilization (1–1200 A.D.) can be credited with bringing the art of using molds to perfection. Much evidence of Mochica ceramic art has been found in the Moche valley. As Professor Christopher P. Donnan states in his article on Mochica ceramic technology:

Molding might be called the basic technique of Moche ceramics. It played a part in the production of almost all ceramic objects. Moche molds are rare, since they were never a burial item. . . . The molds were made of fired

Fig. 1.19 A Chimu seated figure stirrup bottle, dating from 1100–1500 A.D., and the mold that was used to make the bottle. Private collection; photography courtesy of the Museum of Cultural History, University of California, Los Angeles

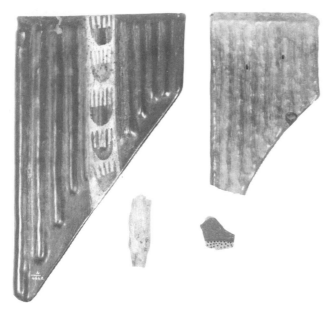

Fig. 1.21 Fragment of an Early Nasca panpipe, showing the individually cast tubes. Progressively longer tubes were lined up side by side and encased with a layer of clay to form the panpipe. Cerro Max Uhle, Ocucaje Ica Valley, Peru. 4.7 cm wide. Courtesy of the Lowie Museum of Anthropology. University of California, Berkeley

Fig. 1.22 Interior view of a broken panpipe, showing the untouched clay surface characteristic of slip-cast pieces. An Early Horizon panpipe of Ocucaje 10 phase. Piñilla, Ocucaje, Ica Valley, Peru. 5.7 cm long. Courtesy of the Lowie Museum of Anthropology, University of California, Berkeley

Fig. 1.20 *Top left*: Nasca polychrome panpipe from a burial. Ocucaje Ica Valley, Peru. 16.6 cm wide. *Top right*: Earliest known type of slip-cast panpipe in Peru. Upper Ica Valley, Peru. 10.7 cm wide. *Lower middle*: Fragment of a mold for casting panpipe tubes. Topara drainage, South Coast, Peru. 7.2 cm long. *Lower right*: Fragment of a conical sieve used to remove coarse particles of clay and sand from the slip. Canets Valley, Peru. 3.6 cm wide. Courtesy of the Lowie Museum of Anthropology, University of California, Berkeley

clay which had been formed over an actual object such as an ear of corn, a squash, etc., or over a pottery matrix.

Two-piece molds were the most common form, although one-piece molds were also used. When a vessel was too complex to be produced in a single two-piece mold, as was frequently the case with highly elaborate forms, it was made in sections which were later joined together. The molds themselves never became more complex than two piece molds.[10]

Professor Donnan also discusses the Moche potters' use of stamping:

Two general rules which governed the use of stamps by the Moche potters can be formulated. First, never more than one stamp was used on any one vessel. Second, there was an attempt at symmetry or balance. If one side of a vessel is stamped, the other side should be stamped also; or if the vessel is spherical, an odd number of stamped impressions can be produced on it, but they

must be evenly distributed. Only in jars which have a face stamped on the neck is there an exception to this rule.

Stamping was done in two ways. The most common way was to place the stamp against the outside of a vessel while the clay forming the side was still soft and malleable. The potter then reached inside the vessel and pushed the side outward against the stamp. When the stamp was taken away from the outside, the impression was left in relief on the vessel wall.

The second way of stamping vessels was to press the moist clay into a stamp and then press the stamp against the outside of the vessel. The clay inside the stamp sticks to the vessel wall and remains attached to it when the mold is taken away.[11]

The stirrup bottle mold shown in Figure 1.19, also from the Moche valley, was made during the Chimu period (1200–1450). Note that the outside of the mold has clay retainers that would permit the mold to be held together tightly with a rope. In all probability, the potter pressed the two pieces of the mold separately and then tightly roped them together, to press the seams and complete the forming of the piece. The mold has no bottom, which permits the two pressed halves to be joined by luting. The stirrup is joined from the inside of the pressed piece to assure a good bond, and then the bottom is added.

An especially interesting aspect of the use of molds in early South America is the use of slip casting techniques to produce hollow clay pipes or tubes. Examples of these are the panpipes from in the Moche valley, shown in Figures 1.20–1.22. Professor Lawrence E. Dawson, in an authoritative article entitled "Slip Casting, A Ceramic Technique Invented in Ancient Peru," describes these pipes as follows:

Ancient Peruvian pottery panpipes consist of a series of tubes which are made separately and stuck together by adding clay on the outside. In some periods the tubes were perfectly straight and of uniform diameter from one end to the other, while at other periods they were segmented, consisting of sections of different diameters. The slip casting process was used only to make the tubes; the joining and finishing was a separate operation done by hand.

My conclusion that the Peruvian panpipe tubes were slip cast is based upon investigations in the field and museum laboratory, in the course of which I observed minute details of fabrication with a microscope and experimented with duplication of the process. There are two characteristics of the tubes which show that they were made by slip casting: untouched inner surfaces and thin walls of uniform thickness.[12]

The fact that ancient Peruvian potters slip cast the tubes for panpipes is quite remarkable, both from an historical and technological standpoint. Nevertheless, slip casting played no part in the development and use of molds for ceramic reproduction. The potters of the Mediterranean world, the potters of the Oriental world, and the potters of the Western hemisphere fully understood the value of the fired clay mold and used it in reproducing ceramic objects and in forming relief decoration on the surface of pottery. Using a fired clay mold became the standard way to produce and decorate ceramic objects that were not suited for wheel production.

THE DEVELOPMENT
OF PLASTER MOLDS

There is no doubt that molds have been around for as long as man has worked with clay, and the same can be said for plaster. The plaster of Paris we use today is calcined gypsum. Historically, however, both limestone and gypsum have been used to make various types of plaster and mortar. Chapter 3 describes in more detail what plaster is and how it is made. Here, a historical review of the development of plaster molds and their use in ceramic production is presented.

The Ancient World

Long ago, man discovered that clay changes into a new substance when heated past red heat. Man also discovered that certain rocks, after heating, could be crushed into a powder, and that adding water to this powder, resulted in a thick liquid that turned into a hard rock-like material upon drying. This liquid could be used as a cement to seal objects together. These two discoveries were of monumental significance for all of civilization. The first discovery provided ceramics for vessels, brick, furnaces, containers for fire; the second provided material to hold structures together, to seal walls, to make houses, to cement blocks of stone in pyramids, etc.

The term "calcinization" refers to the heating of inorganic substances to a temperature that forces the release of some or all of the chemically bound water from the substance. Ancient man knew nothing of what was happening chemically when certain rocks were heated, but he did realize and use the results of the process of calcining both limestone and gypsum.

"Gypsum mortar" was used by the Egyptians for mortar in building the pyramids. In his book *Ancient Egyptian Materials and Industries*, Lucas states that gypsum mortar was used in preference to lime mortar because fuel was scarce and gypsum could be calcined at a lower temperature than limestone.[13] Lucas also indicates that the Egyptians used gypsum mortar as a lubricant to aid in the final placement of individual stones, knowing that when the mortar hardened it would become rock-like.

Although the Greeks were familiar with the process of calcining gypsum, they never used it as a mortar in constructing their stone buildings.[14] The Romans were the ones to carry the calcining process a step further with the development of hydrolic cement, a mixture of calcined calcium carbonate and a volcanic sand called puzzolona.[15] The development of hydrolic cement made possible the construction of the Pantheon,[16] the marvelous systems of aquaducts, and many other architectural wonders of the Roman world.

The civilizations of the Mediterranean obviously knew how to calcine gypsum, and there is even a reference in Pliny's *Natural History* to sculptors using plaster models. However, there is no apparent evidence that plaster was used by Greek potters as a mold making material—and for good reason. If in fact the Greeks of the 5th century B.C. used plaster to make molds, the molds would not last very long. The elements of nature and the water-absorbing characteristics of plaster would result in the total disintegration of the molds. On the other hand, ancient molds of fired clay are relatively abundant, simply because the fired clay did not disintegrate, but lasted through the ages. Because plaster disintegrates, the question as to whether Greek, Roman, or Egyptian potters actually used plaster molds cannot be definitively answered. The important facts, however, are that potters used molds and that the knowledge of plaster was universal.

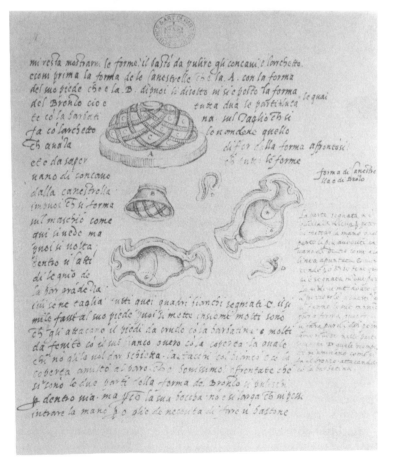

Fig. 1.23 Reproduction of folio 18 from Piccolpasso's *Three Books of the Potter's Art* (1545). On this page, Piccolpasso explains how plaster molds were made and used by Italian potters of the mid-16th century. Courtesy of the Victoria and Albert Museum, London

Sixteenth-Century Italy

The first historical record of plaster being used by potters is Piccolpasso's account, published in 1545, of how plaster molds were made by Italian potters in the middle of the 16th century.[17] Piccolpasso states in his *Three Books of the Potters Art* that he received all his information about mold making from Signor Vannuccio Beringuccio's *Pirotechnia*, published in Venice in 1540. In the 8th book of the *Pirotechnia*, Beringuccio discusses how plaster was made and how it was used in molding many kinds of objects such as cannon and bells; he does not discuss using molds for ceramic production. Piccolpasso's reference to Beringuccio as the authority on plaster mold making suggests that making plaster molds was a standard procedure and not an unusual or new one.

Piccolpasso is the first to discuss the use of plaster molds by potters. His description of how molds were made is worth quoting:

Now that I have discussed thus far the work on the wheel I intend to give some account of the making of moulds of plaster and the manner of giving shape to the clay in this process. You must know in this connection that the plaster must be fresh and not too much burnt, well pounded and well sifted; then it is soaked in warm water and carefully stirred with the hand and broken up from the solid consistency it acquired when put into water. When it has thus been dissolved it is thrown upon any sort of relief or intaglio, provided that the

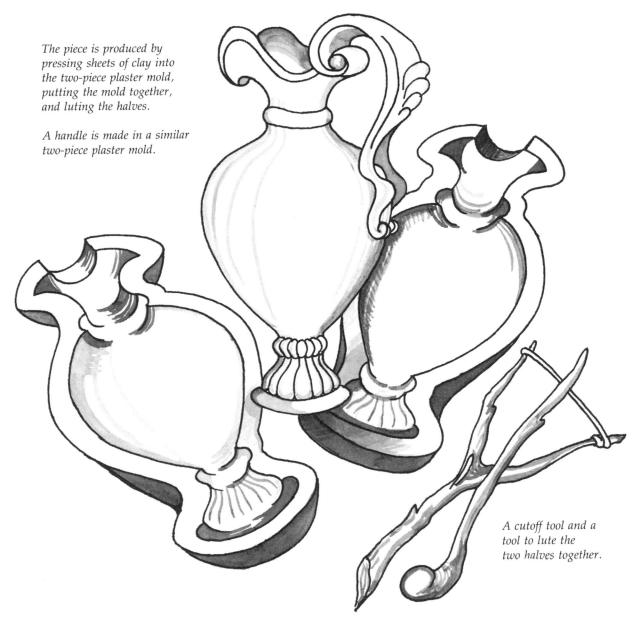

The piece is produced by pressing sheets of clay into the two-piece plaster mold, putting the mold together, and luting the halves.

A handle is made in a similar two-piece plaster mold.

A cutoff tool and a tool to lute the two halves together.

Fig. 1.24 A plaster mold as described by Piccolpasso.

recipient be of fresh clay. When the plaster has taken hold, the clay is carefully removed and the mould will be found clean and smooth so that wares can be made in it, as will be explained. I will not expatiate much on this matter, because in the Pirotechnia *of Signor Vannuccio Beringuccio, Sienese nobleman, in the 8th book, where he treats the moulding of various reliefs, all that can be said about making moulds is to be seen. For whoever wishes for full knowledge will have recourse to the studies of this gentleman where he will find all he desires.*

Piccolpasso describes how the molds are used by putting a batt (sheet) of clay into the mold and pressing the batt into all the features of the mold. He also provides an excellent description of how the batt is made using two rails and a copper or bronze wire to cut the clay ball into thin sheets. How to trim the excess clay in the molds and how to put together the two halves with slip are also described in detail. His description of the preparation of slip for bonding handles and other pieces onto a vessel is unusual enough to quote:

You take either very dry clay or some of the very soft clay left over when you work on the wheel on the stick G, which seems like ointment. With this is mixed cloth fluff, then they are well stirred and worked into so soft a state that they stick bravely, provided that the two pieces of ware that are being attached together are equally dry or equally "green," otherwise nothing will be done.

Piccolpasso's description indicates that the potter mixed a fiber in the slip to improve its bonding action when it was to be used to "glue" together pieces of molded clay. Adding fiber is still practiced today by potters who incorporate shredded nylon in clay mixtures to increase the toughness of the clay.

A reproduction of folio 18 from Piccolpasso's book is shown in Figure 1.23. This page warrants inspection by anyone interested in mold making technology. One of the most interesting features is the dotted line on the shoulder of the mold. Piccolpasso states that "the part marked * is that which is removed so that the hand can be inserted;. . ." He clearly means that if the hand or a joining stick cannot reach inside the mold, then this is the area where a hole is made so that the two parts of the piece can be put together. Notice also that the two-piece mold would produce a vessel that is enclosed on top, so that the hole at the shoulder would be quite necessary to insure that the bonding of the two parts was well done and would not come apart when the piece was dried, glazed, and fired.

The technology described by Beringuccio in the *Pirotechnia* suggests that plaster was used in many trades. The casting of bells and the making of decorative moldings for interiors are among the many subjects that Beringuccio writes about. Piccolpasso gives Beringuccio all the credit for detailing the methods used in mold making with plaster. Since plaster was used by many civilizations, and the various technologies discussed by Beringuccio were the "state of the art" in many trades, it is logical to assume that potters of 16th-century Italy were making pots in

plaster molds in a manner handed down from their ancestors.

The Staffordshire Potteries

According to Simeon Shaw (*The History of the Staffordshire Potteries*, 1829), plaster molds were shown to the Staffordshire potteries in 1743:

Information that the French manufacturers employed moulds of Plaster of Paris, caused some of the Burslem potters to have moulds formed of Plaster stone; the specimens evincing greater ingenuity in the workman, and the prevalent desire to improve the Art. The correction of this error introduced an important improvement; providing a fresh branch of manual employment, and supplying great facilities for manufacturing the choicest productions of taste and ingenuity. Mr. Ralph Daniel, of Cobridge, happened to visit a porcelain manufactory in France, where among other information relative to their processes, he ascertained that moulds were formed by mixing Plaster of Paris in a pulverulent state with water. He obtained a mould of a large Table Plate, which on returning home he exhibited to all the Potters, and explained the discovery, and its attendant advantages, and quickly moulds were introduced. The manufacturers were eager to possess moulds, because of the numerous productions which with great facility could be formed in them, yet not be produced by the wheel and lathe; and others which did not need either; and also the quickness with which the clay acquired, what potters call the green state.[18]

Shaw continues with a description of how plaster of Paris is made, stating that the calcinization process is called "boiling." He then describes the nature of plaster of Paris and its peculiar adaptability to the needs of the potter:

When the mass has been . . . deprived of its water [by calcinization], it is rendered so miscible with that fluid, that on receiving its own proportion of water it condenses such a quantity, as almost immediately to become changed into one compact and solid mass. Hence when used, the fluid is quickly poured, into moulds for states, or busts: and [into] round models or blocks to form moulds for the potters—usually for articles not circular, and for teapots, saucers, plates, dishes, etc. This property of so quickly absorbing moisture, causes the plaster moulds to be most peculiarly adapted to the purposes of the Potter; for as the moulds can be kept dry by placing them on shelves around a stove, they very readily absorb the water from the clay impressed into

them, and the Articles are more easily delivered or quit from the moulds, in a fit state for finishing, than would be conjectured by persons not acquainted with the Art.[19]

These excerpts from Shaw, although rather long, are of the utmost importance, primarily because Shaw established a relatively close date for the introduction of plaster molds into the potteries of England. Several

Fig. 1.25 This camel teapot (c. 1745) is an excellent example of the fanciful pieces executed by Staffordshire potters of the mid-1700s using plaster of Paris molds. Most production molds were pressed, not slip cast. Courtesy of the Nelson-Atkins Museum of Art, Kansas City, Missouri, Burnap Fund

Fig. 1.26 Bottom view of the camel teapot, clearly showing the seam where the two halves of the teapot come together. Courtesy of the Nelson-Atkins Museum of Art, Kansas City, Missouri, Burnap Fund

points raised by Shaw deserve special attention. First, the use of plaster for molds had apparently been going on for some time in the potteries that Ralph Daniel visited. Second is Shaw's reference to the English potters forming molds of plaster stone. Shaw seems to indicate that the potters attempted to cut molds or models from a block of gypsum believing that this was the material used by the European potters. This might possibly be where the term "block" came from (a block mold being a mold from which to make molds, or a first mold from the model). Thirdly, the description of the use of the plaster molds uses the term "impressed," and that undoubtedly refers to the mold being a press mold and not a mold for any other purpose, such as slip casting. (Slip casting could not be done efficiently until effective methods of deflocculation were developed in the late 19th century.)

The fourth aspect of interest is Shaw's use of the term "plaster of Paris." In Piccolpasso's and Beringuccio's books, plaster is simply "plaster," not from Paris. However, when Shaw reports about Ralph Daniel's trip, the term "plaster of Paris" is used. Plaster of Paris is the term used today for the material that is high-quality calcined gypsum.

The last aspect that needs to be amplified is Shaw's statement that the use of plaster molds provided a fresh branch of manual employment. Undoubtedly, Shaw realized what impact this new method of making molds would have on the pottery industry: a new trade of plaster mold maker had come into being. Simultaneously, factory production techniques changed from production throwing on the potters wheel to an increasing use of plaster molds. (It should also be noted here that the eventual semi-omation of the production of wheel-thrown pieces and the all-important improvement of the casting procedure via deflocculation were both made possible by the use of plaster molds. These subjects are discussed later in this chapter.) The change in production techniques, and the increase in the quantity of production, necessarily had an effect on the pottery work force. Shaw is again worth quoting on this matter:

Up to 1740, in each manufactory, all the persons employed were, the slip-maker, thrower, two turners, handler, (stouker), fireman, warehouseman, and a few children, and, to be really useful to the master, and secure sufficient employment, a good workman could throw, turn, and stouk; and which he practised in each week at two or three different manufactories. But the White Stone Ware, now experiencing such a demand, its manufacture extended the whole range of the district; and the manufacturers introduced the custom of hiring each workman to serve only one master, and practise only one branch of the Art, while workmen for the different branches, were so much in requisition, that persons from distant parts, and especially from the neighbouring villages, were hired and settled in the towns . . .[20]

The subject of the introduction of plaster molds into England would not be complete without offering two paragraphs from the renowned ceramic historians, Warren E. Cox:

Earthenware, metal or stone molds had been used in making earthenware and not accomplishing any higher quality of aesthetic appeal. Now models were carved from alabaster and a series of clay impressions were made to form a master mold from which working molds could be made in any quantity. The pouring was done with liquid clay and washed around the inside, then left to dry. Any thickness could be obtained by repeating the process. When all is finally dry the mold is taken apart, the sutures trimmed but the original artist's work is thrice removed from the finished article and shrinkage and loss of detail and loss of all the subtle hand quality was the result.

This was bad enough but about 1750 Ralph Daniel brought "Plaster of Paris" which was the final step in the industrialization of the Staffordshire potteries, that industrialization which was the main cause of the death of ceramic art in so many places, as we have found out. It would certainly have been far better had tea never turned the eyes of rich men upon the humble pottery wares, for it was this which made the "improvements," the methods of quantity manufacture and the final squeezing of it for pennies that ruined it completely as an art in the short space of time between 1750 and 1800.[21]

Fig. 1.27 The pressing department of a porcelain factory in France, circa the mid-19th century. From Brongniart's *Traites des Arts Céramiques ou des Poteries.*

No doubt Cox's interpretation of 18th-century ceramic production techniques is derived from Shaw, but it is a mistake to assume, as Cox does, that slip casting was common practice in England before 1750. Indeed, the method of slip casting he describes is one of the methods least likely to succeed, especially on a production basis.

It also seems unsporting that tea alone must bear the blame, if blame must be cast, for the wide use of plaster molds in the English potteries. What is more likely the cause is that the Industrial Revolution had caught up with the English potteries, and they were simply doing everything possible to make pottery successfully and competitively. Their product was in great demand, and the use of plaster molds probably permitted the production of certain pieces in the quantities needed. Cox is correct in that the potteries turned out vast quantities of ware. However, Cox's opinion that no pottery of any artistic worth was produced in England after the introduction of plaster molds, or until after the beginning of the 19th century, seems rather intolerant.

England welcomed the Industrial Revolution with open arms. The introduction of plaster molds made possible the mechanization of clay manufacturing processes. The introduction of transfer printing techniques for decoration and of methods for making powdered flint (silica) to add to clay bodies also helped propel the potteries into a new era.

Plaster vs. Fired Clay Molds

Plaster molds differ in a number of important ways from fired clay molds, and an understanding of these differences is necessary to grasp the effect plaster molds had on the pottery industry. Piccolpasso provides a great deal of information about the methods used to make plaster molds in 16th-century Italy. However, he does not mention the fact that plaster molds wear out from use and must be replaced; nor does he mention the need for a better system to make molds than that of returning to the original piece every time a new mold is required. In spite of the disadvantage of wear, plaster molds have many advantages over fired clay molds:

1 Plaster molds absorb moisture much faster than fired clay molds.
2 Plaster molds do not have to be fired to be used. Clay molds, although they could be used in a dry form for a few pressings, must be fired to be used.
3 Plaster molds are made more quickly than clay molds; plaster can be used almost as soon as it hardens.
4 Plaster molds do not shrink. A fired clay mold will shrink at least 10%, or possibly 15%. When using a plaster mold, only one shrinkage occurs, and that is in the casting. When using a clay mold, both the mold and the casting shrink.

The disadvantage of all plaster molds is that the surface wears away through the action of the clay in pressing or casting, and the molds must be discarded and replaced with new ones. (A fired clay mold, on the other hand, can last forever.)

Master, Block, and Case Molds

To facilitate the replacement of plaster molds, and to minimize wear on the original model, plaster molds for production ware are made in a series of steps that involve fabricating intermediary molds from which the new plaster molds are readily reproduced.

The method of making plaster molds in the English potteries of the mid-1700s is similar to that used today and is well described by D. Towner in his book, *World Ceramics*:

The introduction of plaster of Paris moulds, about 1745, produced an outburst of fanciful modelling such as the teapot illustrated here in the form of a camel. The method employed was to fashion the required object in the solid, usually from alabaster; intaglio moulds were then made from this in common clay by pressing, block or master moulds being then cast from these and glazed with salt. From this hard body a series of intaglio moulds of plaster of Paris could be made and in them the finish articles were cast. The casting process consisted of pouring slip into the assembled plaster mould, whose porosity absorbed the water, leaving a thin lining of clay. This would be repeated until the clay lining was sufficiently thick, when, after it had dried, it would be detached from the mould. In this way an almost limitless number of objects of the same pattern could be obtained, the plaster mould when worn out being replaced from the salt-glaze block-mould.[22]

It is unlikely that slip casting was as common as Towner implies because effective methods of deflocculation had yet to be developed. However, Towner's description of the procedure used in production mold making is worth reviewing in order to clarify the terms used for the various molds.

The first step in the process described by Towner is to make the original object out of alabaster. Today the term for this object is "model," and although the model can be made from almost any material, it is usually made from plaster.

In the second step, intaglio molds are made from this object out of clay. The accepted practice today is to make a plaster mold from the model. This mold is the first mold from the model, and the accepted name today for this mold is a "block mold."

The next step in the Towner explanation is to make clay "block" or master molds from the clay intaglio molds. These master molds were then fired and often salt glazed. It is these molds that Towner and many others refer to as "block molds." Today they are referred to as "case molds." These are the molds that are used to make the working molds for production purposes.

There is some confusion about the term "block mold." A number of authors refer to the block mold as the mold that is used to make the production molds. However, the general name "block mold" today refers only to the first mold taken from a model. The term "master mold" is sometimes used also for these first molds from the model.

The term "case mold" is used today to describe the molds that are used to make the production molds. Because these case molds are used over and over to reproduce the working molds, the case molds of today are usually made from gypsum-cement instead of plaster. It is also the reason that the block or master molds referred to by Towner were salt glazed. Case molds can also be made from other suitable materials such as epoxy resins, fiberglass, and rubber compounds. A soft metal can be used for detail when necessary.

In an effort to keep our terms straight, it may be easier to refer to the mold-making process as a one, two, three (or positive, negative, positive) process: that is, model (positive), block mold (negative), and case mold (positive). The word "mold" is often dropped in discussing these three steps: model, block, and case. The case molds are then used to make the production or working molds. The first mold from the model (that is, the block mold) is often stored so that a new model can be made if necessary.

Pressing clay into plaster molds to form elaborate vessels or other objects became the dominant method of pottery making in Europe. The popularity of the products necessitated increased production, and the styles that gained popularity tended to be those that were suitable for production in molds rather than on the potters wheel. The "presserman" was a highly skilled craftsman, a master of the art of press-

Fig. 1.28 A 19th-century presserman at work, with his "whirler" on the table in front of him. Note the liberties apparently taken by the artist: none of the molds shown, which are round, would be used to make the rectangular fluted teapot being assembled. This teapot, and the other rectangular dishes on the shelves, would be made in rectangular molds sectioned at the corners to avoid interfering with the fluting. (From a little book called "The Potters Wheel and How It Goes Round in the Nineteenth Century," by W. Harris, published by Burroughs and Mountford, the Potters, in Trenton, NJ.)

ing large sheets of clay into multi-sectioned molds to create fancifully designed tureens, teapots, and so on. Until the development of deflocculants, which made slip casting practical, press molding was the standard system for shaping forms that could not be thrown on the wheel.

With the introduction of the plaster wheel to create models that are round, as if they were thrown on a potters wheel, the future of hand throwing on the potters wheel for mass production was doomed.

On the plaster wheel, a model is turned out of plaster in the same way that plaster is turned on a lathe, that is, the plaster is cut away until the correct shape is achieved. From this one "master model," suitable blocks are made for production, either by pressing or casting. Because the plaster wheel has a vertical axis (as does a potters wheel), an accomplished plaster wheel modeler can create intricate shapes such as deep fluting and many-sided pieces that would be unreasonable to throw on a potters wheel.

SLIP CASTING

The development of plaster molds went far to mechanize the production of pottery and minimize the role of throwing on a potters wheel. When the problems of working with liquid clay were solved, and casting of multiple molds became standard, the potters wheel all but disappeared from the large factories.

One of the first authors to attempt to describe slip casting was Simeon Shaw, who wrote about the Staffordshire potteries in 1829. In 1832, the Rev. Dionysius Lardner, an American, provided a very detailed description of slip casting that deserves quoting:

Casting is now employed only for the formation of irregular-shaped vessels, where much nicety is required, and which need not have much strength. The casting operation is performed by intimately mixing the united clay and flint with very pure water to the consistence of cream. On pouring this dilution into the mould, the plaster quickly absorbs water from that portion which lies in contact with its surface, hardening it to such a degree, that on the central and still fluid part being poured off, a coating of clay will remain attached to the mould. This coating having been allowed further to dry during a short time, a second charge of diluted clay, but the consistence of which is much greater than the creamy fluid first used, is poured in, and adds to the substance of the first deposit. Having remained in the mould sufficiently long for this purpose, the remainder of the semi-fluid is poured off, and the mould, with its contents, is set in a stove: when sufficiently dry to allow of separation, the article is taken from the mould, and left until it is brought to the green state, when all imperfections are rectified by the workman, whose skill is exerted to render the vessel as smooth and as perfect as possible.[23]

The process is obviously a time-consuming one, ill-suited to mass production. Furthermore, until relatively recently, slip casting has been beset with technical problems. William Burton[24] has clearly pointed out the problems of casting with slip—problems that have plagued potters from the earliest times. Clay and water mixtures tend to separate if they are not kept in constant motion, and casting by pouring liquid clay into a mold was difficult because of the settling of the clay. The slip had to be poured into and out of the mold many times. If the mold were filled only one time, then the clay would not come out of the mold satisfactorily. Because of the difficulties caused by the tendency of the clay particles to settle, until the 19th century, potteries preferred to use molds as press molds instead of slip molds.

Undoubtedly, many attempts to solve the settling problem were made between 1750 and 1800. However, the first written evidence of someone tackling this problem appears in Alexandre Brongniart's treatise on ceramics, in which he states that in 1844 a certain M. de Bettignies added 3% potassum carbonate to his "casting pastes" so that the clay would better adhere to the mold.[25] Brongniart's description uses the term "dessiccation," which suggests that the clay was thicker or denser when cast. The term "deflocculation" is not used. Brongniart also reports that a potter named Tendelle was casting successfully as early as 1790 (but there is no mention of the suspension problem being solved) and that Sevres began slip casting in 1814.

The history of deflocculation was summed up quickly by Johnson and Norton in the *Journal of the American Ceramic Society* in 1941. In it they say:

It is difficult to state with any degree of accuracy exactly when the action of alkalis or basic salts on clay pastes was known. This action, however, undoubtedly was studied by many potters long before its commercial application was revealed. Brongniart tells of a M. de Bettignies who, in 1844, used 3% of potassium carbonate with his "casting pastes" to give necessary 'adherence" to the mold. This "adherence" probably refers to a firmer cast that would result from the use of deflocculated slips.

The first public announcement concerning the use of electrolytes with clay pastes for the precise purpose of increasing the fluidity of the slip must therefore be attributed to Goetz, who applied for a patent in Germany on October 22, 1891. A portion of the translated patent reads as follows:

"Preparation of casting slips for porcelain, earthenware, and clay products by the addition of

sodium carbonate or bicarbonate, with or without cinabar, whereby the slip will pour more readily.

After this patent was granted in 1894, other patents followed on the use of various electrolytes as deflocculants, such as water glass. Weber was granted a patent for the manufacture of articles made from fire-clay-grog mixtures by the casting process in Germany during 1903. Thus, soon after the beginning of the 20th century, the use of deflocculants in the preparation of casting slips, substantially as they are known today, was common knowledge.[26]

The adoption of the slip-casting process depended upon a combination of two factors. The first is the development and use of plaster molds (potters realized that, for production purposes, plaster was a much better choice for molds than clay; the real need for plaster molds did not occur until the potteries began to industrialize). The second factor is the solving of the slip suspension problem by deflocculation with electrolytes. After this problem was worked out, slip casting for factory mass production became a reality.

SPINNING MOLDS, JIGGERS, AND JOLLIES

We have already seen that certain bisque molds used by the Greeks, Romans, and Chinese were shaped round in such a manner that the mold could be revolved on a turning wheel as the potter pressed the plastic clay against the mold. The Romans used this technique in making Arretine relief ware, and the Chinese perfected the system to the extent that "carved" bowls could be mass produced using this system. Burton points out that there is substantial evidence that English potters in the late 17th century made large plates upside down on a turning mold.[27] The surface of the mold had incised lines that imparted a pattern in the plate. This pattern was then used to guide the potter as he applied the slip trailing decoration. Ronald G. Cooper, in his book *English Slipware Dishes; 1650–1850*, goes into considerable detail concerning the use of these molds:

Thus it was that early in the eighteenth century, some potters were using the same methods that their fathers had known, while others were devising workshop methods of a more mechanical nature. The most important of these changes was the use of moulds whereby clay dishes could be made more rapidly and with greater precision than by throwing. The earliest use of moulds (in the reign of George I) by such potters as Samuel Malkin and John Simpson produced ware in which the ornament was skillfully contrived in relation to the new clay technique.

These moulds were incised with lines of ornament, V shaped in section and approximately one sixteenth of an inch deep which resulted in a corresponding impressed relief pattern of raised lines on each dish made. Such lines incorporate a toothed ornamentation which adds considerable vitality to the quality of decoration as well as facilitating the removal of the clay dish without damaging it or the mould. The raised patterns were then individually embellished by the potter with additional coloured slips, somewhat comparable to the technique of cloissone enamel on copper.[28]

Examples of these plates are shown in Figures 1.29–1.32. In the close-ups, it is possible to see the

Fig. 1.29 Plate by Samuel Malkin, c. 1712, made in a fired clay mold with an incised pattern carved into it. Colored slips were used to fill in the design. Courtesy of the Nelson-Atkins Museum of Art, Kansas City, Missouri, Burnap Fund

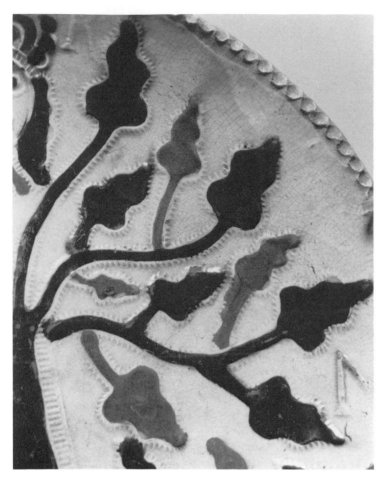

Fig. 1.30 Detail of the Malkin plate, showing the raised pattern caused by the incised lines in the clay mold. Courtesy of the Nelson-Atkins Museum of Art, Kansas City, Missouri, Burnap Fund

Fig. 1.31 A Staffordshire plate, c. 1660–1690. A roulette was probably used to make the pattern in the mold. Courtesy of the Nelson-Atkins Museum of Art, Kansas City, Missouri, Burnap Fund

raised "toothed" ornamentation resulting from the incised pattern in the mold. The delineated areas are filled in with colored slips. Using this method, it would be possible to make the plate in volume and have unskilled workers fill in the design.

The significant point about the molds is not the decoration or ornamentation of the finished ware, but that in making the plates or vessels the mold was turned at considerable speed. The spinning mold is the important phenomenon that separates this form of pressing from the pressing of "plastic" (non-round or fanciful) shapes. Furthermore, it was the spinning mold that led directly to the development of the jigger and jolly system of mechanically forming clay products.

When the potter used a rapidly turning mold to form a vessel, one surface was always controlled by his fingers (perhaps aided by a wooden rib of some sort) and one surface was controlled by the mold. All of the prerequisites for the jigger and jolly system were now present: a mold, probably made of plaster, that fit into a chuck on a wheel, and a worker skilled in pressing clay onto the surface of the spinning mold while shaping the other surface of the vessel with the fingers or a wooden rib.

The development of the jigger and jolly process was an obvious next step. The worker realized that a mechanical arm operating on a pivot on the center axis of the wheel could be brought down over the batt of clay, and this arm could move the clay much more quickly and more effectively than his fingers could. The worker soon realized that a foot for the vessel could be formed if a profile of the foot were cut into a template attached to the mechanical arm. Thus the jigger and jolly system was born.

The development of the jigger and jolly process needed only one more machine to make efficient production possible. Rapid production of anything depends upon a steady supply of raw material—in this case relatively round and uniform flat disks of plastic clay. Pressing balls of clay into disks by hand was too slow to meet the demands of this new mechanized process. Therefore, a machine to press the pieces of clay into thin disks was developed. It was a simple device similar to the jigger arm, that simply pressed pieces of clay into round, flat disks, or batts, of clay.

Various ways to speed up the process of making batts, putting the batt onto the jolly head, and forming the piece with the pressure of the jigger arm were constantly being developed. Soon the jigger and jolly process became a team operation. Usually three men were employed: one to furnish the clay and make the batts; the jiggerman who actually made the pieces on the machine, and a third to remove the mold with the piece on it to a drying area.

The jigger and jolly system was well established by the middle of the 18th century. Who actually invented it is not recorded; however, in all probability, no single person was responsible, because the method naturally evolved from the needs and inventiveness of the potters.

Figure 1.33 illustrates the jigger and jolly set-up. The jigger is the arm with the profile plate on it that comes down over the mold and thus forms the top surface of the piece. The jolly is the turning head, which has a chuck that the mold fits into. The terms "topside" and "inside" are rather ambiguous because in use either the jigger or the jolly could form the inside or the outside of a piece. It is typical to form a plate upside down, with the jolly head containing a mold of the "inside" of the plate and the jigger arm bearing a template to shape the back and rim of the plate. In forming a cup or bowl, the opposite is true: the jolly holds the mold to form the outside of the cup or bowl, and the jigger shapes the inside.

Before the jigger and jolly took over the production of plates, cups, and bowls, the "thrower" was the central man of a throwing team. The thrower worked at his potters wheel, while two assistants brought and prepared clay pieces for him to throw (a third assistant removed thrown pieces to the drying racks). Such a team could produce hundreds of pieces per day. With the introduction of the jigger and jolly, the team continued, but the thrower became a "jiggerman," and the quantity of wares produced per

Fig. 1.32 Detail of the Staffordshire plate showing the colored slips in the areas delineated by the incised pattern. Courtesy of the Nelson-Atkins Museum of Art, Kansas City, Missouri, Burnap Fund

day increased dramatically. This system also enabled the rapid production of oval-shaped pieces by using an eccentric on the jolly shaft to guide the jolly and mold in an oval path. Prior to this development, anything oval-shaped had to be pressed.

A related development that affected pottery production was the introduction of the pug mill or auger extrusion process to prepare plastic clay. The auger extruder was the standard machine used to make brick and tile, and the machine was also used to process a plastic body for jiggering. Again, exactly when auger machines were first employed in pottery and brick manufactories is not known. The auger principle itself is thousands of years old; however, its application in a pug mill to furnish clay for jiggering represents a technical advancement in pottery making, because it increased both the quality of the clay and the speed of production. In the 20th century, a vacuum was applied to the pugging process, producing a clay body totally without air inclusions.

Other improvements to the jigger and jolly system were made over the years. The roller jigger is

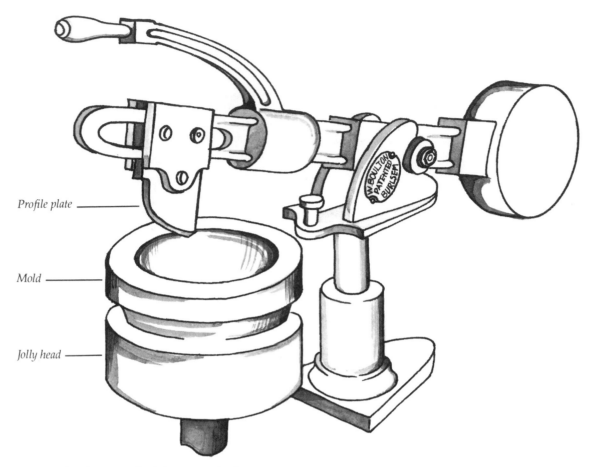

Profile plate

Mold

Jolly head

Fig. 1.33 A typical 19th-century English jigger and jolly.

one. It is simply a jigger with a shaped steel roller in place of the profile plate. The spinning action of the roller shapes the clay much more efficiently than the friction action of the ordinary profile plate. Heated, high-speed rollers have been developed that make for a very fast production system for both positive or negative processes (e.g., cups and casseroles as well as plates). In time, the simple jigger and jolly system has evolved into a totally automatic piece of equipment that operates at very high speed and can produce up to 75 pieces a minute.

AUTOMATIC PRESSES

The "Ram press," which became available commercially in the early 1950s, made possible the rapid production of non-round forms. It is a high-pressure press, and was first developed by Ram Products, Inc., of Springfield, Ohio. The press uses two gypsum-cement dies that have a network of air lines and steel reinforcements. The dies are placed on the press and attached to high-pressure air lines. Plastic clay is placed on the surface of one die, and the press compresses the clay between the two dies. As the dies are separated, air pressure is applied to one of the dies, usually the lower one, which releases the piece from the die. When the dies are far enough apart, high-pressure air is applied to the top die, and the piece drops into the hands of the operator.

Even dies of gypsum-cement, no matter how hard, wear out from the friction of the clay moving against it during pressing. To remedy this, Ram Products has developed fired clay dies that will virtually last forever. Thus an earlier form (fired clay instead of plaster molds) combined with modern technology may become the production system of the near future.

Automatic pressing systems, whether they use dry or plastic clay, depend upon molds (or dies) as the essential element of the forming process. The presses are very efficient and enable a wide variety of shapes to be made. Automatic dry pressing, for example, can produce between 500 and 2000 wall tiles per hour or a bathroom sink every seven minutes. However, because of the high pressure needed to form the pieces, most automatic pressing systems are out of reach for the normal artist-potter.

Man's use of molds to produce ceramic objects has exhibited considerable continuity through the ages. In the past, molds were used to produce objects that could not be made on a potters wheel. History shows that these molds were made from fired clay until plaster was demonstrated to be a superior mold-making material. During the Industrial Revolution, the use of plaster molds became the key to success for the slip-casting and jiggering processes. Today, automatic machinery has taken over processes that potters have done by hand for more than two thousand years. Yet plaster molds are still used even in the most advanced automated processes.

The various techniques of making and using molds should be investigated by anyone interested in forming objects with clay. Molds can be used to achieve unique aesthetic goals, whether the need is for a single object or a thousand. History offers many examples of mold-made ceramics to draw on for inspiration; indeed, some historical pieces exhibit a mastery of technique that is beyond our capabilities today. The clay artist who takes up the challenge of mold making will find that producing handsomely crafted molds not only provides the satisfaction of having done something well, but also that they provide totally new opportunities for expressing ideas in clay.

REFERENCES

1 A. Lucas, *Ancient Egyptian Materials and Industries*, London: Edward Arnold, 1962, pp. 368–369.

2 Bernard Racham, "Pottery and Porcelain," *Encyclopaedia Britannica*, 1951, p. 338.

3 Trude Dothan, "Lost Outpost of the Egyptian Empire," *National Geographic Magazine*, December 1982, p. 761.

4 Gisela Ritcher, *The Craft of Athenian Pottery*, New Haven, CT: Yale University Press, 1923, pp. 28–30.

5 *The Chinese Exhibition*, catalog of the Royal Ontario Museum, Toronto, Ontario, 1974, p. 90.

6 Nils Palmgren, *Sung Sherds*, Stockholm: Almquist & Wiksell, 1963, pp. 331–370.

7 Jennie J. Young, *The Ceramaic Art, A Compendium of the History and Manufacture of Pottery and Porcelain*, New York: Harper Brothers, 1878, p. 244.

8 Warren E. Cox, *The Book of Pottery and Porcelain*, New York: Crown, 1944, p. 391.

9 Ernst Rosenthal, *Pottery and Ceramics from Common Brick to Fine China*, Middlesex, England: Penquin Books, Harmondsworth, 1949, pp. 19–20.

10 Christopher P. Donnan, "Mochica Ceramic Technology," *Nawpa Pacha #3*, 1965, pp. 115–134.

11 *Ibid*.

12 Lawrence A. Dawson, "Slip Casting, A Ceramic Technique Invented in Ancient Peru," *Nawpa Pacha #2*, 1964, pp. 107–111.

13 A. Lucas, *Ancient Egyptian Materials and Industries*, London: Edward Arnold, 1962, pp. 75–76.

14 J. Earl Hadley, *The Magic Powder*, New York: G.P. Putman and Sons, 1945, pp. 7–8.

15 *Ibid*, p. 10.

16 Jasper O. Drattin, *A Brief History of Lime, Cement, Concrete, and Reinforced Concrete*, University of Illinois Bulletin, Engineering Experiment Station Reprint Series, No. 27, University of Illinois Press, June 29, 1943.

17 Cavaliere Cipriano Piccolpasso, *The Three Books of the Potters Art*, London: Victoria and Albert Museum, 1934. Translated from the Italian by Bernard Rackham; a reproduction of *Li tre Libri dell Arte del Val saio* (Veroma: 1545).

18 Simeon Shaw, *History of the Staffordshire Potteries*, Devon, England: 1829; reprinted in 1970 by David and Charles, Ltd., South Devon House, Newton Abbot, p. 163.

19 *Ibid*., pp. 163–164.

20 Shaw, p. 166.

21 Warren E. Cox, *The Book of Pottery and Porcelain*, New York: Crown, 1944, p. 899.

22 D. Towner, "Staffordshire and the Rise of Industrialism," in *World Ceramics*, New York: McGraw Hill, 1968, p. 267.

23 Dionysius Lardner, *A Treatise on the Origin, Progressive Improvement, and Present State of the Manufacture of Porcelain and Glass*, Philadelphia: Carey and Lea, 1832, p. 54.

24 William Burton, F.C.S., "English Earthenware and Stoneware, A History and Description, London: Cassell and Company, 1904, p. 96.

25 Alexandre Brongniart, *Traites des Arts Céramiques ou Des Poteries*, 3rd ed., Vol. 2, Paris: P. Asselin, 1877, p. 469.

26 Johnson and Norton, "Fundamental Study of Clay: 11 Mechanisms of Deflocculation in the Clay-Water System," *Journal of the American Ceramic Society*, June 1941.

27 Burton, p. 24.

28 Ronald G. Cooper, *English Slipware Dishes, 1650–1850*, New York: Transatlantic Arts, 1968, p. 99.

Most ceramic studios are already equipped with many of the items needed to work with plaster, and what is not already on hand can readily be purchased or fabricated. It is essential to emphasize at the outset, though, that having the right set-up is equally as important as having the right tools. It is a relatively simple and direct procedure to sit at a potters wheel and produce beautiful pottery, using the minimum of tools and equipment. It is a totally different problem to attempt to make quality plaster molds in a situation unprepared for the process. Unfortunately, this aspect of mold making is often neglected. Quality plaster molds cannot be made in a setting that has not been prepared for it ahead of time. The procedures for mold making are relatively simple and can be carried out in almost any ceramic studio, provided the studio has been suitably organized for it. Otherwise, mold making can turn into a frustrating, messy, and unsuccessful venture. With proper preparation, and following the correct procedures outlined in this book, success is almost guaranteed.

Because of the importance of proper preparation, this chapter could just as easily have been called "Getting Ready to Make Molds"—because that's what this chapter is all about.

CHAPTER

2

Tools and Equipment

THE PLASTER SHOP

The plaster shop, whether a separate facility or a specially prepared area in a ceramic studio, is where all mold-making activities take place. A room or area of 300 square feet can be made into a fine plaster shop for one or two artists. It should be well-lit, preferably with natural light from windows, and be adequately wired and ventilated (to assure sufficient drying of the molds). Figure 2.1 shows an efficient layout for such a shop. It is equipped and arranged so the artist can enter with a design drawing and leave with the model, block molds, case molds, and first working molds for production.

The equipment for the shop will be itemized and discussed in the next section. For the moment, however, note that the table is the center of the mold-making activities; the plaster wheel is in a secondary location. The workspace and equipment shown in this layout are arranged to promote the easy flow of

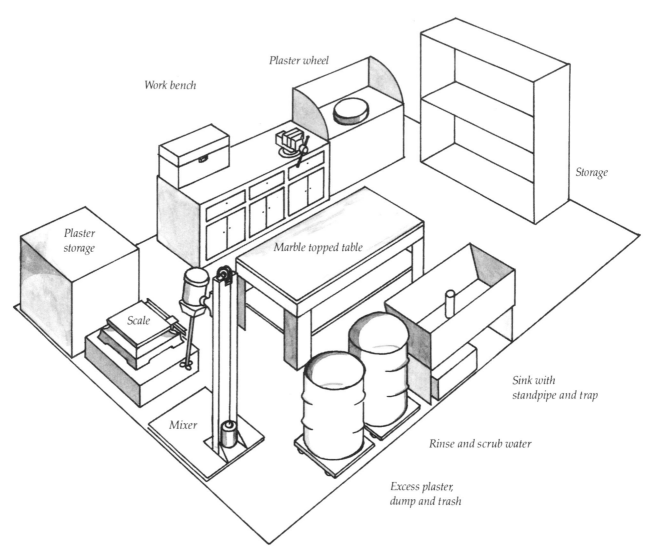

Fig. 2.1 The plaster shop.

work, from weighing out the plaster to drying the molds. The equipment must be arranged to match the sequence of procedures used in mold making. Otherwise, the shop will quickly become chaotic. So the watchword when setting up a plaster shop is "Plan ahead!"

TOOLS AND EQUIPMENT

Mold makers are often tool addicts—and in this they resemble the woodworker more than the potter. The mold maker maintains a diverse stock of tools for cutting, carving, and shaping plaster. Occasionally a special implement is needed for a particular task, and it must be made from scratch or by modifying another tool. Master mold makers seem to be adept at this, so perhaps a good term for them is "mold mechanics." The basic set of mold makers tools, however, are commonplace and readily available.

The equipment and tools listed below represent the minimum amount needed for mold making. We'll begin with the major pieces of equipment, and then move on through the various tools and accessories.

Major Equipment

Most of the major pieces of equipment for the plaster shop are shown in the plaster shop layout (Figure 2.1). These are:

1 A sink with running water. Ideally, it should be a large deep sink with a stand pipe in the drain, a sediment trap in the drain pipe, and both hot and cold running water.

2 A marble-topped table. The table should be at least 3′ × 6′, 26″ to 30″ high, and sturdy enough to hold a 1½″ thick marble slab (but the table should jiggle slightly when pushed with your hip). Marble is the ideal surface and is seemingly standard, but formica, stainless steel, and heavy plate glass are also completely satisfactory. The table should be carefully leveled after it is placed in the room. If large, heavy molds will be made, a second, lower table, 20″ to 26″ high, will be a welcome addition. This table can be small, but it must be sturdy. The lower height permits large amounts of plaster to be poured much more easily.

3 Storage for plaster and shelves for the models and molds. Some large shops use a plaster bin that holds several hundred pounds of plaster. This type of storage is not suitable for small shops because the plaster will not be used that rapidly and will take on moisture from the air.

4 A dependable scale that can weigh up to 100 pounds. (A kitchen scale typically has a limit of 25 pounds.) A platform scale is more satisfactory than a hanging one because the plaster bucket can be put directly on the platform.

5 A power mixing system. This can be a portable electric drill with a 24″ shaft and a propeller, or it can be a permanently mounted variable speed mixer that can be raised and lowered into position. The drill can be variable speed; however it must achieve at least 1200 rpm. (Power mixing systems are discussed in more detail in Chapter 3.)

6 Heavy-duty workbench with vise to serve as additional work and storage space.

7 A plaster wheel or heavy-duty potters wheel for turning the models and molds. Sometimes a wood lathe is used for this purpose, but it is much more awkward to use than a plaster wheel. How to make this important piece of equipment is described in a separate section in this chapter.

8 Two 50-gallon open drums or heavy-weight plastic trash containers. One is used as a trash container for excess plaster; the other is filled with water and serves as the primary rinse and scrub for the plaster bucket.

9 A source of compressed air. This is useful for all kinds of tasks, from cleaning molds to separating sections of molds.

Tools for the Tool Box

The following list of tools comprises a "starter set" for model and mold making. Most of these tools are readily available from ceramic or woodworking supply houses or hardware stores, and most fit easily into item #1—the tool box.

1 A tool box, of appropriate size and design to store tools in an orderly manner. It should have many small drawers because most mold makers tools are not very large (see Figure 2.2).

2 Turning tools. A variety of turning tools are shown in Figure 2.3 and 2.4. You will want at least the three shown in Figure 2.4. The best-quality turning tools can be purchased from woodworking supply houses such as Leichtung Fine Tools in Cleveland, Ohio (see Sources of Supplies). These tools are called "shave hooks" and are much better quality than the average turning tool found in most ceramic supply catalogs. The Milligan Hardware & Supply Company of East Liverpool, Ohio, a major supplier of the pottery industry, also carries high-quality turning tools.

3 Two quality steel calipers, one inside and one outside (Figure 2.5). These calipers should be good quality and the tension should be capable of adjustment. A 10″ or 12″ caliper is much better than a small size for the first purchase. A school compass that uses a lead pencil is also good to have because it can hold an indelible pencil.

Other types of calipers should be mentioned.

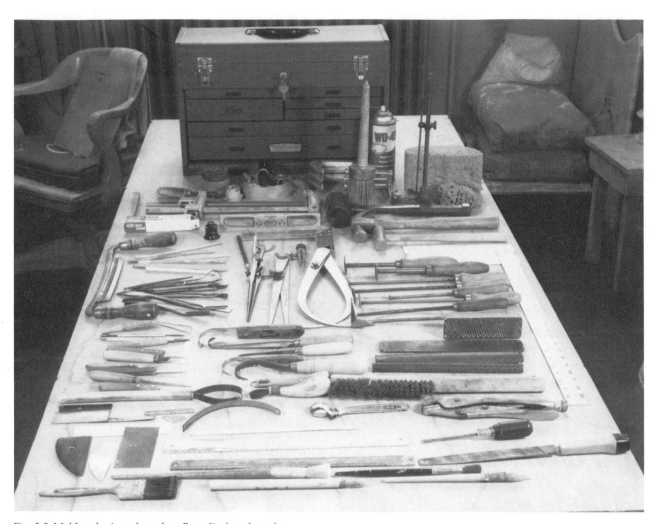

Fig. 2.2 Mold maker's tools and toolbox displayed on the shop's marble-topped table.

Fig. 2.3 Various tools for turning plaster. The two heavy-duty tools in the back are woodworker's shave hooks. The two bent tools on the left are for cutting interior shapes.

Fig. 2.4 Woodworker's shave hooks used to scrape plaster for final shaping.

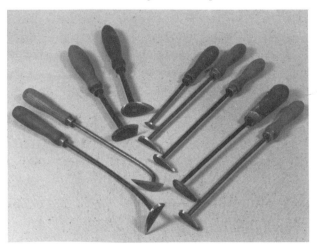

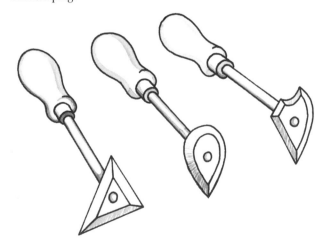

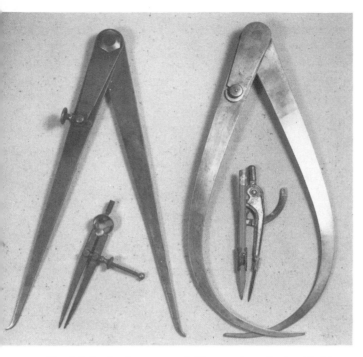

Fig. 2.5 A school compass, dividers, and good sets of inside and outside calipers are necessities. The caliper on the right is a transfer caliper, which can be set, opened, and closed again to the original setting.

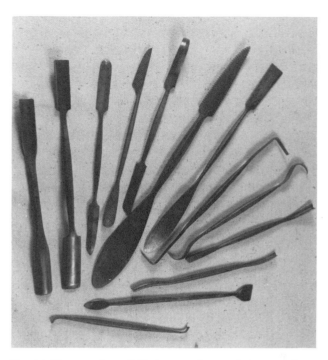

Fig. 2.6 Plaster tools available in ceramic or sculpture supply houses are valuable for mold making.

A Vernier caliper is a very accurate measuring device. A transfer caliper is designed to permit measuring, opening the caliper for referral to another dimension, and then reclosing at the first measurement. A quality divider is also an excellent tool for assuring accuracy in the molds. These last three items are found in professional mold shops and should be purchased as the need arises.

4 Wooden clay working tools of various shapes to aid in making clay models or molds.

5 A group of steel plaster sculpture tools (Figure 2.6). The more the better.

6 Two potters fettling knives, one a tempered blade and the other untempered so that the blade can be bent to fit whatever shape is needed (see Figure 2.7).

7 A knife that is curved at the end so that hemispherical natches can be cut in the mold (Figure 2.8). The natches serve as "keys" to fit a two-piece mold together.

Fig. 2.7 A wide variety of knives should always be kept in the tool box. The knife on the left is a potter's knife, or fettling knife, with the blade sharpened and tapered. This is a stiff blade, not a soft blade. The rest of the knives are all made from paring knives.

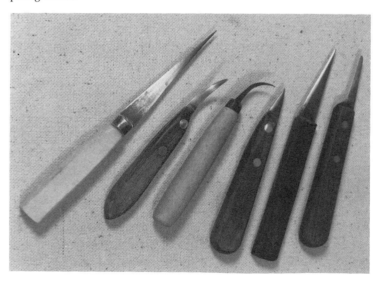

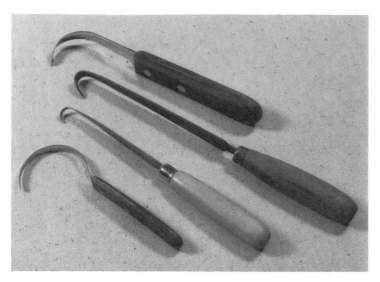

Fig. 2.8 A group of knives for cutting natches into the mold to key the pieces together.

Fig. 2.9 Hacksaw blade scrapers and other tools. The curved tools are made by heating a 5"-long piece of hacksaw blade with a torch to dull red and bending the blade around a steel pipe. The blade is then reheated to cherry red and plunged into water to harden the steel. In the tools at the top, the ends of the blade are inserted in a slot cut on the end of a reed or wooden dowel; the blade is epoxied in place and wrapped with nylon string. The handle is then inserted in ¾" plastic hose.

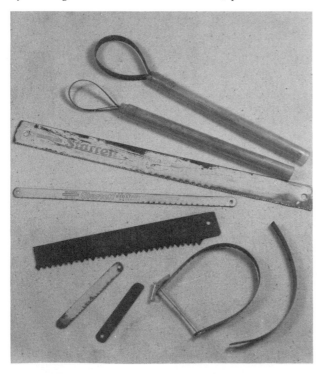

8 Scrapers (Figure 2.9). Scrapers range from metal potters ribs to power hacksaw blades. Scrapers can be cut from tempered sheet steel with tin snips, filed to shape, and then sharpened with a stone. Hacksaw blades make excellent scrapers. They can be bent to shape by heating with a torch to remove the temper and then, when the metal is dull red, bending the blade around a steel pipe. The tool is retempered by the same heating process (to dull red) and then quenched in water. Power hacksaw blades are very valuable tools. These blades are extremely sturdy and are made from high-quality steel. The back edge of the blade can be sharpened to form a long stiff scraper. Rubber scrapers, such as potters ribs or rubber kitchen spatulas, are also necessary.

9 Files. Files are used for sharpening tools and for filing plaster. A good bastard steel file is used for tool sharpening, and sometimes is used on the surface of plaster. Stanley Sureform Tools have become a standard. All three shapes (round, half round, and flat) are necessary (Figure 2.10). In shaping plaster molds, the Sureform rasps are used without the handle. Otherwise they clog very quickly with plaster and are difficult to clean.

10 Hammers and saws. A regular carpenter's hammer and a large rubber mallet are used in separating molds from mold boards (Figure 2.11). A cop-

Fig. 2.10 Stanley Sureforms, originally designed as woodworking rasps, have become mandatory tools for the mold maker. They are normally used without the handle to prevent clogging.

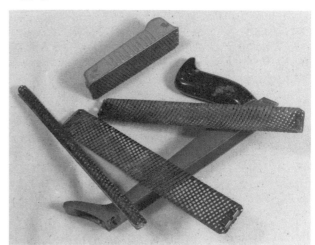

ing saw is valuable for cutting shapes out of plaster or wood. Hacksaw blades, used without the frame, are excellent plaster cutters.

11 A good-quality level, at least 9″ long (Figure 2.12).

12 A good-quality carpenter's square or tri-square, at least 6″ long on the ruler or blade side and with a wide enough base so that it can stand up on the base. A level enclosed in the base is an asset. (See Figure 2.12).

13 A good-quality carpenter's square at least 24″ on the long side is very useful in the long run. The small shape, however, can make do with a tri-square and steel ruler.

14 Rulers. These should include standard rulers as well as an expandable carpenter's rule.

15 Plaster batch calculator. This calculator and the shrink calculator discussed below are indispensable to the mold maker, and both are packaged with this book. The plaster batch calculator is used to accurately determine the amounts of plaster and water needed for any size batch of any consistency. It is very simple to use and assures consistent, high-quality results. Its use is described further on page 51.

16 Shrink calculator. The second device included with this book is the shrink calculator. It enables the user to determine exactly how big to make a clay piece to assure an end product of the required size, in spite of shrinkage during manufacturing.

The calculator has two functions. The first is to determine the amount of shrinkage that occurs in a particular clay body during the manufacturing process. The amount of shrinkage is expressed as a percentage from 1% to 40%. Years ago the U. S. Gypsum Company made a beautiful shrink ruler with nicely detailed brass ends on it. This ruler was marked off in units representing three shrink values (8%, 10%, and 12%) as well as in standard 1″ demarcations. Such a ruler, although useful, is good only for those specific shrink values. If a particular clay body had a 14% shrink, the correct shrink ruler had to be painstakingly calculated or else guessed at. The shrink calculator that comes with this book has no such limitation. It will quickly determine any percentage

Fig. 2.11 Hammers for the mold maker: a standard claw hammer for nailing or taking mold boards apart, a rubber-tipped hammer with both hard and soft rubber heads, and a large rubber-encased mallet for pounding mold boards apart.

shrink from 1% to 40% and permit making the corresponding shrink ruler.

The shrink calculator also contains a metric scale for determining the shrinkage percent on a 10-cm test tile. However, by following the printed direc-

Fig. 2.12 The tri-square (right) and a torpedo level (left) are essential tools for mold making. A surface gauge (center) is a very fine tool for a professional mold shop, but a tri-square with a wide base, a small clamp, and pencil can make an adequate substitute.

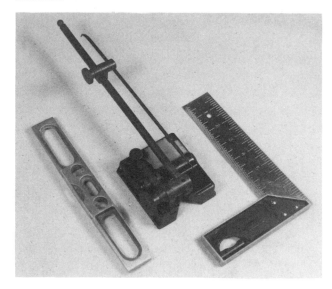

tions on the calculator for making the larger test tile, a small mark on the test tile for 10 cm is all that is necessary for testing the shrinkage in metric units. It does not make much, if any, difference which scale is used; however, it is easier to see the reading on the larger (nonmetric) scale. It also may be advisable to make several tests of the same clay body in order to get an average shrinkage value.

The shrink calculator can be used no matter what process is applied to the clay (throwing, casting, pressing). If the same clay body will be used for both throwing and casting, two separate tests should be made, one using plastic throwing clay and another using a casting made with deflocculated clay.

The second function of the shrink calculator is to use the determined percentage of shrink to make a shrink compensating ruler. The ruler is expressed in "inches," but they are larger than standard inches by the percentage of shrink determined for that clay body. This compensating ruler, or shrink ruler, is then used to make a piece in clay that will be the required size after drying, firing, etc.

Fig. 2.13 Furniture clamps, whether the bar clamps shown here or the pipe type, should be bought and used in pairs. This shows the proper use of furniture clamps in securing four plaster mold boards.

A shrink ruler can be made from almost anything that has a straight edge and can be marked upon. The blank side of a wooden school ruler is ideal. Be sure to indicate the shrink value (e.g., 13%) on the ruler.

In a mold making shop, the shrink ruler is mainly used to make a model of the correct size before the molds are made. If the model is the correct size as determined by the shrink ruler, then the end product will be correct size. In a production throwing shop, the shrink ruler is used to determine the size of the item that is thrown. The shrink ruler offers a very convenient way to assure that pieces fit together even though they are thrown at different times.

After use, the shrink calculator should be wiped clean of any clay and stored in the tool box until needed again.

17 An indelible pencil. This item is mandatory. It is a pencil that marks purple on plaster. Buy several from an art supply house and put them away. Laundry marking pens, felt tip pens, ballpoint pens, and colored pencils are not satisfactory.

18 A variety of brushes. These range from small bristle brushes used to clean up molds to large mold maker's brushes.

19 Other small tools. Many other tools are handy to have in the tool box. These would include a small block plane, drawknife, bit brace, tin snips, pliers, wrenches, heavy-duty scissors, surface gauge, a small wood carving set, a set of pattern files, vise grips, etc. If you continue to work in plaster, this list will grow automatically over time.

20 Sponges. The natural sponges are preferable to the synthetic ones.

21 Duco-Cement is useful for gluing broken pieces of plaster together.

Other Tools and Accessories

Of course, not everything the mold maker uses fits into a tool box. Here are a number of other items indispensable to the mold maker's craft:

1 Furniture clamps. Two or four furniture clamps, either the kind that fit on steel pipes or a set of bar clamps (Figure 2.13) are ideal. They should be at least

24″ long and the clamp should be 6″ deep. Four of these clamps, which are used to secure all sorts of mold board set-ups, will serve a shop very well. When the mold is very high, however, these clamps must be used in conjunction with rebar or band clamps.

Many mold shops use rebar clamps, made of bent concrete reinforcing rod, for retaining mold boards (Figure 2.14). These clamps are easily made from $\frac{1}{2}$″ or $\frac{3}{8}$″ diameter concrete reinforcing rebar stock. The rebar clamps shown in Figure 2.14 are made by heating the rod with an acetylene torch and bending it around a pipe until the desired shape is achieved. After bending, the rod is reheated to a dull red and plunged into water to temper the steel. The rubber ends hold the clamps in position at any angle of use.

Although C clamps should be one's last choice for mold board clamps, they come in handy at the workbench and are quite useful when used with the particular type of mold board shown in Figure 2.15 (see item 3 below).

2 A furniture band clamp is essential for securing round mold set-ups, and it is very useful for securing tall mold boards, as shown in Figure 2.14.

(Note how small squares of plaster are used to assure that pressure is applied in the right places.) You will probably find more use for the band clamp than for the rebar clamps.

3 Mold boards. Mold boards are used to form the outside shape of the mold. They should range in size from 6″ × 12″ to perhaps 12″ × 30″, and they are usually made in matching pairs. A professional mold shop will have a collection of mold boards for all sizes and shapes of molds. The boards can be made from $\frac{3}{4}$″ marine plywood or standard plywood. Both surfaces should be thoroughly sealed to make them waterproof; formica or other stable plastic material can be glued permanently to one side.

One style of mold board works especially well with C clamps (see Figure 2.15). The boards are made in matching pairs by length, and each board has a 2″ × 2″ block carefully glued and nailed at one end. The blocks must be placed so the boards stand perfectly upright and so that the end of the board is perfectly flush with the 2″ × 2″ block.

For small molds, plaster mold boards are usually more convenient to use than wooden ones.

For molds that are not straight-sided, heavy

Fig. 2.14 Many mold shops use rebar clamps made of concrete reinforcing rod. The ones pictured here offer more tension than the usual simple U-shaped rebar clamps. In this mold board set-up, it takes four clamps to secure the boards. Because the mold boards are tall, a band clamp is used at the base.

Fig. 2.15 Four C clamps are combined with four specially constructed mold boards. This is a versatile and excellent system.

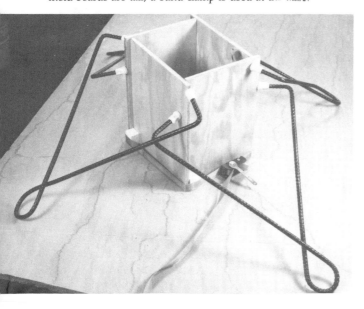

roofing paper, tarpaper, light-gauge sheet aluminum, heavy plastic (e.g., smooth plastic placemats), or linoleum can be used to form "cottles" for the mold. (The term "cottle" has remained unchanged for over two centuries. The early mold makers needed a flexible material that could be wrapped around the wheel head to form a chamber for the plaster to be poured into. The obvious choice was leather. In fact, leather was ideal. Various widths of leather belting were used. It was thoroughly tanned, waterproofed with mold soap, and held together with rope. These strips of leather were called cottles, and they served the early mold makers very well. The word "cottle" today refers to any flexible material that can be wrapped to form a chamber for casting plaster.)

4 Clamps for cottles and molds. No matter what the cottle material, it must be held in place very securely for pouring plaster. Heavy cord, clothes line, or Velcro straps are best for this job. Strapping with Velcro closures, commonly used to hold slip-casting molds in place, is available through the Minnesota Clay Company or other supply houses. Spring-action clothespins and heavy-duty clamp-type paper clips can also be used to hold flexible materials together. Large rubber bands made from truck inner tubes are also useful for retaining slip-casting molds, but they are not very satisfactory for production work. Cloth-covered elastic cords (the kind with the hooks on the ends) are very useful for holding two-piece molds together. As already mentioned, a furniture band clamp is an excellent all-around retaining device.

5 Long-handled turning tools. These tools are not standard; that is, you must fabricate them yourself from normal short-handled tools. They are truly worth the effort, however, because the long-handled tools have many advantages over the standard tools, especially when doing serious work on the plaster wheel. The tools pictured in Figure 2.16 are typical of the type of long-handled tools used in turning plaster. The tool on the left is a standard turning tool; it is the same tool that is pictured in Figures 2.3 and 2.4.

To make a long-handled tool, first drill a hole in the end of a heavy-duty wooden handle to accept the metal shank of a standard tool. Simply pull the handle of the standard tool off the shank and insert the shank into the drilled end of the new wooden handle. The total length of the new tool should be from 30" to 36". It must be long enough to be tucked under the right arm; better too long than too short.

The pictured long-handled tools have a metal ferrule and pin securing the steel shank, but this is not necessary. Epoxy glue applied to the shank before it is inserted into the new handle should provide enough bond to keep the tool from twisting in the handle.

The advantage of long-handled tools over standard tools is apparent in Figure 2.17. Before describing their benefits, however, it is necessary to describe the belly stick.

6 A "belly stick" is a necessity for turning plaster. The belly stick is traditionally a long, sturdy wooden stick with a pointed nail on one end and a small wooden plate fastened to the other end. The wooden plate is sometimes padded to make it easier on the stomach during long hours of use. The belly stick shown in Figures 2.16 and 2.17 is a length of $\frac{3}{4}$" pipe with a large rubber stopper on one end and a wooden insert with a pointed nail on the other end. The length of the belly stick is determined by the distance from the back board of the plaster wheel to the stomach of the plaster turner. This particular belly stick is about 36" long. This length gives enough space to move the legs smoothly in turning plaster. When necessary, the belly stick is simply removed from one spot and placed in another by forcing the pointed nail into the back board of the plaster wheel. The back board will soon become punctured by a multitude of small holes.

In Figure 2.17, a belly stick is shown placed just under the sternum, and the turning tool is held in both hands. This position is a much steadier one than any position possible with a standard short-handled tool. It is a triangular stance, with the corners of the triangle being the stomach, the left hand on the working end of the tool and the belly stick, and the right hand anchoring the end of the tool on the hip or under the right arm. With a standard short-handled tool, both hands hold the tool securely against the belly stick. The advantage of the long-handled tool is that it permits much steadier and smoother action when cutting plaster.

Fig. 2.16 Five long-handled turning tools, with a standard turning tool (a shave hook) on the left. The turning tool on the far right is a cut-off tool for deep cutting and removing a model from the plaster wheel head. The "three-in-one" tool with exchangeable heads (just to the right of the shave hook) was made by Pat McGuire of the Ceramic Engineering Dept. at the University of Illinois. A belly stick lies on top of the turning tools.

Fig. 2.17 The long-handled turning tool is supported with the left hand and the belly stick. The right hand supports the end of the tool, and it is anchored on the hip or tucked under the right arm. Movement is made with the legs and the right hand. This position, made possible by the long-handled tools, provides far steadier smoother turning action than is possible with standard tools.

7 Plaster mixing buckets. Plaster buckets with spouts and handles are ideal containers for mixing plaster. Many styles are available, and all are suitable, except one: the kind that has a depression in the bottom that forms a hand hold when the bucket is poured. This type is hard to clean and should be used as a last resort. An old-fashioned galvanized coal bucket is an excellent choice for mixing larger batches of plaster, and it cleans up easily.

You will want to have on hand a variety of containers, ranging in size from 1-quart plastic mea-

suring pitchers to 5-gallon buckets. (The galvanized coal bucket holds much more than 5 gallons, but pours larger than 3 gallons are very heavy and difficult to handle, especially for a novice.)

8 A timer, such as a simple kitchen or photographic timer.

9 Dust mask. Very little dust rises when plaster is sifted carefully into water. However, some dust is inevitable, and wearing a nose and mouth mask is a wise precaution.

10 Soaps and other separating preparations. When the second half of a mold is to be poured, a resist must be applied to the surface of the first half; otherwise, the two halves will not separate. A standard resist for this purpose is English Crown Soap, obtainable from most ceramic supply houses. A thick brown jelly, it must be diluted with water prior to use (usually 1 cup of English Crown Soap to 1 quart of water). Heating the water increases the dissolving rate. The resulting liquid should be stored in a covered container. A natural sponge is used to apply it to hardened plaster. Many other top-quality separators or resists are on the market now, and any one of them could serve the purpose—the choice depends upon personal preference. (Undoubtedly, the number of new products is due not to the needs of the ceramic industry, but to the needs of the plastic industry.) These various materials are listed in the Sources of Supplies.

11 Water-based clay and oil-based clay. The plaster shop should have both kinds of clay available. Water-based clay should be in plastic form, easy to handle. It is possible to buy any kind of clay body, pugged, de-aired, and packaged in 25-pound plastic bags, usually two bags to a 50-pound cardboard box. For plaster work, choose a light-colored clay in preference to a dark-colored clay most dark clays obtain their color from iron oxide, which stains the plaster badly). The important point is that the clay be plastic and readily formed into coils, slabs, or whatever shape is needed. Water-based clay should be stored in very tight plastic bags, two layers of plastic, and in a covered container.

The general term for oil-based clay is *Plastelene*. It is a clay that is combined with oil to form a never-drying, plastic material. It comes in various colors for children's modeling kits, but the most common color is green. For industrial purposes, it comes in various hardnesses and colors, usually green or brown. It is used by the automobile industry for making large-scale models of automobiles. The very hard, brown type of oil clay is too stiff to use in a plaster shop. The mold maker uses the standard green oil clay to fill spaces, help retain mold boards, and make models.

During use, the Plastelene sometimes gets mixed with bits of plaster, and these plaster bits make the Plastelene hard to manipulate. To make sure that plaster scraps don't get mixed into the clay, (whether oil or water-based), the clay should be washed off thoroughly as soon as it is taken from the particular job it was used for. If a great amount of plaster is spilled onto water-based clay, the clay should be discarded.

Water-based clay is much cheaper than oil-based clay, and it should be used more liberally than the oil-based clay in mold work. Highly refined and smooth surfaces can be achieved on both clays. The oil-based clay can be polished to a glass-like surface by using a drop or two of water and polishing with a spatula or other tool.

12 Rubber mold compounds are useful for making flexible case molds (molds for making molds), and they are discussed in Chapter 18. A number of companies supplying quality compounds are listed in the Appendix.

Tool Maintenance

Clean, well-maintained tools are a necessity. If plaster is left to harden on any metal tool, the tool will tend to rust where the plaster is. This soon makes the tool worthless. Cleaning hardened plaster from the tool with a wire brush and lightly coating the tool with WD40 or a rust-preventive spray should make the tool last a lifetime. This also applies to wooden and plastic tools.

In working with plaster, most of the work is a matter of "taking away" instead of "adding on." The "taking away" is scraping, planing, filing, carving, sanding, and polishing. The tools used for these purposes must be sharp enough to work the plaster efficiently. Knives, turning tools, and scrapers become dull with use, and they must be periodically sharpened.

A sharpening stone is used to sharpen knives. For sharpening scrapers, a piece of silicon carbide kiln shelf does an excellent job. The procedure for sharpening scrapers is much different than that for sharpening knives. Scrapers are sharpened so that the narrow edge forms a flat surface perpendicular to the side of the scraper. By sharpening the scraper so that the edge is flat, the scraper then actually has two sharp edges. To sharpen a scraper, hold it upright on a clean kiln shelf that has been moistened with water and rapidly move it back and forth (Figure 2.18). Make sure that the scraper is held perpendicular to the shelf; any wobbling will cause a rounded edge.

Turning tools are usually sharpened only on the beveled surface. Most knife-like tools are sharpened on two sides with files and a sharpening stone in a normal manner.

After the tool is sharpened, apply a light coating of WD40 or a silicon rust preventive such as Sterrett M1 Lubricant. This is especially important if the tool is to be put away and not used immediately.

THE PLASTER WHEEL

There is no doubt that the occasional mold maker can get along without a plaster wheel, but a plaster wheel is essential to any mold shop that functions as part of a production pottery. A master mold maker in a production shop is usually a master on the plaster wheel as well. The skills needed to use a plaster wheel creatively are relatively easy to learn. With a little practice and understanding of the molding process, the artist will discover that the plaster wheel offers exciting opportunities for creative ceramic production.

Unfortunately, a plaster wheel is seldom, if ever, found in studios of individual potters, or even in ceramic training situations. Although there is a growing interest in mold making, very few schools offer the clay artist any opportunity to learn about the creative possibilities of a plaster wheel. Hopefully, when its importance is realized and its creative pos-

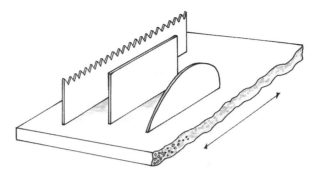

Fig. 2.18 Scrapers are sharpened on a piece of moistened silicon carbide kiln shelf. The scraper is held perpendicular to the shelf to create two sharpened edges on the tool.

sibilities better understood, it will become as common as the potters wheel.

Converting a potters wheel to a plaster wheel is one way to obtain this piece of equipment at reasonable cost. Since the kick wheel is used in so many ceramic studios, a standard Randall kick wheel with motor drive attachment was chosen to be converted to a plaster wheel (Figure 2.19).

Before undertaking the conversion, it is important to understand the limitations of the kick wheel and the primary requirements of a plaster wheel. The Randall kick wheel places the potter in a seated position so the feet can kick the wheel to obtain the momentum necessary for throwing. The seated position is perhaps as historic as the throwing process itself. The motor drive attachment enables the wheel to gain momentum without kicking.

A plaster wheel, on the other hand, must be operated from a standing position. There should be as little vibration as possible when the wheel turns with the weight of plaster on it. The wheel must be able to turn freely when necessary. (This is why a kick wheel is a better choice for conversion than a direct-drive or belt-drive power wheel. The free rotation of the large flywheel is very important on the plaster wheel.) Furthermore, the unit must be powerful enough to turn at 100 to 200 rpm even under the considerable load exerted by cutting plaster with turning tools. (Thus the motor drive is a necessity.)

The conversion of the kick wheel to meet the above requirements was accomplished as follows:

1 The seat post and seat were removed and a vertical pipe was installed to support the work table

Fig. 2.19 The conversion consists of rebracing the wheel structure, relocating the top bearing, and replacing the seat post with a pipe to serve as a corner brace.

of the wheel. This pipe also supports two angle braces (Figure 2.20).

2 The bowl and head were removed and the top bearing was raised 3″ to eliminate any shaft vibration. This was done by inverting the bearing and placing a 2″-square channel on the bearing bracket. The bearing was placed as close to the head of the shaft as possible.

3 A large angle iron was bolted onto the lateral pipe supports of the wheel with U bolts. Two smaller

angle irons were bolted to the lateral pipe supports near the top bearing and at the base of the seat post flange. See Figure 2.20.

4 A smaller angle iron was U-bolted across the back vertical piping on the right side of the wheel in a position similar to the angle iron that braces the motor on the left side.

5 The wheel was moved to its desired position in the shop and a new table with high back boards was constructed on top of the former table. The new

table is made of $\frac{3}{4}''$ plywood and is thoroughly sealed with sealer to resist moisture and plaster build-up. The pipe that replaced the seat post supports the outer corner of the new table. (See Figure 2.21.)

6 The standard chuck-type head was returned to the shaft and a large plaster head was cast on it. The plaster head was cast in three layers, each interlocked with the others. The first two layers are of gypsum-cement and the third (top) is of pottery plaster. The head weighs about 70 pounds.

7 The head and wheel were accurately leveled. (Figure 2.22.)

8 The top surface of the plaster head was cut so it is about 36″ from the floor.

The conversion results in a very satisfactory plaster wheel. It is remarkably steady and vibration-free, it has a much greater momentum because of the large plaster head, and, finally, it has adequate power for turning plaster. The cost of the conversion is under $50 if all new material is used; angle iron can be purchased at a scrap yard for much less.

Do not skimp on the angle iron. Heavy, larger angle irons do a far better job of bracing than do lighter, smaller irons. The purpose of this bracing is to eliminate vibration in the pipe structure of the wheel. Without the bracing and the relocation of the bearing, this wheel would not be satisfactory for use as a plaster wheel.

Many brands of potters wheels can be successfully converted to a plaster wheel. The most important thing to aim for is vibration-free, rapid rotation during the process of turning plaster.

A good plaster wheel found in factory mold shops usually has a variable speed system on it in preference to a one-speed direct drive wheel because a free-moving wheel is an advantage in model and

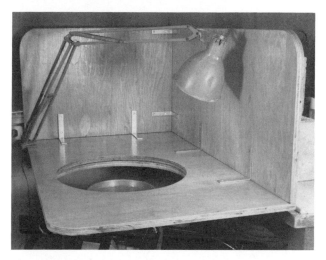

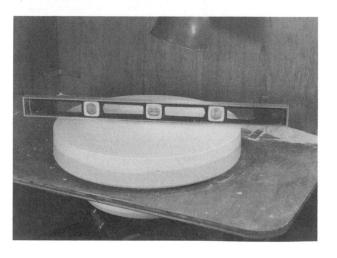

Fig. 2.20 A Randall kick wheel with motor drive attachment was chosen for converting into a plaster wheel. The wheel is shown here prior to conversion.

Fig. 2.21 A new table was made with high back boards to support the tools used in the turning process.

Fig. 2.22 A large head is cast in the head of the potters wheel.

mold making. If the wheel has to be rotated with power everytime it needs to be moved a few degrees, then the direct drive is a considerable handicap.

An ideal plaster wheel should give ample power at all speeds up to perhaps 150 rpm, and be a free wheel when working on a model in detail.

The variable speeds are not often used, however, because the experienced turner can use the wheel effectively at one speed. A speed of 100 rpm is a good speed to work plaster with. However, on the converted Randall kick wheel with motor drive attachment, a constant speed of 100 rpm is difficult to obtain. If the motor drive is continually in contact with the wheel, then the speed of the wheel continues to increase until the wheel is spinning much too fast for turning plaster. Since this modified wheel has the weight of the large plaster head to help maintain momentum, the motor drive can be used sparingly and enough speed for cutting all but the heaviest cutting can be easily maintained. Although this particular aspect of the converted wheel may seem a drawback, it is far preferable to a direct-drive wheel because of the free action of the wheel.

One's adeptness at working with plaster can make the difference between success and failure in producing high-quality, usable molds. The thought of working with plaster seems to arouse one of two reactions in the novice mold maker. The first is that plaster is an invaluable aid to the ceramist, a unique material, ideal for use in creating either a single press-molded piece or a production run for several hundred. The second reaction is that plaster is very messy, it clogs the drains, and is more trouble than it's worth. This book is dedicated, of course, to the former position. Following the procedures outlined in this book should erase any apprehension among newcomers to plaster. "Messes" are easily avoided if simple precautions are taken seriously.

This section has been carefully worked out to assure that the procedures are presented clearly and accurately. It has also been reviewed and approved by the United States Gypsum Company, the foremost producer of plaster in the world.

As we read in Chapter 1, plaster has been known and used for many thousands of years. Today, as in past eras, plaster is indispensable to the ceramic and building materials industries. It is also used extensively in foundries, glass factories, dental labs, and in jewelry making. It is produced in a wide variety of formulations, each having specific characteristics to meet the needs of a specific process or product. By varying the constituents of the plaster and the amount of water added to the mix, plaster can be formed into building materials (e.g., plaster board) or it can be formed into a rock-hard material that can be made water resistant. The plaster of Paris used by the ceramist or sculptor can have the density of a sponge or a stone, depending on how much water is mixed with it.

3

Working with Plaster

HOW PLASTER IS MADE

Historical methods of calcining gypsum differ little, in principle, from modern production methods. Beringuccio's *Pirotechnia*, published in Verona, Italy, in 1540, contains a fine little woodcut of a plaster kiln in use (Figure 3.1). Diderot's *Encyclopaedia*, published in Paris between 1751 and 1765 (about the same time that plaster molds were being adopted in the English

Fig. 3.1 Woodcut from the 9th book of Beringuccio's *Pirotechnia*, published in Italy in 1540. The plaster kiln is on the left; the structure on the right is probably a ceramic kiln. Actual size of the woodcut is 2″ × 4″.

potteries), includes a description of the manufacture of plaster as well as an illustration of a plaster kiln in use (Figure 3.2). This illustration shows a three-chambered plaster kiln. In the chamber at the left, gypsum is being heated or burned to the point of calcination (240° F). The middle chamber is probably cooling down, with the bricked-up end wall partially removed to speed up the cooling process. The chamber at the right is awaiting a load of gypsum.

Gypsum is a white mineral (calcium sulfate) found in deposits in the earth. North America has many deposits of gypsum, but few are large enough for commercial consideration. The United States Gypsum Company operates the world's largest industrial plaster processing facility at Southard, Oklahoma. Briefly, the mining and production process is as follows:

1 After relieving any overburden, the gypsum rock is blasted loose (Figure 3.3).
2 These rough and various-sized pieces of gyp-

sum are then transported to large crushers (Figure 3.4).
3 The crushing is done in several stages. During crushing, the small rock-like pieces of gypsum are screened out to be used in the manufacture of Hydrocal or other gypsum-cement products (Figure 3.5). The final stage is crushing the gypsum to a flour-like texture.
4 The finely ground gypsum, called "landplaster," is then loaded into 30-ton "kettles" and calcined at 240° F (Figure 3.6). During the calcining process, the gypsum is mixed constantly by huge rotors, or sweeps, inside the kettles.
5 The plaster is removed from the kettles, reground to a flour consistency, and normally packaged in 100-pound paper sacks (Figure 3.7).

The process of calcining is carefully controlled to ensure removing the correct amount of water from the crushed gypsum. If the heating of the gypsum is prolonged or is too hot, the end product is termed

Plate 277 Mining Gypsum

Vol. 1, Architecture, Maconnerie, Carrier Platrier.

Fig. 3.2 Gypsum mining and calcining in 18th-century France, as illustrated in Diderot's *Encyclopaedia*.

"dead plaster;" if it is not hot enough, the plaster can be reprocessed correctly.

The formula for pure gypsum is $CaSO_4 \cdot 2H_2O$. The calcining process drives off $1\frac{1}{2}$ molecules of the water of crystallization. The formula is then $CaSO_4 \cdot \frac{1}{2}H_2O$. Calcining produces a product that is 94.12 pounds calcium sulphate and 5.88 pounds combined water per 100 pounds of plaster. When water is mixed with the plaster, causing it to set, the reverse action takes place. The calcium sulphate hemihydrate ($CaSo_4 \cdot \frac{1}{2}H_2O$) recombines with water, reforming the original calcium sulphate dihydrate ($CaSO_4 \cdot 2H_2O$).

The United States Gypsum Company produces more than 30 different types of plaster and gypsum-cements. The term "gypsum-cement" refers to gypsum products that are produced with pressure and heat. Various types of high-strength gypsum-cements are formulated by controlling the exact type of raw materials used and the amount of heat and pressure.

The main difference between plaster and gypsum-cements is easily revealed by comparing the amount of water used to make a typical mix. In plaster, a mix of 70 (70 pounds water to 100 pounds plaster) is typical to produce a usable consistency. In

Fig. 3.3 Modern-day gypsum mining. After the overburden is removed (dark material in background), the gypsum is blasted loose and loaded onto trucks for transport to the processing plant. Courtesy of United States Gypsum Company, Chicago, IL

Fig. 3.4 Gypsum rock is unloaded into the primary crusher at the Southland, Oklahoma plant. Courtesy of United States Gypsum Company, Chicago, IL

Fig. 3.5 Gypsum is sorted by size for use in the manufacture of Hydrocal® gypsum-cement. Courtesy of United States Gypsum Company, Chicago, IL

Fig. 3.6 Kettles, holding up to 30 tons, are used to calcine gypsum in the manufacture of U.S.G. industrial plaster. Courtesy of United States Gypsum Company, Chicago, IL

Fig. 3.7 U.S.G. No. 1 Pottery Plaster is bagged for a trip to the weigh station. Courtesy of United States Gypsum Company, Chicago, IL

gypsum-cement, typical ratios are 45 to 25 pounds water to 100 pounds gypsum-cement, which produces a rock-like product.

PHYSICAL CHARACTERISTICS OF PLASTER MOLDS

In Chapter 1 mention has already been made of a number of features of plaster molds that make them preferable to fired clay molds. The most important differences are that plaster molds do not need to be fired, their shrinkage is not a factor that needs to be normally considered, and they absorb moisture from clay or slip much faster than do fired clay molds. It was the absorptive capacity of plaster that guaranteed it a place in the potteries of earlier centuries for use as press molds and slip-casting molds. Indeed, plaster is the only practical material for slip-casting molds.

Plaster is a boon to the mold maker for a number of other reasons, as well. First of all, it forms a smooth, durable surface suitable for the reproduction of very fine detail. Plaster has no grains or lumps; it is quite plastic at one stage and hard at another, so it can readily be poured, paddled, carved, sanded, and polished. Thus it is the ideal material for working into shapes of all kinds with all manner of surface texture.

Another important physical characteristic of plaster is its coefficient of expansion. Plaster has a low coefficient of expansion, which means that it expands very little after setting. But it *does* expand, however slightly, and this factor must be taken into consideration in the design of one-piece molds. Otherwise, there is the possibility that the mold will not release. For most applications, simple precautions are sufficient to allow a proper release of one-piece molds. However, when the depth of the model requires a very deep mold with almost vertical sides, then the amount of expansion is critical and must be determined before the mold is made. Once the expansion of a particular mix is known, then that mix can be depended upon to react the same way every time. This subject is covered more thoroughly in Chapter 19.

Another factor that deserves further consideration is that plaster molds are subject to wear. This wear is most pronounced in molds used for slip casting; however, even molds for pressing plastic clay soon show evidence of wear, especially if there is any detail in the mold. The finer and more detailed the product, the more wear on the mold. Typically, 25 to 200 pieces can be cast from a single slip mold. If the product is very detailed, then the mold probably will not last 25 uses before a marked diminishing of quality can be seen. The mold should then be discarded.

In using plastic clay, wear on the mold is usu-

ally not noticed until several hundred pieces have been made. In this case, a constant check of the size of the piece is important if quality is to be maintained. The finished pieces will actually increase in size as the mold proceeds to wear. This type of wear is caused by abrasion of clay materials that are harder than gypsum.

A final point: the deflocculants in clay slips may attack the surface of a mold. If the formulation of the slip is incorrect, and if too much deflocculant is used, a dark scum often forms on the surface of the mold and on the cast piece. This can be corrected by reviewing the slip formulation and by correcting the amount of deflocculant.

PREPARING A BATCH OF PLASTER

This section offers a number of general guidelines for the correct mixing of plaster for making molds.

The Plaster Batch Calculator

A plaster batch calculator, produced by the United States Gypsum Company, is enclosed with this book. Learning to use it will greatly simplify the process of determining the correct amounts of plaster and water needed for any particular batch. At first glance, the plaster batch calculator may seem complicated. Actually, it is a very simple device, easily mastered in a few minutes (see the instructions printed on the calculator). Using this calculator will assure high-quality, consistent results time after time.

Some mold shops rely on a chart that tells the amount of plaster to add to an amount of water. This type of chart is satisfactory if only one consistency of plaster is used in the shop. The advantage of the batch calculator is that it determines—in a matter of seconds—the correct amount of plaster and water for *any* desired consistency.

Using the batch calculator makes it unnecessary to resort to premeasured containers for mixing small batches of plaster. If a small batch is required, a simple method is to fill a container with enough water to fill the mold set-up; then weigh the water. One movement of the sliding scale on the calculator will reveal the correct amount of plaster required for that amount of water at your chosen consistency.

In calculating the amount of plaster needed for a specific mold, using the batch calculator will probably yield more plaster than is actually needed to fill the mold set-up. This is correct and not a mistake; more plaster is much better than too little, and the excess is simply thrown away.

The minimum amount of plaster that the calculator can calculate is roughly 5 pounds of plaster and water; that is, 2 pounds of water to 3 pounds of plaster at a consistency of 67, which is a normal ratio to use in mold making.

A final note concerning use of the batch calculator: The batch calculator is based on cubic feet or percentage of a cubic foot to establish the amount of plaster needed. It will take some time and experience to think in terms of cubic feet rather than quarts and gallons. To give you some perspective, a cubic foot of plaster is probably more plaster than will ever be needed in one pour in a studio or small shop. If a cubic foot is needed, it is not a one-person operation. It takes two people to handle this much plaster for pouring molds. Also, the pressure created by this much liquid plaster is tremendous, and the cottles or mold boards must be constructed with this in mind.

One-half cubic foot of plaster is a cylinder approximately 12" high and 8" in diameter— roughly the size of a large plastic bucket. One-half cubic foot of plaster cannot be mixed in one of these buckets; there is no room at the top for mixing. A half cubic foot of liquid plaster weighs slightly more than 50 pounds. This amount of plaster can be lifted and poured into a mold board or cottle by one person, but, nevertheless, 50 pounds of plaster can make one giant-size mess if it is not properly handled.

Consistency

The amount of water used in preparing plaster for mold making will determine the hardness and absorbency of the mold. The less water used, the harder and stronger the mold. The harder the mold, the less absorbent it is. The water/plaster ratio is commonly referred to as "consistency," and it is expressed in parts of water per 100 parts of plaster by weight. That is, a consistency of 70 is 70 parts water by weight

to 100 parts plaster by weight. The number 75 indicates a water/plaster ratio of 75/100, which will produce a softer, less durable mold. The number 65 indicates a ratio of 65/100, which will produce a harder, denser mold. Typical consistencies in mold making range from 60 to 75. At values much lower than 60, the plaster is no longer workable as a mold. (The plaster batch calculator lists recommended consistencies for various types of plaster.)

"Peaking" and Using Premarked Containers

Many people are familiar with the routine of sifting plaster into a container of water until the plaster "peaks"—that is, until the amount of plaster that is sifted through the fingers forms a mountain of plaster in the water with the "peak" rising above the water surface. This procedure for arriving at the right proportions of plaster and water is standard in producing plaster to be used for sculpture because consistency is not of major consequence.

In a mold shop, or in making molds that are to be used for producing ceramics, the requirements are much more stringent. If a two-piece drain mold is made with different plaster-to-water ratios for each side, then the mold will produce a drain casting that has one side thicker than the other. A very unsatisfactory mold will result because of this variation. Even when making press molds or drying batts, a standard consistency of plaster will produce higher-quality results, and the mold or batt will have a longer useable life. What often happens in the peaking procedure is that the worker is distracted or interrupted and he loses track of how much plaster is being sifted into the water. When sifting is resumed, the proper "peaking" can never be obtained because the plaster has become saturated and loses its "mountain" formation in the water.

Granted, it is a nuisance to weigh small amounts of plaster every time a small batch is needed. However, the importance of consistency makes it mandatory that a standard be maintained. By using two plastic containers that have been marked for the amounts of water and plaster needed for small batches, the correct consistency of every batch can be maintained. Plastic containers are plentiful, and it is easy

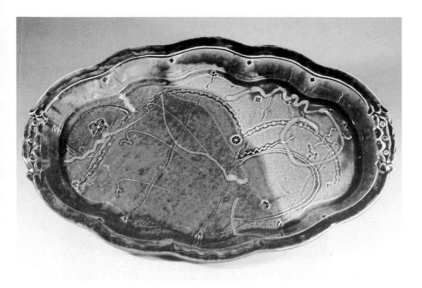

Scott Frankenberger, Battle Ground, Ind. "Platter," 2"x15"x20". Made in a Styro-foam press mold.

Pressed tile from the Starbuck-Goldner Studio, Bethlehem, Pa. Right: Petal Pattern; below: Double Curves.

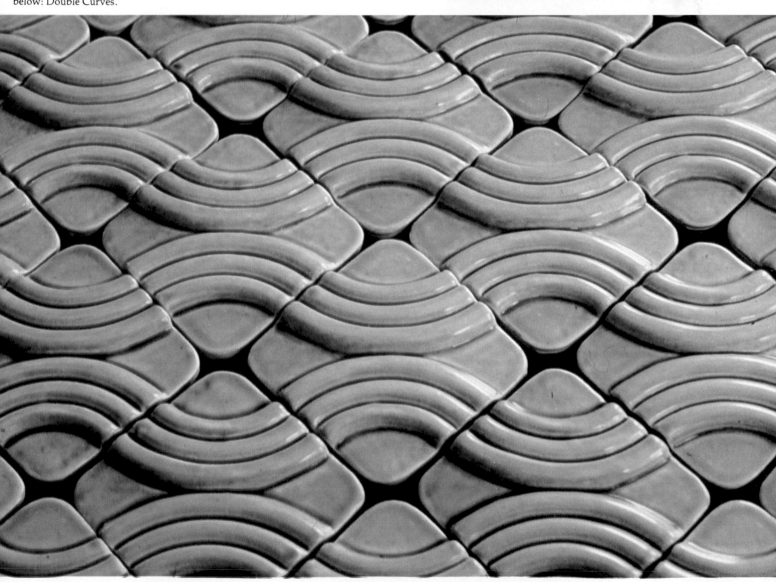

Paula Winokur, Horsham, Pa. "Gothic Lady." The artist uses a face mold to create her "dream boxes." The same mold is used for each face, but the facial characteristics are altered while the porcelain is still very plastic. Small press molds are used to embellish the area surrounding the face. The rest of the box is slab built.

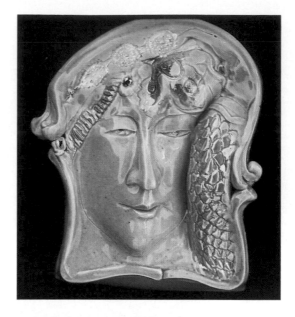

Thomas Hoadley, Pittsfield, Mass. Press-molded Nerikomi jar, 11" h. Nerikomi is a Japanese technique that starts with combining colored clays into a block from which thin slices are cut. Each slice bears the pattern of the "marbled" colored clays. The clay slices are pressed into a two-piece plaster mold, the mold is assembled, and the jar is luted together.

Andrea Gill, Kent, Ohio. "Vine Leaf Vase," 30"x20"x8". "All of my work is earthenware cone 04. Pieces are constructed out of press-molded parts that are hand built together. There is no slip casting involved. The molds are formed from clay shapes, cast with a thin face coat of plaster, a layer of burlap strips soaked in plaster, and covered with another thin layer of plaster. The thickness needs to be only about ³/₄". The areas where the parts fit together are thicker to allow for a good sized set of keys, as large molds require larger keys.

Ron Fondaw, Miami, Fla. Top: "Pressed Tile," 18"x18"; bottom: "Oatt," 21"x27"x7". "A combination of techniques are used for the construction of my work. I begin with a plaster mold which is assembled from many pieces, some cast and some cut out on a band saw. Into the mold I apply a veneer of porcelain slip, into which I cut out and inlay colored slips and/or oxides. I then press in rough clay of different tones. This is fired to a temperature of approximately 2100° F (cone 01). In this firing some of the veneer peels away. Next the Egyptian paste is inlaid and glaze is applied to some of the areas and fired to 1800° F (cone 07)."

to keep two or three matching marked sets in the shop.

One procedure that is even faster is to use two matching containers, one for plaster, which is always to be filled to the rim, and one for water, which has a hole pierced in the side at the level that gives the proper proportion of water for the filled plaster container.

Both these procedures eliminate weighing yet assure the correct ratio of water to plaster.

Stages of Setting

Plaster goes through several different stages after it is mixed with water, and the succession is a rapid one. It quickly changes from a liquid to a plastic material, then to a near solid when it can no longer be manipulated by hand, and then to the final set-up where crystallization takes place and heat is generated.

The plastic stage is the "workable" stage, when the plaster can be manipulated as desired. It can be paddled into shape or carved quickly with large tools that scoop away the "cheesy" plaster. Once the plaster enters the final set-up stage, it should not be paddled, hammered, or given other rough treatment because of the danger of cracking the plaster.

One must become familiar with the normal set-up time of the plaster and learn to work with it in making molds. However, at times it is advantageous either to accelerate or retard the setting time with the use of additives. For accelerators, the Unites States Gypsum Company suggests potassium sulphate or terra alba (ground) gypsum. Common table salt can also be used as an accelerator. Recommended retarders are U.S.G. Commercial Plaster Retarder or U.S.G. Sodate Retarder. Sodium citrate, obtainable at most pharmacies, is the ingredient used in U.S.G. Sodate Retarder. Sodium citrate is very effective and is used only in minute quantities. Accelerators and retarders should only be used when truly necessary, however, because they all weaken the casting.

The Mixing Routine

One of the most important things you can do to help assure success in working with plaster is to establish a proper mixing routine and repeat this routine every time you mix plaster. The following guidelines should be used in setting up a successful routine:

1 *Always use a clean container to mix the plaster in.* Many suitable plastic pouring pails are available. It is always easier to pour from a spout than from the edge of a standard pail. Another excellent container for mixing is an old fashioned, galvanized coal bucket. To facilitate easy clean up, it is a good idea to treat the container with a coating of WD40, silicon spray, or one of the excellent mold-release sprays. Spray on a light coat, then rub it off.

2 *Always weigh out the water first and then add the correct amount of plaster by weight.* No matter how much experience a mold maker has, the correct ratio can be achieved only by weighing. Normally room-temperature water is fine. The cooler the water, the slower the set; the warmer the water, the faster the set. (Some shops use softened, deionized water at a constant temperature.)

3 *It is always better to make the plaster batch larger than necessary and discard the excess plaster after the pour.* It is a good idea to save the sacks that the plaster comes in. Tear off the top completely and place the sack near the pouring so that after the pouring is made the excess plaster can be poured directly into the empty sack. Then proceed to clean up by rinsing and scrubbing the plaster bucket in a rinse tank, *not a sink!*

4 *Never put large amounts of plaster into the water without sifting the plaster through the fingers or a very coarse sieve.*

5 *Always time the procedure so that each mixing and pouring is the same.* The actual mixing time will vary between 2 and 5 minutes, depending on the density of the mix. However, a 2-minute "slake" or soak period is required before mixing can begin. This slake period is important because it permits the plaster to become completely saturated with the water prior to mixing.

6 *Hand mixing of plaster is satisfactory for batch weights under 5 pounds; any batch over 5 pounds should be power mixed.*

7 *In hand mixing small amounts of plaster, it is essential to stir the plaster quickly, yet not forcefully enough to whip air into the mix.* It is usually best to place the hand near the bottom of the bucket and move the fingers rapidly in an oval pattern. Do not stir so that the hand comes out of the bucket with each stroke.

8 *A mechanical mixer must be powerful enough to thoroughly mix the saturated plaster and water within 2 to 5 minutes. But the mixing action must not be so vigorous as to force air into the mixture.* Whenever the mixing action creates a marked vortex or whirlpool effect, air is likely to be entrapped in the plaster and the mold will contain air pockets. If splashing occurs, the mixing action is definitely too vigorous. Some experienced plaster workers like to hand mix the final 30 seconds of mixing in order to feel the consistency with their fingers.

For a comparison of a number of different power mixers, see the separate section on mechanical mixing devices later in this chapter.

9 *If high-quality molds using a high-density mix are required, then mixing under vacuum is recommended.* If plaster is mixed in a vacuum, then there is no danger of entrapping air in it. A number of manufacturers offer mixing machines that provide a vacuum during mixing. The resulting molds are absolutely without pinholes, and the life of the mold is considerably increased.

10 *Plaster is ready to pour at the moment mixing is complete.* "Marking" is a traditional, and usually trustworthy, method for judging when the plaster is ready to pour. When a finger trailed over the surface of the plaster leaves a slight wake or trail, that is the moment to pour the plaster. To produce high-quality molds, it is important to learn the exact amount of mixing time it takes to produce the desired result. Once the "moment to pour" is established by experience, then mold quality is relatively simple to maintain. With further experience, however, both early and late pouring techniques can be used to advantage.

11 *The pouring action should be smooth and steady, without interruption.* If the batch is large, it is often better to pour rapidly against a board placed into the mold set-up so that the plaster does not hit the mold

boards with too much force. Pouring plaster against a board or shaft of some sort before it hits the mold form disperses the stream of plaster without causing bubbles. Some mold makers agitate the table while the plaster is being poured. This habit is excellent, but it takes practice. After the pour, the table should be agitated with the hip to force air from the plaster.

12 *After the pour, the plaster should be opaque and the surface should turn glossy; the glossiness soon disappears and the surface becomes dull as the plaster begins to set.* A word of caution: Heat is generated as plaster sets, and proper caution is always warranted. In a large batch of plaster, the internal temperature reaches over 150° F, high enough to cause serious burns. Although this warning may seem to overemphasize the danger, every year people are burned by hot plaster.

13 *If water rises to the surface of the plaster after the pour, this indicates that the plaster has not been mixed sufficiently or that the water-to-plaster ratio is not correct.* The problem of rising water is rather common, but it must not be ignored if quality is to be maintained. To eliminate the problem, the first step is to mix a little longer and more thoroughly. If that doesn't correct the problem, then a review of the water-to-plaster ratio is called for. Both the correct mixing time and correct consistency are important for quality work.

14 *Normal clean up.* Discard the excess plaster in the mixing container into a suitable trash container or an empty plaster sack; then wash the mixing container off in a primary rinse water. A production shop would have several plastic plaster mixing containers and would not wash the container after use, but would let the plaster set fully and then clean the container by bending the plastic. Clean up should be as thorough as the rest of the mixing procedure. Old, hard plaster left on containers or equipment can flake off and fall into a batch of plaster. These hard pieces of plaster act as accelerators and speed up the setting action of the new batch. If hard pieces of plaster wind up on the working surface of the mold, the mold will not respond correctly and the casting will be flawed.

15 *Emergency clean up.* Sometimes when pouring plaster, something goes wrong and liquid plaster is suddenly everywhere except where it should be. The easiest way to clean up such a mess is to let the plaster set until it is cheesy. Then take a large scraper and scrape large quantities of the plaster into a waste bucket. The plaster is most easily handled when it has just begun to set up. Work rapidly to get all the plaster into the waste container. If a cottle or mold board has slipped, causing the plaster to escape, the cottle or mold boards must be cleaned thoroughly and prepared again, because any old plaster left on them will flaw the new mold.

If liquid plaster is accidentally spilled onto clothes, the cloth should be flooded with water to dilute the plaster before it hardens into the fibers.

16 *It is best not to use old plaster that has been sitting around the shop for 3 to 6 months.* Plaster is dated on the sack, and if the plaster is over 6 months old, the set and working time will change, as will the consistency, but the quality of the plaster after set will not be altered. If it sits open in a room, plaster has a tendency to take on water and become lumpy; it should not be used.

17 *Pouring new plaster onto old plaster produces an area on each side of the bond that is harder than either pouring. This must be taken into consideration whenever you pour fresh plaster onto old.* New plaster adheres to old plaster very well, especially if the old plaster is moistened and roughened. However, the old plaster absorbs water from the new plaster and, therefore, causes it to become harder at the bonding surface. When making large drying batts or thick press molds, this factor is of little concern. However, in repairing molds or in model making, the difference in hardness created by pouring one layer onto another is totally unsatisfactory.

The way to avoid this is to plan an interlocking system on the first layer so that when the second layer is poured, it will be held in place by a physical lock. Seal the surface of the first layer as you would do in casting a two-piece mold. The result is a surface that has no hard areas in it, and one that can be worked or used without problems. This technique is especially important in model making where pieces need to be added without affecting the character of the plaster.

18 *Plaster can be tinted to reduce eye strain.* White plaster is quite beautiful, but there are occasions where the whiteness or glare makes it difficult to see contours or a seam between two layers of plaster. To help overcome this problem, plaster can be tinted to enable a clear definition of two layers of plaster. One of the easiest stains to use is Rit fabric dye. Simply add a suitable color dye (royal blue or bronze green) to the mixing water until the water is quite dark, then proceed with the mixing. The result is a pastel-colored plaster on which it is easier to see separation lines and details.

MECHANICAL MIXING DEVICES

Mechanical mixing is commonly done using a variable speed electric motor. In the professional mold shop, the mixing unit is permanently mounted on a device that enables the mixer to be lowered into the mixing container at the correct angle for efficient mixing and then raised, out of the way, after the mixing is completed. The Lightnin® Mixer, supplied by the Mixing Equipment Company (see Sources of Supplies), seems to be standard. Until recently, the standard impeller for these mixers was a three-blade, 25°-pitch propeller, available in various diameters. In 1983, the Mixing Equipment Company introduced the A310 mixing impeller. A three-bladed impeller with blades resembling the wings of a jet plane, it is 50% more efficient than a regular impeller. The A310 design will undoubtedly replace the standard three-blade propeller.

A Lightnin variable speed mixer with an A310 impeller of the proper diameter would be the ideal mixer for all plaster mixing. However, mechanical mixing can be successfully accomplished using less "sophisticated" methods. One method is to use a variable-speed drill, which can be purchased for under $40.00. A $\frac{3}{8}$" or $\frac{1}{2}$" drill chuck should be chosen in preference to a $\frac{1}{4}$" sized chuck if a new drill is purchased. The larger chuck accepts a larger-diameter shaft for mixing, and the larger diameter shaft has less tendency to vibrate and will maintain its straightness better than a $\frac{1}{4}$"-diameter shaft.

The main drawback to power drills is that at 1200 rpm (the usual maximum speed) and with the

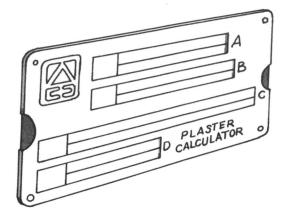

1. *Calculate correct quantities of water and plaster for desired consistency and mold size. All calculations are in pounds.*

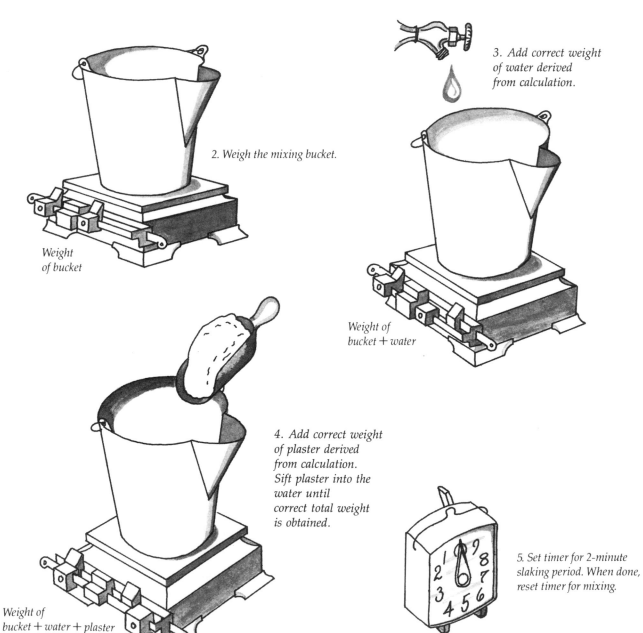

2. *Weigh the mixing bucket.*

Weight of bucket

3. *Add correct weight of water derived from calculation.*

Weight of bucket + water

4. *Add correct weight of plaster derived from calculation. Sift plaster into the water until correct total weight is obtained.*

Weight of bucket + water + plaster

5. *Set timer for 2-minute slaking period. When done, reset timer for mixing.*

Fig. 3.8 Preparing a batch of plaster

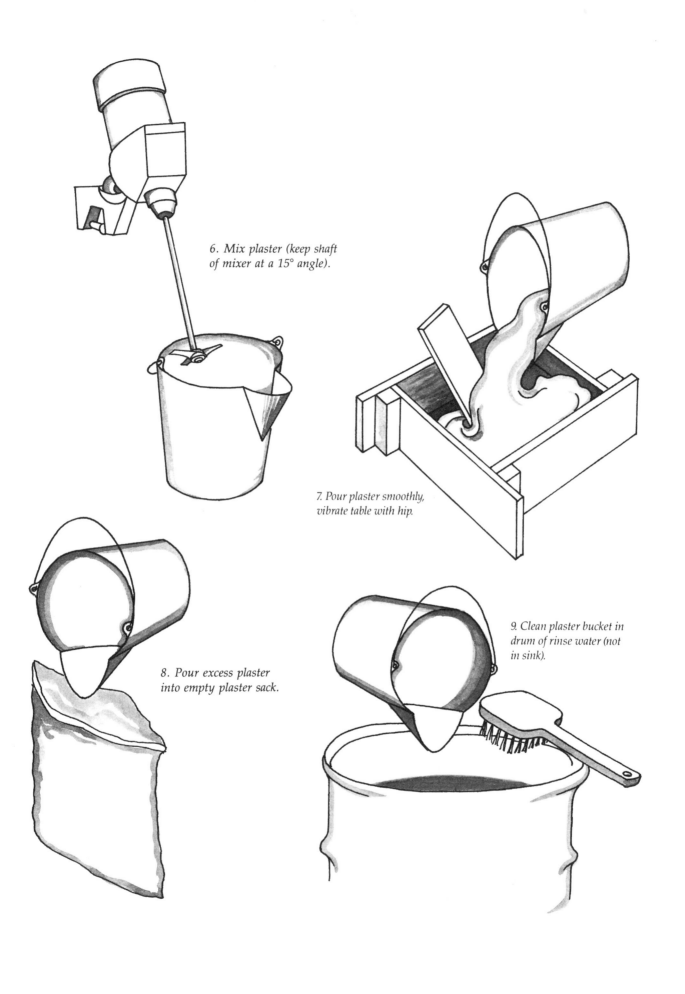

6. Mix plaster (keep shaft of mixer at a 15° angle).

7. Pour plaster smoothly, vibrate table with hip.

8. Pour excess plaster into empty plaster sack.

9. Clean plaster bucket in drum of rinse water (not in sink).

standard 3″, three-blade propeller, they simply do not mix larger batches of plaster (over 50 pounds) fast enough. They are effective for mixing small batches, but to efficiently mix 50 pounds at this rpm, a larger-diameter propeller is needed, and these are usually available only from professional suppliers.

Several other types of readily available (or readily fabricated) propellers were tested for their mixing effectiveness. They were all tested using a ⅜″ variable speed electric drill and a ⅜″ × 24″ stainless steel shaft that was tapped on the end to accept nuts and washers if necessary. The propellers tested are shown in Figure 3.9.

The first type of propeller tested was a Sears paint mixer, consisting of a ¼″ × 12″ shaft with two three-blade propellers placed 3″ apart on the shaft. The first propeller is at the end of the shaft, and the second is 3″ above it. This is an excellent mixer for gallon cans of paint. As is, it is ineffective in mixing plaster in any amounts over about 1 gallon. However, by increasing the pitch of the blades to an angle approaching 30° or more, the mixer is much more effective. (The blades are aluminum and can be bent

with a pliers.) One must make sure the angle of both propellers forces the plaster down. Nevertheless, the short narrow-diameter shaft limits the effectiveness of this mixer.

The second type propeller was the standard 3″-diameter, 25°, three-blade impeller described earlier. This impeller is effective for most studio mixing, the only disadvantage being that to be really effective the rpm of the shaft should be higher than the drill motor can supply. There are two ways to achieve really good mixing at 1200 rpm with this style of propeller. One is to purchase a larger-diameter propeller. The other is to add a second 3″ propeller about 4″ up the shaft from the first. Either of these methods will produce a mixer that is very effective for almost any size batch of plaster.

The third type of propeller tested was the rubber disk type. A 5″-diameter disk proved to be tricky to use. It did not compare to the impeller-type mixer for effective mixing.

The fourth type of mixer was the A310 impeller fitted on the ⅜″ shaft of the drill. At speeds approaching 1200 rpm, this propeller mixed plaster quicker and more efficiently than did the standard 3″ blade propeller. This design is excellent for any mixing, and it is much more efficient than normal propellers. The only drawback to the A310 impeller is that, due to the design of the blades, it could cut through plastic buckets with ease if not operated with adequate caution. One model in the A310 series of impellers comes with a ring guard around the ends of the blades, and this model would be a good choice for purchase when one is seriously setting up a mold making facility.

The fifth type of propeller tested was a rubber propeller made from ⅛″-thick rubber sheet. Three identical 2″ × 4″ rectangles were cut from the rubber. The rectangles were then epoxied together in a slightly spiral shape (see Figure 3.9). A ⅜″ hole was drilled into the exact center of the propeller, and it was fitted onto the ⅜″ shaft of the drill. This simple-to-make mixing blade was very successful, especially at low speeds. Small amounts of plaster could be mixed quickly and large amounts (over 5 gallons) could be handled with ease. This propeller will wear out over time, but for general studio or individual use, it seems to be quite satisfactory.

Fig. 3.9 Five mixing impellers for mixing plaster. From left to right: The new A310 impeller from Mixing Equipment Company; the standard 3″ propeller from Mixing Equipment Company; a rubber disk for mixing plaster from Permaflex Company; a typical paint mixer as purchased; an impeller made from ⅛″ sheet rubber. On the right is the ⅜″ shaft used with all impellers, except the paint mixer.

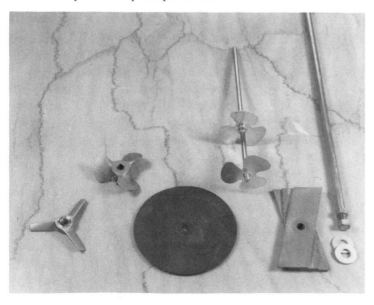

One mixer that was not tested is the one that looks like a cage, with two mixing rings connected by vertical mixing vanes. Generally, this is an excellent design, but for plaster mixing it seems that it would be difficult to keep clean. With an open impeller, cleaning the blades is accomplished easily by immersing the mixing shaft in the rinse barrel and running it for a moment.

If the power mixer forces the plaster mix out of the container, it is possible that the motor is turning in the wrong direction (reverse) or that the pitch or angle of the propeller blades is reversed. The mix should be forced down, whether mixing is done by hand or with a mechanical mixer. Waves of plaster should never come out of the container during any mixing procedure. *All mixing action should force the material down, not up.*

The guidelines presented in this chapter should be considered as guidelines to freedom. These are guidelines that will open the way to successful, satisfying work with plaster. Detailed routines of how to make and use plaster molds follow in the next chapters. For the most part, two plaster products are used, both from United States Gypsum Company; they are Puritan Pottery Plaster for mold and model making and Ultracal #30 for case making. In some instances, Georgia Pacific K 59 Industrial Plaster was used because its off-white color was an advantage in photographing certain procedures.

Part II: Press Molds

Dick Evans, Milwaukee, Wis. "Landscape Bowl," 15" dia. Thin pieces of porcelain are built up on the surface of a bisque-fired hump mold. The mold is thrown on the wheel, trimmed smooth, and fired. The foot is thrown directly on the piece.

POSITIVE AND NEGATIVE FORM

Mold makers work with the concepts of "positive" and "negative" form every day: their basic routine consists of reproducing a positive three-dimensional model (cup, plate, sculpture, etc.) by making a negative image of it (the mold) and then casting or pressing the final positive product. If this were all there is to positive and negative forms, there would be little room for confusion over the terms and little interest in positive and negative form as an area for creative expression. However, many variations in the use of positive and negative forms are open to the clay artist working with molds, and the interplay of positive and negative form represents an area rich with creative possibilities.

Exploring positive and negative form is a good starting point for experiencing some of the possibilities inherent in using molds. In addition, it provides an opportunity to introduce one of the most ancient systems of surface decoration: the stamp.

Figures 1.13 and 1.14 in Chapter 1 show Roman stamps used to impress an image into a clay mold. Stamps similar to these, made of metal or clay, were used to produce the magnificently detailed Arretine bowls of the Roman Empire. In this case, the steps were model, mold, product; that is, the stamp is the model; the bowl-shaped mold with the negative impression of the stamp is the mold; and the product is the bowl bearing a positive relief figure that is the exact image of the stamp.

Consider now the stamps shown in Figure 4.1. These are Egyptian stamps dating from perhaps 500 years before the Roman stamps discussed above. These stamps are not positive. They are negative forms made by pressing a little ball of clay over a fired clay model. The results on the product are the same as in the Arretine ware, because the negative stamp is used directly on the surface of the piece of pottery, producing a positive relief on the product. The Roman stamp is one step further removed from the end product. Elementary as these procedures seem, it often takes careful thought to determine how to proceed in producing the desired end product using a system of molds.

Stamps and Sprigg Molds

Fig. 4.1 A group of fired clay press molds from Egypt, dating from after the 4th century B.C. These molds were probably used as sprigg molds rather than stamps. Courtesy of The Oriental Institute, University of Chicago

MAKING A STAMP

The photographs in this chapter show the procedure for making positive and negative stamps and their use in decorating a clay surface. Plaster is the ideal material for a stamp because it is easily worked, it makes a clean impression in the clay, and it is easily separated from the clay.

The first step is to make a plaster blank from which the stamp will be carved. Figure 4.2 shows a blank being made by partially filling a plastic cup with plaster. When small amounts of plaster are

needed, it is best to mix more plaster than required for the particular job and use the excess plaster to make plaster batts or sheets for future use. The reason is that very small amounts of plaster and water are difficult to weigh precisely enough to assure the correct consistency, nor are small amounts usually mixed long enough. By mixing a larger batch, it is easier to maintain a correct ratio of plaster to water (small errors make less of a difference) and to achieve thorough mixing. When making a plaster blank for a stamp, the amount of plaster actually mixed should be perhaps three or four times what is needed for

Fig. 4.2 A plastic cup is partially filled with plaster to form a blank for the positive mold. Excess plaster is poured into the mold form in the background.

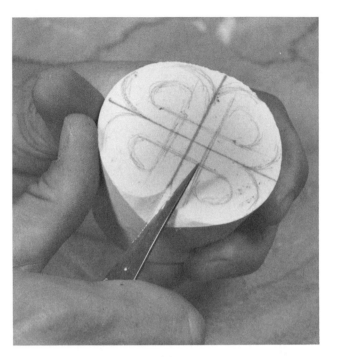

Fig. 4.3 After the plaster blank is filed flat, a pattern is drawn on it and carved with a sharpened potters knife.

the cup. In this instance, the excess plaster was poured into the mold set-up seen in the background of Figure 4-2. Thin sheets of plaster are used as templates in mold making (see Chapter 15). These thin sheets of plaster are made by pouring excess plaster directly on the marble surface of the work table. After the plaster has set up, the thin sheet is stored away for future use.

After the plaster blank has set, it is removed from the cup and filed flat with a Sureform blade. Then the desired pattern for the stamp is drawn on the level surface with an indelible pencil. The pattern for this stamp is derived from themes common to many cultures. It can be described as a knot or as an endless over-under double line. Many cultures have developed this sort of decoration to a high degree of refinement. Numerous pattern books are available to anyone interested in learning about the history of pattern or in adopting traditional patterns for per-

sonal expression. Myer's *Handbook of Ornament* (Dover Press) is an excellent book filled with handsome line drawings of historic decorative patterns.

The first step in establishing this knot design on the stamp is to divide the available space into quarters. The next step is to repeat the pattern four times, once in each quarter. Then the carving begins. Figure 4.3 shows how the pattern is carved into the plaster blank with a sharpened potters (fettling) knife. After the general shape has been carved as a positive form, the over-under character of the lines is carved. The main carving tool is the sharpened fettling knife. The carving is further refined with small steel potters trimming tools, scrapers, and sandpaper. Figure 4.4 shows the completed carving.

In carving a positive design for a stamp, it is important that there be no undercuts or rough areas in the carving that will prevent the stamp from being easily withdrawn from the clay. Look carefully at the carved design in Figure 4.4 and notice the beveled surface behind the carved lines. This surface reflects the design and produces a secondary image that will become apparent upon pressing the stamp into clay.

The stamp created by the carving is a positive form; that is, the design stands out in relief. When a positive stamp is pressed into clay, the result is a negative form. To emphasize the difference between positive and negative, another mold is made, using this positive stamp as a "model" and a plastic cup as the mold form. First the positive stamp is dressed with mold soap and polished slightly with a cloth.

To "dress the mold" means to seal the surface so that after plaster has been poured over it and has set, the model and mold will separate. English Crown Soap is commonly used for this purpose, but a number of other excellent products are also available (see Sources of Supplies). To dress the mold, the mold soap is thinned with water and applied with a natural sponge; then a lather is worked up and rinsed off with water. This process is repeated three times. After the third application and rinse, the surface of the model is burnished to a waxy shine with a cloth. The dressing can be tested by putting a drop of water on the surface of the plaster. The water should bead up and not disappear into the plaster. If the water does not bead, repeat the dressing and rinsing process

Fig. 4.5 After the positive relief is dressed with mold soap, a plastic cup (minus the bottom) is fitted snugly over it as a cottle for casting the negative stamp.

Fig. 4.4 The finished carving, after refinement with scrapers and sandpaper.

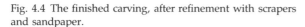

until it does. If the mold soap is not *thoroughly* rinsed off, the plaster may have a spongy consistency. Dressing a mold or model is mentioned repeatedly in this text because it is one process that beginning mold makers seem to fail to do successfully; with the result that their models and molds are difficult to separate.

After dressing the mold, a plastic cup is wedged onto it and plaster is poured into the cup (Figure 4.5). After the plaster has hardened and is cool to the touch, the cup is removed. Figure 4.6 shows the two molds after they have been separated. These molds represent a positive and a negative image of the same design. As soon as the plaster is sufficiently dry, the molds are ready to use.

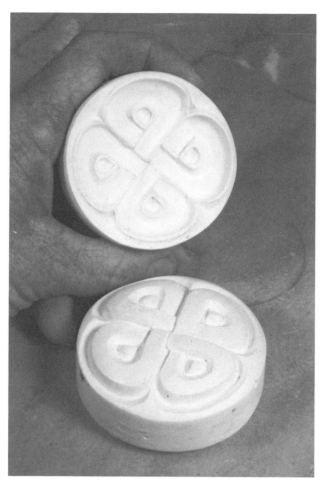

Fig. 4.6 When the plaster has hardened, the molds are separated. The result is two stamps—a positive and negative image of the same design.

THE STAMPING PROCESS

The form to be decorated (either thrown or slab) is first marked off into equal parts to assure correct placement of the stamp. The divisions are made by lightly scoring with a potters knife. Figure 4.7 shows the scorings and how the stamp is placed against the clay surface. A registry mark at the top edge of the stamp assures the correct orientation of the image. A registry mark, which is especially important when stamping an all-over, repeat design, can be made with indelible pencil (as shown), or it can be carved into the plaster.

In this example, the negative press mold is being used to impart a positive image to the clay surface.

In spite of its name, the press mold is not pressed forcefully into the clay. In fact, the opposite must occur: the clay is pressed into the mold. The distinction is an important one because one method means success and the other leads to difficulty in achieving a quality product. On the initial contact of stamp and clay, the stamp is pressed *slightly* into the clay surface, but then all pressing action from the outside ceases. This initial pressure will distort the piece slightly. Now the hand on the inside of the

Fig. 4.7 A thrown form is marked off into equal parts to assure correct placement of the stamp. First the negative mold is pressed lightly onto the surface of the clay, but thereafter all pressing is from the inside, into the mold.

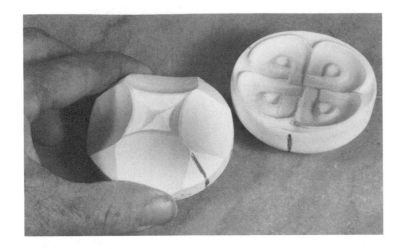

Fig. 4.8 A design is carved on the back of one of the stamps in order to fill the spaces left between the repeating circles.

Fig. 4.9 The little design is used to achieve an all-over pattern. Note the registry mark on the stamp.

piece pushes the clay into the mold. The stamp is held steady while the fingers of the inside hand fill every detail of the stamp with clay.

Withdrawing the stamp from the clay surface after pressing is sometimes tricky. If the stamp sticks into the clay and is difficult to remove, wait a short while so that the plaster has more time to absorb moisture from the clay. Then attempt to remove the stamp. It should withdraw without difficulty, and the next pressing should go more quickly.

In Figure 4.7 a registry mark can be seen on the top edge of the mold stamp. This mark is necessary to assure the features of the design are orientated according to the desired effect. It is especially important that a registry mark be used when stamp-

Fig. 4.10 The positive mold is used on another thrown form in the same manner as the negative stamp, but it creates an indented, rather than raised, design.

ing all-over, repeat designs such as this one. This mark is made with an indelible pencil; however, any indication, such as a carved line or a notch, serves just as well.

In stamping an all-over pattern using a round design, a space is created between the repeating circles. In Figure 4.8, the back side of one of the stamps is carved with an image to fill that space. Figure 4.9 shows the use of this "filler" design. It is lightly pressed into the clay surface at the correct position, and the clay is fully pressed into the stamp from inside the piece.

In Figure 4.10, the positive stamp has been used to decorate another thrown form with negative images. Even though this piece was not as fully pressed as the other, it is readily apparent that the negative stamping produces a very strong pattern in which the "negativeness" all but disappears. This visual

Fig. 4.11 Three stamped pieces, one made with a negative stamp (left foreground) and two with positive stamps. Both types of stamps produce a strong relief pattern.

effect of strong positive relief created with negative impressions is also evident in the piece on the right in Figure 4.11, and it is one of the main points to be made in this section. It is often not entirely clear just how some pressed designs are created—that is, whether they were made with positive or negative press molds. Hopefully, by reviewing this presentation, the artist can apply the different effects of positive and negative stamping to create more inventive and personal decorative pieces of his or her own.

PRESSING DEEP RELIEFS

One stamping method that works successfully is to initially press all the designs into the clay very lightly, and then repeat the pressing. On the second pressing, press the stamp fully. If the design is a very deep relief, then perhaps three or even four pressings will be required. The registry mark on the stamp is essential for repeated pressings. Such multiple pressings are required to get deep relief. A single pressing could stretch the clay wall to the breaking point. Also, in a single deep press, the stamp will stick into the clay surface quite firmly and a long wait will be required for the stamp to free itself from the clay.

With a small amount of practice and a lot of

ideas for three-dimensional patterns, it is easy to press very deep relief patterns. It is also possible to press positive and negative forms on the same piece, relating the designs so that their combined effect is one of very high relief.

Generally speaking, the deeper the relief on the stamp, the thicker the clay on the piece. The wall of the piece must be stretched into the form on the stamp, and if there is insufficient clay, then the features of the stamp cannot be realized. It is difficult to deeply stamp thin-walled pieces without the clay cracking or splitting. Nevertheless, the decorative possibilities of this cracking and splitting during deep pressing are worth investigating, and this approach might have interesting results.

SPRIGG MOLDS

The mention of sprigg molds automatically brings to mind Wedgwood and Blue Jasper Ware, which ex-

Fig. 4.13 Clay is pressed firmly into every detail of the mold. Excess clay is removed with a scraper or knife, leaving the surface flat and smooth.

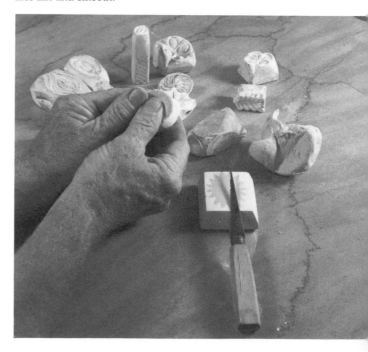

Fig. 4.12 A limestone sprigg mold for decorating pottery, dating from after the 4th century B.C. Courtesy of The Oriental Institute, University of Chicago

Fig. 4.14 The spriggs drop out of the mold in a few minutes and are placed on a damp piece of plaster. The surface of the pot and the back of the spriggs are moistened slightly to assure good bonding.

Fig. 4.15 The sprigg is picked up with a knife blade or damp brush and carefully applied to the pot.

Fig. 4.16 A group of press molds carved from scraps of plaster. The five molds in the foreground are for sprigging. The flat shoulder permits the pressed clay to be scraped level.

emplify the technical mastery of sprigging. Examples of Blue Jasper sprigging can be seen in museums everywhere, and, in fact, they can be purchased in hundreds of retail outlets around the world.

Wedgwood, a Blue Jasper Ware, has come to be a general term for relief decorations applied to a colored body, usually blue. The reliefs have a classical theme and are characterized by incredible detail. Sprigging has a much more ancient past, however. Figure 4.12 shows an Egyptian sprigg mold, made of limestone, dating from sometime after the 4th century B.C. The limestone surface is carved in intaglio fashion to produce decorations for pottery. The stone is relatively soft and absorbent and can be carved with harder materials such as flint or basalt.

The sprigging technique presented in this chapter differs little from that employed by Wedgwood. Wedgwood used intaglio metal molds to create the reliefs; the molds presented here are made from pieces of plaster batt. Of course, much more refined detail can be achieved by using metal molds as opposed to carved pieces of plaster. Yet, hopefully, what is presented here can be directly applied in the studio by almost anyone reading this book.

Figure 4.16 shows a group of press molds made from scraps of plaster. The five molds in the foreground are for sprigging. They were flattened with a file after being carved. This flat shoulder permits the clay to be scraped level with a spatula or a knife so that the sprigg has a flat back that can be applied to the surface of a pot.

Figure 4.13 shows the mold being filled with clay. To ensure the best possible bond between sprigg and pot, the clay used for the spriggs should be similar or identical to that used for the pot. The clay must be pressed firmly into the mold to assure that every detail of the mold is filled. Excess clay is scraped from the mold with a spatula or knife, leaving the surface flat and smooth. In a very short time the small relief is ready to drop out of the mold onto a dampened piece of plaster (Figure 4.14). The spriggs must be kept damp and pliable so they can be applied to the pot. It is best to press all the spriggs needed for the project at once and keep them damp until needed.

The pot in Figure 4.15 has a dark slip on it. Before applying the sprigg, the surface of the pot is dampened so it will act as a binder. The sprigg is picked up with a brush or knife, the back is moistened slightly, and it is placed on the damp surface of the pot. Care must be taken in applying spriggs of contrasting colors to the pot surface, because too much water or scrubbing with a sponge or brush will cause the clays of the spriggs and pot to blend together, spoiling the crispness of the color contrast.

After the sprigg has been applied to the pot, the piece is carefully dried in order to assure a secure bond. If cracks occur, they can be filled with a slip of the same clay body.

Press molds such as these, made from normal consistency plaster, should last about 50 impressions before noticeable wear occurs. The impression of a worn press mold is less sharp, and the detail begins to disappear. When wear occurs on these decorative press molds or sprigg molds, additional use can be derived from them simply by sharpening the carved lines with a knife or scraper.

The possibilities for surface decoration that sprigging offers the clay artist are often overlooked today. Sprigged decorations can be as strong or as delicate as the artist desires. The imagery can be classic or contemporary. The relief can be deep enough for a half-relief figure or it can be delicate enough to indicate translucent flower petals. Sprigging offers a wide range of decorative possibilities, and the entire concept is open to anyone working in clay who is searching for new ways to express ideas.

CHAPTER

5

Hump Molds, Mushroom Molds, and Jacks

HUMP MOLDS

A hump mold is a positive form over which clay is pressed and shaped. Since the process is positive to negative, the inside surface of the end product bears the image and shape of the hump mold, and the outside surface is available for unlimited alteration while the clay is still on the mold.

The hump molds pictured in Figure 5.2 are typical of the many different shapes that might be used in the studio. All of them are solid plaster except the two largest molds, which are hollow. Plaster hump molds the size of these largest ones (approximately 12″ × 12″ × 24″) must be hollow because of the problem of weight. If they were solid, they would be too heavy to use conveniently.

A basic (solid) hump mold is very simple to make. Most of the small hump molds pictured in Figure 5.2 were made by simply pouring plaster into a hemispherical plastic bowl. It is relatively easy to alter the resulting hump mold to any desired shape with a Sureform blade. If a plastic bowl is not available, then a thick bowl can be thrown on the potters wheel, dried, and filled with plaster to produce a satisfactory hump mold. The clay wall of the bowl should be extra thick to withstand the pressure of the liquid plaster.

The procedure for making hollow hump molds is described in detail later in this chapter.

MUSHROOM MOLDS

Mushroom molds are simply hump molds with a "stem." Mushroom molds can be advantageous, depending upon the project. In pressing clay on a flat-backed hump mold, the pressing must end somewhere short of the edge of the mold to permit ready handling of the pressing and the mold. On the mushroom molds, however, the stem permits the clay to be pressed all the way to the edge of the mold, and the edge can be used as a guide to cut away the excess clay. Or the clay can be draped completely over the edge of the mold. Using a long stem and a large batt of clay raises some interesting possibilities for "draped" forms.

Since it is easier to make flat-backed hump molds

Fig. 5.1 Donald E. Frith. Porcelain bowl made by throwing thin sheets of clay onto a hump mold. The foot is thrown on a wheel.

Fig. 5.2 A group of plaster hump molds. The two largest molds are hollow.

than mushroom molds, it is most practical to make a number of hump molds and convert them to mushroom molds as the need arises. The conversion process is a simple one:

First, a circle is drawn on the flat surface of the hump mold, using a compass and indelible pencil. This circle will guide the placement of the locking cavity and the cottle for the stem. Then a cavity is carved into the back of the hump mold (see Figure 5.3). This will serve to lock the stem of the mushroom into the mold. Next, the hump mold is secured in a nest of water-based clay, carefully leveled, and thor-

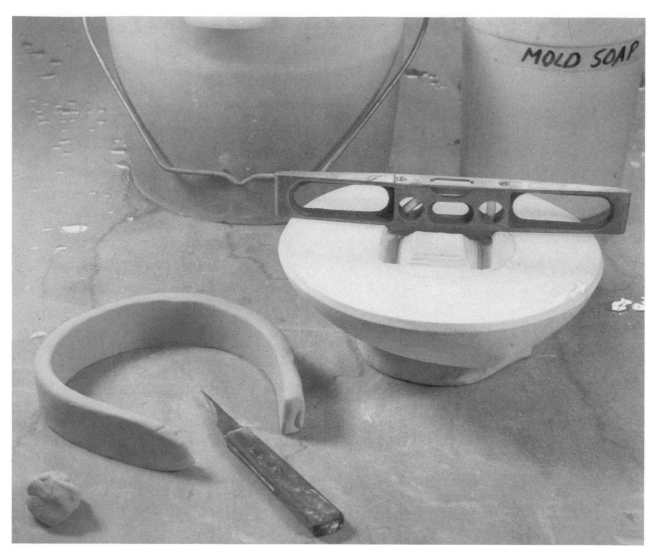

Fig. 5.3 To convert a hump mold to a mushroom mold, a locking cavity must first be carved into the back of the mold. The mold is then secured in a nest of clay, leveled, and dressed with mold soap.

oughly dressed with mold soap. Then a cottle of water-based clay is placed on the circle and filled with plaster (Figure 5.4). After the plaster has set, the cottle is removed and the edges of the hump and stem are beveled with a knife or rasp (Figure 5.5). Then the mold is set aside to dry.

MAKING A HOLLOW HUMP MOLD

The problem in making a large hump mold is that it must be hollow, yet the plaster must be thick enough to properly absorb moisture from the clay and to withstand the pressure of clay being pressed against it. The solution is to build up layers of plaster and fabric over a wire armature and shape the mold with a template. (A Styrofoam core can be used instead of a wire armature; in fact, Styrofoam is an excellent substructure for large hump molds.)

Figures 5.6–5.12 illustrate the procedure for making a regular oval hump mold on a wire armature. The mold is 12″ high, 12″ deep, and 24″ long. First, the profile of the oval base (12″ × 24″) is developed on a large piece of paper folded in quarters.

Fig. 5.4 The clay cottle is put in position and filled with plaster.

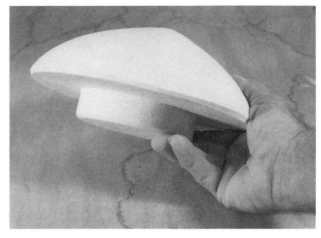

Fig. 5.5 After the plaster has set, the cottle is removed and the edges of the stem and mold are beveled.

(Only one quarter of the oval need be drawn since the shape is symmetrical.) After the one-quarter profile is drawn satisfactorily, cut the paper through all four layers. Unfold the paper pattern, check the accuracy of the oval shape, and correct it if necessary. Refold the pattern and transfer the one-quarter oval outline to a thin sheet of plaster (Figure 5.6). Then cut the plaster profile with a piece of bandsaw blade. Notice in Figures 5.6 and 5.7 that the one-quarter oval is carefully positioned in a corner of the plaster sheet and the outside, straight edges of the template are cut perfectly square so that the oval profile can always be aligned correctly on its axes.

Figure 5.7 shows the axes and the outline of the oval base drawn on the marble table top with a china marking pencil. The axes lines are drawn parallel to the edges of the table, and the oval is placed so that it is easy to work on both sides of it. (In making smaller molds of this type, it is easier to work on a plaster plate, as described in Chapter 7.)

Figure 5.8 shows the clay cottle that is used to form the base of the oval mold. Although the thick walls of the cottle are adequate for retaining liquid plaster, an additional safety measure is taken by wrapping the cottle with nylon cord and securing the end of the cord with half-hitches and a large clip.

The armature for the mold is made out of $\frac{1}{2}$-inch galvanized wire mesh. The mesh is cut into strips measuring about $2\frac{1}{2}'' \times 24''$, and the strips are formed into half-oval shapes conforming to the pattern drawn on the marble surface.

For the base casting, three of the half-oval strips of wire mesh are assembled as shown in Figure 5.8 and fastened with wire pulled from the mesh. A flat piece of mesh is used to reinforce the base of the mold. Notice that the gap between the cottle and the mesh ring is approximately 2 inches. This will be the

Fig. 5.6 The quarter profile for the hump mold is transferred to plaster board and cut with a bandsaw blade.

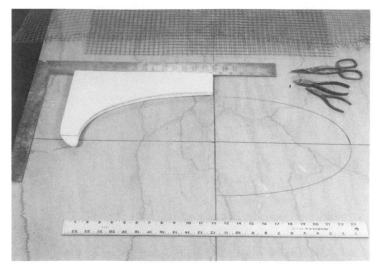

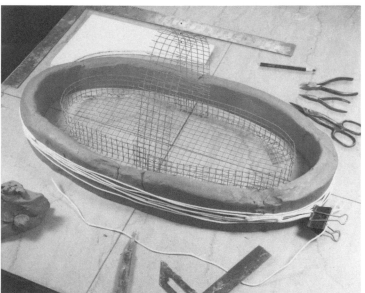

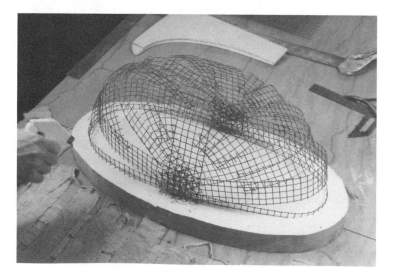

thickness of the plaster in the finished mold. Plaster is now poured into the cottle to form the base for the mold. After the plaster is set, the cottle is removed.

The next step is to complete the armature using more strips of wire mesh that have been formed into half-oval shapes. See Figure 5.9 . Strips of terry cloth toweling are soaked in water, carefully separated, and placed near the mold, ready to be dipped in liquid plaster and put on the armature. This preparation and placement of the cloth strips is very important because they must be applied to the armature quite rapidly. The last preparatory step is to spray the plaster base with water. Although the base should still be rather moist at this point, a final spray of water will assure a good bond between the new and old plaster.

To begin building up the mold, the wet terry cloth strips are soaked in liquid plaster and placed on the mesh armature. Excess plaster is scraped up from around the edge of the base and troweled onto the surface of the mold (Figure 5.10). A second layer of plaster-soaked cloth strips is then applied on top of the first layer. Cheese cloth, not terry cloth, is used for the second layer. The first layer is sprayed with water before the second layer is applied.

In making a large hump mold, whatever the core structure, it is important to use the plaster-saturated fabric strips for the first two layers of the mold because a shell mold of this size needs more structural reinforcement than is provided by the plaster alone. Plaster-saturated fabric is very durable, especially if several layers are used. The first layer is usually made of heavier fabric such as canvas or terry cloth, and the second or final layer can be of a finer fabric such as cheese cloth or an old shirt. Each layer must set up before the next layer is applied, but the whole operation is continuous, and the plaster is kept damp.

After the two layers of plaster-soaked cloth strips have been applied, the mold is covered with two

Fig. 5.7 The axes and outline of the oval are drawn on the marble table top with a china marking pencil.

Fig. 5.8 A clay cottle is secured with nylon cord, and the armature is built up using strips of wire mesh.

Fig. 5.9 After the base is cast, the armature is completed. Water-soaked strips of toweling are arranged for ready access.

more layers of plaster. As each layer is applied, it is carefully shaped by the template. When applying the second and last layer, however, more plaster is applied than necessary so that the excess can be carefully scraped down to the exact shape of the profile while the plaster is still in the plastic stage. Be sure to make the last layer of plaster thick enough so that the final shaping and filing does not expose the layer underneath.

Figure 5.11 shows how a Sureform blade is used to do the final shaping. When used without the handle, the blade can bend according to the curve required. Control of the surface shape is easy to achieve if the template is constantly referred to. As shown in Figure 5.12, the template is placed on the short axis of the oval and rotated from horizontal to horizontal, or 180°. The form created by this profile is actually one half of a flattened sphere. The form itself is quite beautiful.

The finished hollow mold is light enough to permit it to be moved from place to place in the studio. Because of the flat base, it can be set on a wheel head for turning while working, or it can be set on a potters wheel so that a foot can be thrown directly on the pressed piece.

A hump mold of this scale can produce interesting pressed pieces ranging in size from a few inches to the full 24″ length and 12″ width and depth. A clay form of this latter size is already relatively large, and if other forms are added to it, it is easy to produce pieces that exceed 48″ × 24″. This is indeed a large clay form. Of course, it is much easier to use only a portion of a large hump mold to create pieces that are on a scale of 18″ × 12″ or smaller. Pressed forms of this size pose very little problem in assembling, drying, and firing.

A natural follow-up to making a large hump

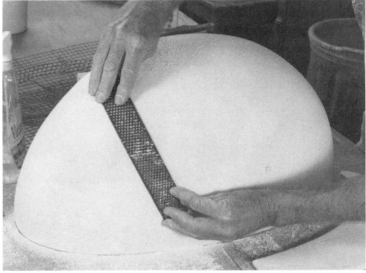

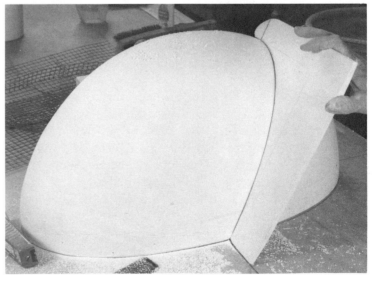

Fig. 5.10 Two layers of plaster-soaked strips of cloth are applied to the wire armature. Excess plaster is scraped up and troweled onto the surface of the mold.

Fig. 5.11 Two layers of plaster are added to the mold. The last layer is thicker than required so that it can be shaped to conform to the template.

Fig. 5.12 To check the shape of the mold, the template is rotated from its axis over the surface of the mold. During planing, the template must be constantly moved from one position to another to check the results.

Fig. 5.13 A thin sheet of porcelain is ready to be thrown or placed on the hump mold. In the upper left is the foot that has been thrown in preparation for assembling the pressed form. The foot is thrown upside down so that the rim can begin to dry and the joining area will stay damp.

mold such as this is to make the negative of the mold. To minimize the weight, the negative mold should be made by building up layers of plaster to form a shell. Casting the negative mold in mold boards set up in a square around the oval hump mold would require a large amount of plaster and would result in an extremely heavy and unwieldy mold. Needless to say, the positive hump mold must be thoroughly dressed with mold soap before work on the negative mold begins.

It would also be possible to cast a negative mold consisting of a series of interlocking rings, each cast upon the other in a clay cottle that rests on the previous cast layer. These plaster rings could serve singly as ring molds or they could be stacked and used as a negative oval mold. To carry this thought one step further, positive hump molds could be cast in layers using the negative ring molds as mold forms. These positive oval-shaped layers could be then used as molds to make products that nest together.

A large hump mold such as this one offers almost unlimited possibilities for creating a variety of pressed, draped, or constructed clay forms. One freeform, "action" approach to using this hump mold is taken in the next section.

HUMP-MOLDED BOWL OF THIN PORCELAIN SHEETS

Figures 5.13–5.15 show the construction of a hump-molded vessel that is built up from small, thin sheets of porcelain that have been thrown out on a plaster batt and then thrown or placed on the mold. The idea behind this approach is to take advantage of the color and translucency of thin sheets of porcelain when fired to maturity and to produce a form that is a direct result of spontaneous actions. This technique might truly be called "action potting" since the spontaneous act of throwing out the clay to make a thin sheet is so apparent in the finished piece.

First the foot or base for the bowl is thrown on a potters wheel. It is thrown upside down so that the end that is to come into contact with the hump-molded piece is at the bottom, on the batt. Figure 5.13 shows the pedestal foot on the batt next to the hump mold.

Next, several pieces of porcelain are thoroughly wedged and formed into small balls of various sizes.

Fig. 5.14 The foot is firmly pressed to the form after several layers of clay have been built up. A small hump mold placed on the foot keeps it from distorting and slows down the drying.

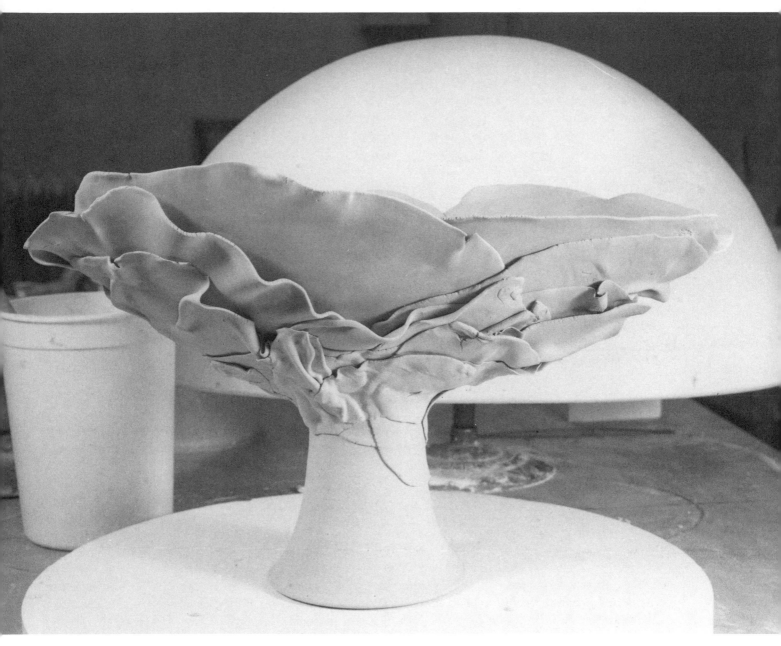

Fig. 5.15 The finished piece can be taken from the hump mold in a short time.

Each ball of porcelain is then rolled out on a plaster batt to a sheet less than $\frac{1}{8}''$ thick. The shape that the sheet of clay takes upon rolling out is left unaltered. Neither the shape nor edges are controlled other than by the rolling action itself. It is important that the porcelain be rolled out on a large batt so that it becomes less plastic as it is worked.

After the sheet of porcelain is rolled out, it is picked up and thrown out onto the surface of the plaster batt in such a way that the sheet spreads thinner and thinner with each throw. To get the desired results, the clay must be carefully thrown toward the batt at a very low angle. Only in this way will the clay spread out and become thinner. Actually, the process of making thin slabs of clay by repeatedly throwing out the clay onto a surface is an ancient one. The phenomena is closely related to the classic way of preparing pizza dough by repeatedly tossing it into the air and catching it in such a way that the dough stretches into a thin, even sheet.

The important feature of this process is not that very thin sheets of clay are made, but that during the thinning process the piece of clay is left unaltered. As the clay becomes thinner, interesting shapes occur and often cracks and holes appear; all these imperfections are left intact. (On the other hand, care must be taken not to completely destroy the sheet during the throwing action.)

The bowl itself is formed by throwing the thin sheets of porcelain against the hump mold. No extra water or slip is used for bonding. The form can be built up rather rapidly, and the delicate sheets of porcelain reinforce each other as more are added. No correcting or altering of the individual sheets is done. Soon the hump-molded piece takes on the appearance of an upside-down cabbage with the leaves opening up.

The foot is put in place after a firm area is made with the sheets of porcelain. The foot is simply pressed onto the pressed clay with no slip added for bonding. When the foot is in position, several more sheets are thrown on to reinforce the joining area and to integrate the foot with the pressed form.

After the form is finished, that is, after you are satisfied with the interesting development of all the various layers, curves, folds, holes, and cracks, the whole piece is misted with water and left to dry. Since the plaster works rapidly on the porcelain, the piece can be taken from the hump mold and inverted to its upright position in a short time. Figure 5.15 shows the completed piece after it has dried sufficiently to be self-supporting. After carefully drying, the piece is ready for the kiln.

JACKS

A jack is a template mounted in some fashion that is used to shape moist plaster. Jacks are commonly used to shape large items such as architectural moldings for building interiors, but they also have a place in the mold shop because they are uniquely adapted to making certain types of molds.

In using a jack, either the jack is moved against the moist plaster, or the jack is stationary and the plaster is moved against it. It sounds simple, but establishing what will move and how is somewhat more complicated when producing, for example, a large model of a boat hull.

In this section, a jack system will be used to produce a six-sided, tapered positive press mold.

The design of the jack pictured in Figure 5.16 is very simple. It is made with plywood and two sturdy shelf brackets. A bracket of the type shown is stronger than a bracket made with flat metal. The scraping action of the jack against the moist plaster demands that the device be sturdy. This jack can be slid along the side of a stationary plaster mold, or it can be secured to the edge of a table with C clamps and the plaster can then be moved against the jack. The template used in this presentation is cut from Plexiglas and inserted into the space between the two upright pieces of plywood. After it is located correctly to produce the desired shape, holes are drilled in the Plexiglas through already existing holes in the wood. Bolts and wing nuts secure the profile plate to the jack. Any number of different templates can be used in this jack.

Next to the jack in Figure 5.16 is a piece of plywood that will be used as the base for the mold. Plaster is placed on the plywood, and the jack is moved back and forth along the edge of the plywood to shape the plaster. The thickness of the plywood used for the base of the jack is the same as the thickness of the plywood used for the base of the mold. These two pieces, the jack and the base of the mold, must slide back and forth against each other easily.

To make a six-sided mold, a six-sided plywood base is prepared (Figure 5.17). A core of Styrofoam is used for the mold. The Styrofoam is cut with a hacksaw blade to a shape that is similar to but smaller than (by at least 1 inch on all sides) the intended mold. A few finish nails are driven into the six-sided base and the Styrofoam is simply pushed over the nails to secure it in position. Styrofoam is an excellent core material for a mold such as this, and, because the mold is small, there is no need for fabric reinforcement of the plaster. Styrofoam is an excellent

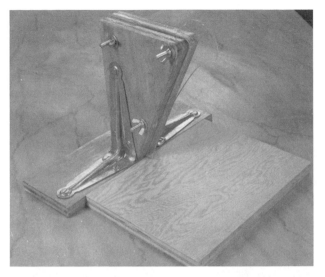

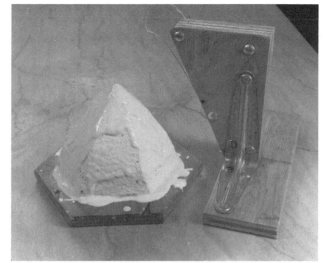

Fig. 5.16 A jack with removable Plexiglas profile.

Fig. 5.17 A hexagonal plywood base is made to serve as a guide for the jack. Styrofoam is used for the core of the mold and is held in place by pushing it over finishing nails that have been driven through the plywood.

Fig. 5.18 The first layer of plaster is brushed well into the surface of the Styrofoam. Any plaster that runs down the sides is troweled back up with a spatula or scraper.

Fig. 5.19 A second layer of plaster is applied to the Styrofoam. This layer is much thicker than the first one, and it is continually and evenly troweled back up to the top of the form.

Fig. 5.20 The final layer of plaster is applied. As it reaches the plastic stage, the jack is moved along the base to shape the plaster. The plaster is sprayed often with water to retard the setting process while the jack is being used.

base for building up the plaster shell. Its porous texture soaks up the first layer of plaster, and the plaster does not run off this surface as it does from a nonporous surface.

Figure 5.18 shows the first coating of plaster on the Styrofoam form. This first layer, which is applied with a brush or spatula, is relatively thin, and it is brushed well into the surface of the Styrofoam. If the plaster runs down the side of the Styrofoam, it is troweled back up with a spatula or scraper. All layers of plaster are put on as evenly as possible so that

there are no underlying bumps of hardened plaster to interfere with the shaping action.

A second coating of plaster is applied (there will be three in all). This layer is much thicker than the first. In Figure 5.19 it is apparent that the plaster is almost touching the template at the base; however, at the top of the mold, it is some distance from the template. When applying the plaster, the extra plaster that builds up at the base is troweled up to the top of the mold. This must be done very conscientiously, using the template as a reference, so that the

Fig. 5.21 The finished mold and a faceted dish made from it.

final layer will be approximately the same thickness throughout. In Figure 5.19 the plaster on the left side of the mold has already been troweled up to the top of the mold. When this second layer is complete, about $\frac{1}{2}$ inch of space should remain for the final layer.

Now the final layer of plaster is put on the mold, and the jack is scraped along the surface of the mold to shape the plaster (Figure 5.20). The jack actually must be moved back and forth along one side of the base several times, and the excess plaster that accumulates on the profile is removed each time. This process is repeated until all six sides of the mold have been scraped to the correct form. As the plaster hardens, the scraping and shaping action continues on all six sides of the base. The plaster surface is sprayed with water to retard the final set so the jack can give the plaster a very exact and polished surface.

When the mold is complete, it is put aside to dry. As soon as the plaster is dry, the mold is lifted off the plywood base and the bottom edge is beveled. The jack is throughly cleaned and the template is removed. After the jack has been cleaned with water and dried off, it is sprayed with WD40 to retard any rust and to oil seal the plywood.

One piece made from this mold is shown in Figure 5.21. In this particular case, a porcelain pot was thrown on the wheel. It has a top diameter the same as the hexagonal mold, and it tapers to a small base. The height of the thrown form is almost the height of the mold. The thrown piece is cut from the wheel and carefully nested over the mold. As the thrown form touches the mold, the sides are sponged so that they conform to the mold. The mold with the thrown form on it is centered on the wheel and a foot is quickly turned on the pot.

This mold can be used in many different ways to shape and alter thrown forms. The outside surface of the positive press-molded piece is also available to receive a variety of decorative treatments. Thus the impact of the final piece depends not on this simple form itself, but on what the artist does with and to the form.

The purpose of this exercise is two-fold. The first is to react to plaster in a spontaneous, active way to achieve a highly patterned surface to be used as a negative decorated press mold. The second is to use this press mold and a traditional hump mold to assemble a sculptural form.

"WET-CARVING" THE PRESS MOLD

To begin making the highly patterned press mold, a large, round batt of plaster is cast, using an aluminum cottle set up like the one pictured in Figure 12.1. When the plaster has set up slightly, the cottle is removed and the flat surface of the soft, cheesy plaster is "attacked" with large, looped tools that scoop out the plaster and form a rough, slightly negative shape. By the time this step is completed, the plaster has set up to a harder state. Then smaller tools are used to carve the plaster (Figure 6.2). Where deep gouges were made with a large tool, a smaller tool is used to accentuate the deep carving with radiating lines. All carving is done in a rapid, spontaneous manner, following no preplanned design. Strong, spontaneous carving results in a strong, active pattern.

Figure 6.3 shows the finished negative press mold. The mold is thoroughly brushed clean of all the carved scraps of plaster, and the whole working area is thoroughly cleaned to insure that no plaster shavings get into the clay during the pressing procedure.

THE PRESSING PROCEDURE

Next, two large batts of clay are rolled out on a heavy cotton sheet. The batts should be about ½ inch thick or less, and they must be big enough to overhang the edges of the press mold. The batts are scraped with a large rectangular scraper to reveal any air pockets; the air pockets are pierced and the air is pressed out with the scraper.

The cotton sheet is used to support the clay batt while it is being transported to and placed on the press mold (Figure 6.4). After the clay is placed onto the mold, the cloth is peeled from the clay and the pressing action begins.

CHAPTER

6

Combining Pressed Decoration and Hump-Molded Forms

Fig. 6.1 Donald E. Frith. Hump-molded and pressed relief stoneware vessel.

Fig. 6.2 As the plaster sets up, large areas are scooped out with looped tools. As the plaster gets harder, smaller tools are used to accentuate the design.

Fig. 6.3 After the carving is complete, the plaster is set aside to dry. Final embellishment of the design is done with a small carving tool.

Fig. 6.4 A thin batt of clay is rolled out on a cloth and placed on the press mold.

A careful description of how to press clay into a relief mold is offered here because, although the process might seem to be an elementary one, it is actually quite involved. Simply put, the clay must be pressed so that it absolutely fills the mold. The clay must bear the exact "print" of the mold. This is harder to achieve than it would appear, and pressings often reveal vacant spots or cracks because the clay was not pressed completely into the mold.

The following is a step-by-step description of pressing a batt of clay into a relief mold:

1 Place the batt of clay onto the surface of the mold and trim the excess clay from the edge.

2 Do not apply water to the clay surface during pressing because this tends to lubricate the surface and turns the "pressing" action into a "smoothing" action.

3 Place the mold on a wheel so that it can be rotated slowly.

4 The first series of pressings is done with the fist or a soft padded mallet. Starting from the center, pound the clay into the mold while the mold is slowly rotated. It is important that a regular pattern of pounding is followed to insure proper pressing of the whole surface of the mold.

5 Rotate the mold in the opposite direction and repeat the pounding from the center out in a spiral pattern. The blows should produce a relatively smooth surface and leave little or no impression in the clay.

6 A second series of pressings is now done using the fingers or a small rubber hammer. Press hard into the clay, leaving indentations, and follow a spiral pattern as was done before. It is a good idea to repeat the pressing in radiating spoke-like patterns after the spiral pattern is

Fig. 6.5 After the clay is pressed into the mold, reinforcing ribs and a thicker rim are added. Then a second clay form is pressed on a large, regular hump mold.

Fig. 6.6 While the two pressed pieces dry, six feet are pressed in a small carved plaster mold.

Fig. 6.7 The two pieces are carefully pressed together, and a roulette is used to strengthen the bond and add a decorative pattern. The feet are attached with slip.

complete. It is important to establish a consistent pattern of pressing, because this will have a great effect on how successful the results are.

7 The last pressing is done with a soft rubber rib. Use the rib in a hard smoothing action to achieve a relatively smooth surface.

8 The results of the pressing will soon be evident. If there are vacant or unpressed parts in the relief, then review the pressing procedure and try again.

After the clay has been thoroughly pressed into the mold, reinforcing ribs and a thicker rim were applied to help support the clay (Figure 6.5). This support is needed because the thickness of the clay varies considerably due to the deep relief pattern. The thicker rim also helps make the bond for the hump-molded section that will be added.

Fig. 6.8 The complete piece is inverted and the mold is removed. Several small holes are cut into the design and one is cut under the rim to permit draining.

PRESSING THE HUMP-MOLDED PIECE

Next, a batt of clay is pressed on a large hump mold. The process of pressing a thin batt of clay onto a hump mold is much simpler than pressing clay into a negative relief. There is usually no need to cut the clay to help conform to the mold. Carefully pressing with a sponge while turning the mold is usually enough to make the clay conform to the mold.

After the clay is pressed onto the hump mold with the sponge, the surface is pressed with a rib. This ribbing assures that good contact has been made between the clay and the mold, and it removes any excess water left from the sponging. The excess clay around the edge of the mold is cut away, and the mold is put aside to dry with the pressed relief mold.

ASSEMBLING THE FORM

While the two molds are drying, a small piece of plaster is carved into a press mold for the feet. The feet will dry in the mold almost as fast as they can be pressed (Figure 6.6). A fan placed nearby will aid the drying action.

When the two pressed pieces are slightly stiff (soft leather stage), they are ready to be bonded or luted together. The hump-molded piece is lifted from the mold and placed on the relief-molded piece. The bond between the two surfaces is made by pressing the surfaces together and smoothing with a rib. Then a roulette is pressed around the rim to assure a strong bond and to provide a pattern (Figure 6.7). (The roulette is a carved rubber caster inserted in a wooden handle.)

The pressed feet are applied with slip. The location of the feet are established with the aid of a compass. Since the feet are hollow, a small hole is pierced in them to assure that they will not pop off during firing.

Fig. 6.9 The completed, unfired piece shows the strong pressed pattern of the mold.

Fig. 6.10 A top view of the unfired piece.

When the clay is firm enough to be self-supporting, the assembled form is inverted and the relief mold is removed. A number of small holes are cut into the relief so the piece may be used as a vase (Figure 6.8). A hole is also pierced under the edge of the rim to enable water to be drained completely from the piece. The finished, unfired piece is shown in Figures 6.9 and 6.10.

This molding and construction process lends itself to production work as well as to creating individualized items. The possible combinations of spontaneously carved press molds and variously shaped hump molds is practically limitless. By changing the depth of either mold, totally different looks can be obtained. The feet or other support can also be infinitely varied. This same process can also be applied to creating a closed form on the vertical plane rather than the horizontal.

This chapter presents a "one-pour" system of making two-piece molds and introduces the use of the base plate as an essential part of mold making. The subject chosen for demonstrating these techniques is a six-sided press-molded teapot.

THE ONE-POUR, TWO-PIECE MOLD

The "one-pour" system of making a two-piece mold is a very easy one to use when the model is made from plastic clay. The model is simply sliced in half, and the two halves are carefully aligned on either side of a Plexiglas separator in the mold board set-up. No keying of the body or spout is necessary. Both top and bottom of the pressed piece are open to assure correct alignment; to facilitate luting, and to make it easier to adapt the mold to other uses.

The handle mold is made with the natches in place. (In the one-pour system, plastic insert natches are used, as shown in Figure 7.10.) The term "natch" is the word used by English and early American potters for the male and female hemispherical keying device that holds the various pieces of a mold in correct registry. In present-day America, the word "notch" or "key" is often used instead. I prefer to use the historical word "natch."

(The term "natch" in English potteries was also used to describe the fitting devices for jigger operations. A male natch was the metal ring on the jigger head that received the jigger mold, and the female natch was the tapered part of the jigger mold that fit into the metal ring. The term "chuck" is used in this text for the tapered opening on the jigger head that receives the jigger mold.)

THE BASE PLATE

The use of a base plate is actually the most important subject treated in this chapter. A base plate is a flat piece of plaster that is marked with lines to aid in establishing the size of the mold and the correct placement of the cottle or mold boards (Figure 7.1). Using the base plate takes the place of marking the same guidelines directly on the marble surface of the work table. Using the base plate simplifies one's work and increases one's accuracy. Moreover, the whole project,

Pressing a Large Teapot

Fig. 7.1 A hexagon and concentric circles are marked on the base plate with an indelible pencil. The surface is then dressed with mold soap.

plate and model, can be easily moved into storage or moved temporarily to make room for another project. The base plate can be reused as often as necessary for other molding jobs. All in all, the base plate is a great convenience in mold making.

Figure 7.1 shows an 18"-diameter, 1½" thick base plate that has been ruled off according to the proposed project needs. In this case, the project is a large hexagonal teapot. The lines are drawn on the plate with an indelible pencil, and the plate is then dressed with mold soap to "set" the lines and waterproof the plaster surface.

MAKING THE MODEL

The teapot body will be constructed using a two-piece, six-sided, tapered mold and shallow hump molds for the top and bottom. The spout and handle are made in separate piece molds.

The model for the teapot is made from a porcelain clay body. The clay is first thoroughly wedged and shaped into a large rectangular plug, which is placed in the center of the base plate. Then the clay is given its six-sided shape using knives and scrapers. The lines on the base plate guide the shaping (Figure 7.2).

The one-pour method of mold making requires that the model be cleanly cut in two, and thus moist clay is the obvious (and most readily available) material to use. But plastic clay, whether water or oil based, has several limitations as a material for model making, and it is essential to be aware of them in order to achieve a high-quality product. First of all, the moist clay model is much more fragile than a plaster model, and much care must be taken to pro-

Fig. 7.2 A six-sided model is shaped from porcelain with knives and scrapers, using the lines on the base plate as a guide.

Fig. 7.3 Sureform blades and various scrapers are used to give final form to the model.

tect the surface from being marred in any way. The clay body must be very thoroughly wedged to remove any air pockets that might appear on the model surface; and the clay should be kept in a semi-moist or soft leather hard state to permit alterations if necessary.

Figure 7.2 shows three scrapers that are essential for the mold maker. The little rectangular flat scraper is not made of thin metal that metal throwing ribs are typically made of. This scraper is made of rather thick steel (18 B.S. gauge), and it is quite stiff. The edges are sharpened in the standard manner, and two corners are rounded off. The other two scrapers are hacksaw blades. The small one in the foreground is a piece of a hand hacksaw blade; the large one is a power hacksaw blade. Both blades have been sharpened as a scraper on the back edge of the blade. Two hands are used to draw the large hacksaw scraper across the model. Smooth surfaces are achieved by alternately scraping first in one direction and then in the opposite direction. Never scrape in one direction only.

Sureform blades are employed to achieve the correct shape for the model (Figure 7.3). The model is smoothed or finished with the back of the hacksaw blade and the rectangular scraper. The top of the model is flattened and will serve as a guide for the depth of the plaster when the mold is poured.

SETTING UP THE ONE-POUR MOLD

Next the model is carefully cut in half with a knife, and a piece of $\frac{1}{8}$"-thick Plexiglas is inserted between the halves. Since the Plexiglas is transparent, the two halves can be matched up exactly. The use of the base plate is quite apparent in Figure 7.4. Four lines have been added to indicate the exact size of the

Fig. 7.4 The model is carefully cut in half, a Plexiglas separator is inserted between the halves of the model, and the two pieces are lined up exactly. The width of the sheet of Plexiglas is indicated by the lines on the base plate.

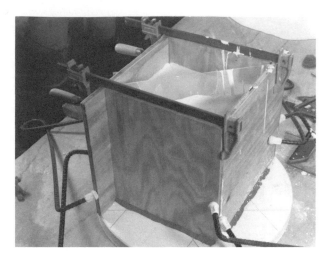

Fig. 7.5 Dressed mold boards are clamped in place on the base plate and the seams are secured with oil clay. Plaster is poured into both sides of the mold at once.

mold. These lines will guide the placement of the mold boards. The outside dimensions of the mold are large enough to give adequate thickness to the plaster. Note that, although the mold set-up is square, the model halves are separated on the diagonal instead of parallel to the sides of the square.

Well-dressed mold boards are set into position, clamped in place, and the seams secured with oil

Fig. 7.6 The edges of the finished mold are beveled to prevent chipping, and a groove is cut on the corners to hold an elastic cord. No natches are necessary in this type of mold.

clay. It is always better to use more clamps than you think are necessary. Most people who have worked with plaster have had the experience of pouring 40 or 50 pounds of plaster into a mold set-up and helplessly watching while the boards or cottle gave way. Maybe this sort of mishap is necessary to demonstrate the great pressure exerted by large volumes of plaster, especially when the mold is tall. Always use too many clamps rather than too few. Figure 7.5 shows two types of clamps being used: rebar clamps and furniture clamps. Because the mold is high, the furniture clamps are quite necessary to secure the sides and to add weight to the boards so that the plaster will not cause the mold boards to float up.

Correctly mixed plaster is poured into both sides of the mold at once. Because the top and bottom ends of this mold are open, plaster is poured just to the top of the model. Once the plaster has set, the mold boards are removed, cleaned, and put away. The model is removed and put in a plastic bag to keep the clay soft. Figure 7.6 shows the finished mold. The outside edges are beveled to prevent chipping, and a groove is cut in the outside corners of the mold to hold an elastic cord. This groove is cut with a round Sureform. Beveling the edges of a plaster mold is important because plaster has a tendency to chip during use, and any tiny chips of plaster that find their way into the clay body will cause trouble. After drying for a few days, the mold is ready for pressing.

In using a traditional two-piece press mold, each half is pressed and the two pieces of mold are then joined and held together with a binding rope. The two pressings are then joined together while the mold holds the pressings securely. In most cases, natches are used to assure proper alignment when the halves of the mold are put together. Since this particular two-piece mold has no top or bottom, the alignment is accomplished without natches simply by putting the mold together on the marble top table.

MAKING THE SPOUT

The spout model (Figure 7.7) is carved from a block of porcelain in a similar manner to the teapot body model. The roughly shaped spout is placed against

Fig. 7.7 A well-wedged block of porcelain is roughly shaped into a spout, which is checked against the teapot body to assure the correct size and design.

Fig. 7.9 The completed spout mold, with beveled edges and groove for an elastic cord.

the model of the teapot body to assure that it is of suitable size and shape. The spout is finished with six sides to carry out the theme of the teapot body. The spout model is completed to the exact design, including the correct angle of fit at the joint before the spares are attached. The spout model is carefully

Fig. 7.8 The finished spout model with spares is carefully cut in half and placed on either side of the Plexiglas. The two plaster mold boards are grooved to hold the Plexiglas separator.

cut in half and carefully aligned on either side of the Plexiglas separator. Note in Figure 7.8 that the line for cutting the base of the spout is clearly shown on the model. There is no such line at the end of the spout in order that a variety of shapes can be cut.

The use of the marked base plate in orienting the model and mold set-up is shown in Figure 7.8. Because this mold is small, plaster mold boards are used for the end mold boards. The plaster is easily grooved to accept the Plexiglas; this assures the exact position and stability of the Plexiglas during pouring. Two standard mold boards complete the set-up. Furniture clamps secure the four sides of the mold, and small coils of oil clay are always placed along the base of the mold to prevent any leakage of plaster. Just before the final assembly of the side mold boards, the boards are given a final dressing with mold soap (being carful not to leave any soap residue or bubbles on the surface).

Figure 7.9 shows the completed mold, with beveled edges and groove for clamping with an elastic band. The mold is set aside to dry a few days. (Actually, a mold of this size can be used as a press mold almost as soon as it is cast. The pressing process is slowed considerably when the mold is damp, but it still works.)

THE HANDLE: USING NATCHES IN THE ONE-POUR MOLD

The handle model is carved from plastic clay in the same manner as was the spout model. Both the rough handle model and the spout model should be placed on the teapot body at the same time to assure that the design of each is correct. Because the handle is more delicate than the spout, extra large spares are added to the rough handle model to aid in handling during final carving and finishing.

The handle mold (Figure 7.10) demonstrates how natches can be incorporated in the one-pour system of mold making. Including natches in a one-pour mold presents a small problem, but it is easily solved by using plastic insert natches from Double A Plastics (see Sources of Supplies). Holes are cut in the Plexiglas the exact diameter required to accept the plastic natches, and the natches are held in place with a tiny ball of oil clay. This procedure for making two-piece keyed molds is very simple. The only precaution is that the natches must be correctly lined up allowing for the thickness of the Plexiglas. That is, since the Plexiglas is $\frac{1}{8}$" thick, the natches must be held $\frac{1}{8}$" apart with the clay; otherwise the mold will not align correctly.

PRESSING THE TEAPOT BODY

The body, spout, and handle molds are now complete. Hump molds for the bottom and the top of the teapot are taken from stock.

Figure 7.11 shows the teapot body mold opened and ready to receive the thin batts of clay. Traditionally, clay is put into a press mold in the form of a thin sheet (batt) instead of as small chunks that are then pressed and bonded together during pressing. To form the batts of clay, the clay is first rolled out on a cloth with a rolling pin or slab roller. Then the clay is carefully scraped with a block scraper to reveal and crush tiny air pockets in the clay. Scraping does not enlarge or thin the clay to the extent the rolling does; however, if thin sheets of clay are required, rolling should always be followed by scraping.

Because the clay batts are so thin, the teapot body is pressed with two batts of clay in each side.

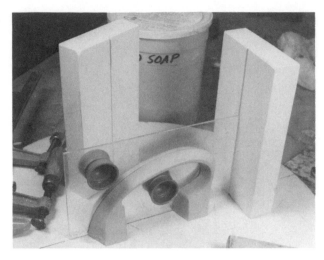

Fig. 7.10 Plastic natches provide the keying system for the handle mold.

(An experienced presserman would simply put a single batt of clay into this mold.) Figure 7.12 shows the placement of the first batt of clay in one side of the mold. After it is pressed in place using sponges and ribs, a second batt will be added to fill this half of the mold. (If the press mold were highly decorated, it would be necessary to press the clay thoroughly with the fingers. This takes skill and practice to get good results.) Any overlap of the two batts is thoroughly pressed to the thickness of a single layer of clay. Any seam that shows on the outside of the piece will be ribbed and sponged away.

After the other half of the teapot body is pressed, the two halves of the mold are fitted together (no slip is used) and held tightly with an elastic cord, as seen in the background of Figure 7.13. The two clay pieces are easily luted together because the ends of the mold are open.

MAKING THE TOP AND LID

The top of the teapot is made on two hump molds, as shown in Figures 7.13–7.15. One mold forms the lid and top, and the other mold forms the inner rims for the lid and top. The hump molds are identical, except that the mold used for the lid is modified to form a cone-like pedestal to hold the bird form that is used for the handle (as seen in Figure 7.21). Making

Fig. 7.11 In preparation for pressing the teapot, thin batts of porcelain are rolled and scraped out on a cotton cloth.

Fig. 7.13 Hump molds are pressed for the bottom, top, and lid of the teapot.

Fig. 7.12 The porcelain batts are pressed into the mold using sponges and ribs.

Fig. 7.14 For the lid handle, a small stylized bird is modeled in clay, and a two-piece press mold is made. A gutter carved into the mold receives and cuts off the excess clay that is exuded during pressing.

the top on similar hump molds assures that all parts of the top conform to design and that they fit properly together.

Figure 7.14 shows the bird form that is used for the lid handle. A model of the bird is made from a small piece of plaster, and it is imbedded in clay to the separation line. The first half is cast and the clay removed; after proper dressing, the second half is cast. The model is removed and a "gutter" for excess clay is cut into the mold. This particular formation also cuts off the excess clay from pressing the two halves of the mold together and it is much better than two-piece press molds without gutters. Usually the gutter design is used for small pressings, but it is standard and necessary when using the Ram pressing.

PRESSING THE SPOUT AND HANDLE

To press the spout, thin batts of clay are pressed into the mold with sponges and ribs (Figure 7.16), and the excess clay is cut away flush with the surface of the mold. Because of the shape of the spout, it is difficult to lute the two halves together, although a special tool could easily be made to do it. However, luting is not necessary. Instead, the halves will be joined with two coats of slip. The two coats are important. The first coat is absorbed by the clay, so the two pieces to be joined are conditioned identically and have similar water content and flexibility. The second coat of slip is the bonding coat. It is applied to both edges, and the two halves are carefully fitted together.

Alignment is easy, even without natches, because the two-piece mold is pressed together in a vertical position, on a flat, smooth surface, such as the marble table top. The edges have enough surface to provide bonding with slip, and as soon as the two halves come together the joint made with slip is complete. Excess slip is sponged away; however, if the right amount of slip is used in the first place, there should be no excess. (In factory production, only one coat of slip is used, but it usually has an added binder such as CMC or a soluble glue, and the water content of the two pieces to be joined are carefully controlled to be nearly identical.) If there are small gaps in the seam, they are easily bonded with a brush, forcing the clay together.

The spout can be separated from the mold almost immediately after the two halves are joined, but, as indicated in Figure 7.17, it is wise to leave it in the mold while checking and repairing the seam, if necessary. The spares at the ends of the spout make for easier handling, and the molded cut-off line shows where to cut off the spare.

The handle mold is pressed slightly over full on each half (Figure 7.18). It is important that the surface of the clay be rough and rise slightly above the surface of the mold. This usually occurs naturally when using a serrated tool to remove the excess clay, but more clay should be added if necessary. Both halves are coated with slip, which fills the rough surface. Then a second coat of slip is applied, and the two halves are brought together. No extra pressure is required to form a bond. The handle can be removed from the mold in a few minutes. This type of mold could benefit from having a gutter, as did the bird mold for the lid handle, but if the pressing

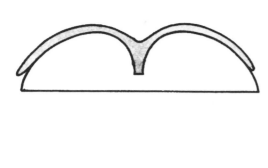

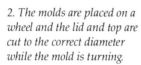

1. Two hump molds are used to press the teapot top, lid, and rims.

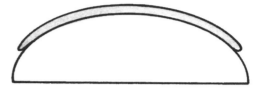

2. The molds are placed on a wheel and the lid and top are cut to the correct diameter while the mold is turning.

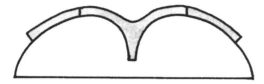

3. The lid rim and top rim are cut in a similar manner.

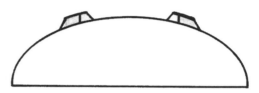

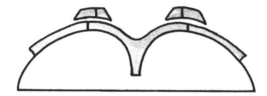

4. The lid and top rims are assembled to the lid and top. Care must be taken when the two rims are attached. Using two coats of slip, the top rim is assembled first, then removed so that the lid rim can be easily assembled.

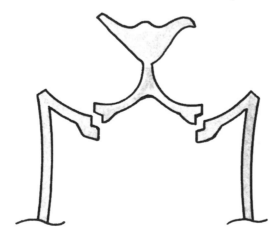

5. The lid is completed with the bird handle. The top is assembled to the teapot body.

Fig. 7.15 Pressing the teapot top and lid.

Fig. 7.16 Porcelain batts are pressed into the spout mold.

is done carefully, as described above, there is little or no excess clay and the bond is sound.

After removing the handle from the mold, it is fettled and sponged. The spares are not cut away until the handle is ready to be put on the body of the teapot.

Fig. 7.17 The two halves of the spout are bonded with two coats of slip. Before removing the spout from the mold, the seam must be checked and cleaned.

Fig. 7.18 The handle mold is pressed slightly over full on each half. The clay surfaces are roughened before being joined with a coat of slip.

ASSEMBLING THE TEAPOT

The first step in assembling the teapot is to place the teapot body on the hump-molded bottom and trim the bottom to match the hexagonal shape of the pot (Figure 7.19). The bottom and body are joined with slip, and the six edges are firmly ribbed and pressed to make the bond. This ribbing gives a more concave shape to the bottom edges, which adds to the design. The sides of the teapot are also ribbed to increase their concavity.

The top is joined to the body in the same manner as the bottom. The top consists of two hump-molded pieces, one of which is a recessed rim on which the lid will rest, and the other forms the visible top of the pot (Figure 7.20). When joining the top, care must be taken not to distort the round opening for the lid. After joining, the excess clay is cut away to match the hexagonal shape of the pot.

The lid is completed by attaching the press-molded bird with slip (Figure 7.21).

After cutting the spares from the handle, the handle is attached using two coats of slip on both handle and pot. (As described earlier, the first coat is a conditioning coat and the second is the bonding coat.)

Fig. 7.19 The body of the teapot is set on the hump-molded bottom, the bottom is trimmed to match the hexagonal shape of the pot, and the two are joined with slip.

To attach the spout, the spares are cut away, the spout is placed against the teapot body, and a light outline is marked on the body. Using the outline as a guide, a hole is cut in the body (Figure 7.22). (An alternative is to cut a series of small holes with a hole cutter, but then the inside edges are more difficult to clean.) The spout is attached to the pot using the two coats of slip system.

The teapot is now finished (Figure 7.23). The clay is in a soft leather-hard stage, which means that it still looks damp, but almost all flexibility is gone. The teapot is left on the hump mold that forms the bottom until it is in leather hard condition. If cracks appear in the joints, they are filled using a very small brush and one drop or less of slip. The slip is carefully put into the joint only, and not all around the area. In repairing cracks in clay at this stage, it is always best to use as little slip as possible and not paint the entire area. If the crack reappears, repeat the slip application.

The finished teapot is removed from the hump mold, carefully sponged, and covered with plastic to permit slow drying.

It would be very easy to make other items with this mold besides the teapot. By pressing and assem-

Fig. 7.20 The top is joined to the teapot with slip. Note that the top is assembled from two hump-molded pieces, one an inside rim and the other the outside visible top of the teapot.

Fig. 7.21 The press-molded bird handle completes the lid. The handle is fitted to the teapot body by cutting away the spares and using two coats of slip. The spout is ready to apply to the teapot body.

Fig. 7.22 A hole is cut following the outline of the spout, and the spout and body are joined with two coats of slip.

Fig. 7.23 The completed teapot is removed from the hump mold that formed the bottom, carefully sponged, and placed on a flat plaster batt to dry.

bling the two halves of the body mold and then cutting the piece to produce two new separate items, such as a creamer and sugar, then one could begin to explore the possibilities of this press system. Various shapes of spouts and handles, and the addition of feet and surface decoration, add to the variety of possibilities.

Press molding obviously offers many possibilities for producing both functional and sculptural pieces. Features such as lids, handles, spouts, feet, and surface   oration can be varied at will, and the assemb'   ig apart, and reassembly of functional or abstract ιυrms is especially fertile ground for exploration.

STYROFOAM PRESS MOLDS

Scott Frankenberger, a young potter from Battle Ground, Indiana, makes press molds out of Styrofoam. Although the procedure that Frankenberger uses is well documented in the September 1982 issue of *Ceramics Monthly*, his inventiveness in the use of Styrofoam and the special possibilities that Styrofoam molds offer a clay artist deserve attention here.

Frankenberger first developed the Styrofoam molds in order to enable a non-throwing assistant to become productive in press molding. He realized that making enough plaster molds for any serious production work would require a separate plaster facility; and his cramped pottery could not accomodate such a move. During his training in ceramics, he had experimented with molds made of wood; but the problems of shaping wood into functional forms suitable for press molding presented even more problems than plaster molds did. Making wooden molds requires wood-working tools as well as power tools, and the wood itself tends to split with time when being used for press molds.

Molds of fired clay were also considered; but they had even more drawbacks than plaster molds. Fired clay molds are heavy, breakable, and unalterable. Furthermore, the process of making them is the same as making pottery (throwing, forming, firing, etc), so making bisque molds would seriously interfere with the daily production of the pottery.

Not feeling bound to traditional techniques or traditional mold materials, Frankenberger soon began experimenting with Styrofoam. He used the blue Styrofoam that is commonly used for housing insulation. It comes in various thicknesses, is incredibly lightweight, and it can be cut easily with a saw or an electrically heated wire. Frankenberger found that after cutting the Styrofoam, he could refine the edges and curves with sandpaper.

Seeing many advantages to this material, Frankenberger began using Styrofoam molds in the late 1970s for pressing such items as shallow plates, baking dishes, and serving trays. He realized that the Styrofoam molds would not absorb moisture from the clay as do plaster molds, but he designed the molds to fit the material available and developed a press-molding procedure that suited his production requirements.

CHAPTER

Styrofoam and Wooden Molds

Fig. 8.1 Scott Frankenberger. Press-molded porcelain jewelry
box, 10″ × 8″ × 2″, made in Styrofoam mold. Courtesy of the
artist.

Figure 8.2 shows 2-inch-thick Styrofoam being
cut into a ring mold with a sabre saw. The blade is
at an angle, and it must move constantly forward to
prevent excess heat from building up that would melt
the Styrofoam. In commercial settings, Styrofoam is
cut with a heated wire. This method has the advantage of leaving no residue or "sawdust" behind because the heated wire tends to seal the cut surface
as it passes through the plastic. This type of Styrofoam is of such a quality that, after cutting, the edges
can be sanded with sandpaper.

Frankenberger is able to cut and finish a mold
in less than 15 minutes. The molds are apparently
durable—he is still using some that are over 3 years
old.

The type of molds shown in the accompanying

photographs are ring molds. They are actually one
piece of a two-piece mold, the second piece being
the plywood board that the ring mold is placed on.
The Styrofoam ring forms the sides of the mold, and
the plywood forms the bottom and serves as a carrier
as well.

To form a pressed dish, thin sheets of porcelain
are first rolled out on a plywood board with a rolling
pin. The rolling is done quickly, and the thickness
is controlled with thin sticks of wood on either side
of the clay batt. Then the sheet is rolled up on the
rolling pin and moved to the mold. Figures 8.3 and
8.4 show how Frankenberger carries the rolled out
sheet of porcelain to the mold. The porcelain sheet
is between $\frac{1}{4}$″ and $\frac{3}{8}$″ thick, and lifting and transporting
sheets of porcelain this thin can be tricky. Franken-

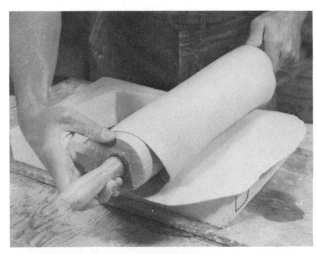

Fig. 8.2 Scott Frankenberger cuts Styrofoam insulation with a sabre saw to make a press mold. After cutting, the edges will be smoothed with sandpaper.

Fig. 8.3 The thin sheet of clay is rolled up on the rolling pin to be moved to the press mold.

Fig. 8.4 The Styrofoam mold is placed on a plywood board that shapes the bottom of the dish and serves as a carrier for the whole unit. Here the porcelain sheet is unrolled over the mold.

Fig. 8.5 The clay is pressed into the mold with the right hand while the left hand lifts and "feeds" the clay into the mold.

berger simply rolls the sheet up on the rolling pin and unrolls it over the ring mold, as a pastry chef would do with a pie crust. His method can be contrasted with the traditional method of rolling the clay out onto a cloth and transferring the rolled clay sheet to the mold by picking up the cloth and clay together.

Another aspect of Frankenberger's clay transferring method is that the clay surface that is face down against the plywood board during rolling is also the surface that becomes the bottom side of the pressed item. In the case of transferring clay sheets

rolled out on a cloth, the clay and cloth are usually turned over on top of the mold and the cloth is peeled away from the clay. This procedure results in the cloth-textured surface being the upper surface in the mold. (This procedure would also probably tear or deform sheets of clay as large and thin as the ones used in these pieces.)

The clay is pressed into the mold with the right hand while the left hand lifts and feeds the clay into the mold (Figure 8.5). If the left hand did not feed the clay this way, the pressing action would cause the clay to stretch and break. This pressing action is exactly like fitting rolled out pie dough into a deep dish.

When the clay is completely pressed around the inside of the mold, the excess clay is trimmed off flush with the top of the mold using a cut-off tool or knife. The trimming must be done very carefully so as not to damage the fragile mold. The thin top edge of the clay piece that results from this treatment is unsatisfactory, in that the piece can warp or crack during drying and firing. Therefore, a rim of porcelain strips is added to the pressed piece (Figure

8.6). The strips are cut with a tool made from a stick of wood with heavy needles driven into it at the desired spacing for the width of the rim (1-inch intervals in this case). The result looks somewhat like a comb.

Before adding the strips, the edge of the pressed piece is pushed down slightly to widen it and textured with a serrated tool (a broken comb works very well). Frankenberger does not use slip to aid in the bonding, but he preconditions the clay by running a wet brush over the edge of the pressing.

The pieces of the rim are joined together by

Fig. 8.6 Strips of porcelain are placed on the moistened edge of the trimmed pressing to strengthen the edge and form a rim.

Fig. 8.7 The rim strips are sliced at an angle to increase the bonding area of the joint. The joints are never made at the corners of the dish.

Fig. 8.8 In the final sponging, care is taken to press the rim firmly onto the edge of the dish.

Fig. 8.9 By the time ten or twelve other pressings have been made, the dish has dried enough to come out of the mold.

overlapping the strips of porcelain and cutting the two on an angle (Figure 8.7). Frankenberger never joins rim pieces at the corners of the dish, and the cut is made at such an angle so as to increase the area of the joint to assure a satisfactory bond.

After smoothing the rim, the piece is given a final sponging (Figure 8.8). Care must be taken to sponge and press the inside of the rim and the wall of the pressing together to assure that a bond between the two has been achieved.

Now the completed pressing is set aside to dry while still in the mold. Although little or no water is withdrawn from the porcelain by the plywood or by the Styrofoam, the pressed piece can be usually removed from the mold by the time ten or twelve other pieces have been pressed (3 or 4 hours). To unmold the dish, it is inverted onto a board (Figure 8.9), and the mold is lifted off. The back is sponged, paying particular attention to the joint between the rim and the wall to assure that a good bond has been made.

The mold is put away in a safe place to await further use. Since the mold has absorbed no water from the clay, its water content is not gradually building up (as is the case with a plaster mold) and it is ready to be used again as soon as needed.

Frankenberger's method for creating the handles for his dishes, in spite of its ancient roots, is quite inventive. His method is to roll coils of clay out on carved linoleum blocks to create patterns on the clay. Two of the blocks are shown in Figure 8.10; one is a series of straight lines and the other is a series of dots. If these blocks were inked and printed on paper, they would simply produce straight lines or rows of dots. However, by rolling a coil of clay on the block with lines, a very appealing spiral pattern is created on the clay. The block with dots produces a tufted effect that resembles tufted upholstery.

To make the handles, porcelain is rolled out in a coil and cut to the correct length for the handles on the dish. A piece of the coil is rolled over the carved linoleum block to impress the image of the block onto the clay. The linoleum block will undoubtedly outlast plaster molds made for similar use. The handle is applied to the edge of the dish in the same manner as the rim: texturing with a comb, ap-

Fig. 8.10 Linoleum blocks, carved in simple patterns, are used to create interesting designs on the handles.

plying water, and placing the handle firmly (but carefully) in position.

The ends of the handles are given a very handsome treatment. Frankenberger blends the ends into the rim of the dish in such a manner that the rim design flows into the end of the handle. This is done for two reasons: the first is that this area is subject to cracking during drying and firing; and second is aesthetic. With the strong pressing and smoothing at the ends of the handles, both problems are solved; the bond is secured and the design is improved.

The finished deep dish is given a final sponging and inspection, and if slip decoration is applied, it is done at this time. The finished product, a deep baking dish or serving dish, is in the foreground of Figure 8.12, with the greenware and the mold in the background.

Frankenberger's use of Styrofoam and linoleum blocks is a creative response to a studio production "problem." He has departed from tradition in order to meet his production needs, while maintaining his commitment to making quality, hand-crafted, individualized pottery items. If his production needs increase, he has the option of increasing his staff and

Fig. 8.11 The handles are applied in the same manner as was the rim, and the ends of the handle are firmly blended into the rim for added strength and visual appeal.

Fig. 8.12 The Styrofoam mold, pressed piece, greenware with slip decoration, and a finished glazed dish.

pressing more Styrofoam molds, or of going to a Ram press, which can produce over 1000 dishes a day if continuously supplied with clay from a pug mill (but this is an expensive alternative for a small operation).

Styrofoam molds have limitations, but Frankenberger has understood these limitations and capitalized on their advantages. He has thoughtfully geared his present production system to meet his personal .aesthetic requirements as well as his production goal—hand-produced pottery of quality materials and workmanship, bearing the distinctive character of the artist.

WOODEN PRESS MOLDS

John H. Stephenson, Ann Arbor, Michigan, works with a mold form made of plywood to create unique sculptural forms in clay. His approach is quite straightforward, yet the products are sophisticated and challenging to the eye.

Figure 8.13 shows one of Stephenson's pressed and shaped clay pieces in a three-sided, box-like plywood mold. Slabs of clay are pressed onto the sides of the mold, and the rounded forms, also built from slabs, are shaped free-hand, working through a hole in one side of the mold. Two things are not shown in this photograph. One is the just-mentioned hole that permits working on the interior of the pressed piece. The other is the frame that supports the mold while work is being done. This frame is shown in Figure 8.14, and how it fits on the mold is shown in Figure 8.15. The frame is designed so that it does not cover up the access hole in the mold, yet securely supports all three sides of the mold.

Figure 8.16 shows two of the "Core Series" that Stephenson made using the three-sided box mold. For each core piece, Stephenson makes two pressings from the mold. The two pressings are positioned with the sides that have access holes facing each other, and they are joined with more clay, which forms additional facets on the piece. Each of the core pieces are stained various colors with colored slips. Stephenson's core series is fascinating because each piece looks as if it has been made by some sort of molding process; yet, upon closer inspection, it is clear that some areas are *not* molded. The use of light-colored slips to accentuate the pressed surfaces and

Fig. 8.13 One of John Stephenson's three-sided plywood press molds with pressed and shaped clay. The mold is 15″ × 17″ × 15″. Not visible is the hole in one of the sides that permits working on the interior of the piece. Courtesy of the artist.

Fig. 8.14 The three-sided frame designed to support the plywood mold. It is roughly 20″ on each side. Courtesy of the artist.

Fig. 8.15 The frame forms a cradle to support the mold and permit access to the inside of the piece through a hole in the third side of the mold. In this photograph, both frame and mold are shown upside down on the table. Courtesy of the artist.

Fig. 8.16 John Stephenson. "Core #2" and "Core #3." Pressed and hand-formed sculpture made in a three-sided plywood mold. Photo by Robert Vigiletti, Precision Photo. Courtesy of the artist.

darker colors on the undulating, hand-formed surfaces intensify the contrast between the pressed planes and the hand-formed surfaces.

Stephenson has developed a unique and supremely simple mold system to express his own aesthetic vision in clay. His work is prime evidence of the creative possibilities to be found in using molds, and hopefully it will inspire and excite others to explore this system or a variation of it in making their own personal statements.

Press molding decorative or structural clay tiles offers the clay artist much room to exercise his or her creative design abilities and ingenuity—as well as to produce a high-quality, functional product with great appeal. This chapter is devoted to press molding tile using plastic clay in a small studio setting. Most commercial tile today is manufactured using dry clay and expensive automated equipment far beyond the resources of the small shop. Flat decorative tiles are made on huge hydraulic presses using steel dies and a granular clay body with approximately 3% water, with added binders and lubricants. Structural clay tiles, usually a hollow brick of some kind with a network of openings resulting from the manufacturing process, are formed on automatic extruders with a clay body that is approximately 15% water. The automatic equipment produces vast quantities of tile at a very rapid rate, and production capacity far exceeds demand. At any one time, the commercial tile industry may operate at about 50% capacity.

Both the cost of equipment and the cost of machining new steel dies are considerable, and tile must be produced by the thousands in order for the manufacturing process to be economical. Therefore, design possibilities are necessarily limited on the large automated equipment. Not so in the smaller studio, where not only tile design but production techniques can be varied to suit the artist's needs.

This chapter presents the work of Beth Starbuck and Steve Goldner of the Starbuck-Goldner Studio in Bethlehem, Pennsylvania. This two-person shop produces limited amounts of custom-designed tile from plastic clay. Both Starbuck and Goldner served apprenticeships at the Moravian Tile Works at Doylestown, Pennsylvania, so they were well prepared to undertake the task of setting up their own custom studio. Each of their designs fits one of the three production systems: (1) deep relief press molds that produce single, three-dimensional tiles; (2) "mosaic" press molds that press multiple flat tiles; and (3) a "stamp mold" process (using a hand-operated lever press). These three systems enable Starbuck and Goldner to produce an almost unlimited variety of inventive designs, ranging from basically flat tiles to sculptural, three-dimensional tiles.

Fig. 9.1 Starbuck-Goldner Studio. "Wedges." Three-dimensional ceramic tile.

DEEP RELIEF TILES

The wedge-shaped tiles shown in Figure 9.1 are made in the V-shaped plaster press mold shown in Figure 9.2. The mold, made from a clay model, is made with pottery plaster at a consistency of about 65. This consistency produces a mold that is sturdy yet still absorbent. The edges of the mold are beveled, and negative natches are included.

The natches enable the molds to be stacked in a series, with the back of one mold in contact with the exposed pressed surface of the tile underneath. This system of stacking insures that all surfaces of the tile dry equally from contact with the plaster surface of the mold. (If only a few tiles are needed, then the stacking feature is not used.)

Stacked molds are not a new phenomenon. Historically, after slip casting became a standard manufacturing method, stacked molds were used to make items such as large platters. The molds were

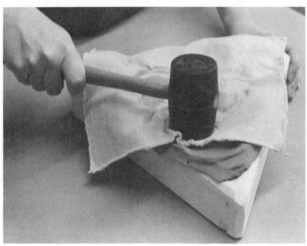

Fig. 9.2 The plaster press mold for the high-relief, V-shaped tiles shown in Figure 9.1.

Fig. 9.3 Clay is forced into the mold with a rubber mallet. The excess clay absorbs the shock of the mallet blows and prevents the mold from breaking. The cloth prevents the clay from sticking to the mallet.

Fig. 9.4 The excess clay is removed with a cut-off wire stretched tightly against the surface of the mold.

Fig. 9.5 A block scraper cleans up the back surface of the tile and pushes back any clay that has pulled away from the edge of the mold.

Fig. 9.6 Part of the back of the tile is removed to permit more even drying and increase the bonding surface. It also makes the tile lighter.

Fig. 9.7 The pressed tile can be removed from the mold in a very short time. The tile is placed on a flat drying board and dried carefully to avoid warping.

made so that, when stacked, both surfaces, top and bottom, served as part of the mold for the clay product. Openings in the molds permitted slip to flow into each mold in the stack. Slip was poured in at the top of the stack and each piece was solid cast. The stacked molds provided a built-in pressure system for the slip, assuring that all the pieces in the stack were cast satisfactorily. This sort of stacked, solid-cast system became obsolete in commercial settings with the introduction of the Ram press, but it is worth considering in a small operation.

Figure 9.3 shows how the plastic clay is pounded into the mold with a mallet. This method achieves much higher pressures than are possible using the fingers alone, and the result is a thoroughly pressed

image from the mold. The cloth is used to keep the mallet from sticking to the clay.

When using a mallet to hammer clay into the mold, it is important to use more clay than is necessary to fill the mold. For these tiles, approximately twice as much clay is about the right amount. The excess clay buffers the mold from the impact of the mallet blows. Were it not for this excess clay, striking with the mallet would result in a great many broken molds. This is a very effective means of pressing tile molds, and the whole process takes much less than a minute.

After the pressing is complete, the excess clay is removed with a potter's cut-off wire (Figure 9.4). It is important that constant pressure be maintained on the cutting wire or it will not cut correctly. A metal scraper removes any remaining excess clay from the surface of the mold (Figure 9.5) and assures that the back of the tile will be flat. The scraper is also used to repair any places where the clay has pulled away from the edges of the mold. Note that the top edge of the scraper, which is held by the hand, is taped for safety.

Figure 9.6 shows a section of the back of the tile being removed with a trimming tool. This accomplishes four things: (1) it makes the tile lighter, (2) it saves clay, (3) it changes the cross-section of the tile to permit faster and more even drying, and (4) it increases the surface available for bonding (the bonding material adheres to the edges of this cut-out area as well as to the outer edges of the tile).

The tile can be removed from the mold almost immediately and is placed on a smooth drying board (Figure 9.7). It is dried under controlled conditions that assure its drying flat. The mold will have absorbed some moisture from the clay, but because the clay has a water content of only about 25%, the mold can be used immediately for another pressing. As the moisture content of the mold increases with each pressing, the time required to release the clay will increase somewhat, too, but since this is a hand operation, it really doesn't matter.

Starbuck and Goldner call this design "Wedges," and its very effective three-dimensional qualities are apparent in Figure 9.1. The tiles are fired to cone 6 in electric kilns, meeting all the standards for tile as required by the installation.

FLAT "MOSAIC" TILES

Another of the studio's production methods is the "mosaic system." This method is a good illustration of the ingenuity of these two artists in matching their studio's capabilities against their production needs. One of the biggest assets they offer their customers is that they can produce a tile pattern of almost any shape or pattern. Since the majority of the installations require a tile that is flat or nearly flat, variety is achieved primarily in the shape and color of the tile.

Figure 9.8 shows the heart of the Starbuck-Goldner mosaic system for creating unusual tile shape

patterns. It is a plaster die that stamps the design on a sheet of clay. A master model is made from a rolled-out sheet of clay. The model must be absolutely flat, because it in reality represents the final product. After this sheet of clay has firmed up slightly, lines are carved into the clay to represent the separation between the individual tiles. The pattern is worked out carefully beforehand, and the carving on the clay is an exact copy of the pattern. The pattern shown in Figure 9.8 is titled "Star and Petal," and it consists of a central unit, the star, surrounded by four identical petal units. In the die, 18 tile units are made, 3 star-shaped tiles and 15 petal-shaped tiles.

To use the plaster die to form a tile, a sheet of clay is rolled out to the desired thickness of the tile. This is done with a slab roller on a piece of plywood cut the same size as the die. Figure 9.8 shows the sheet of clay on the plywood and the plaster die held vertically in back. The outlines on the die are designed so that when the clay is pressed into the die, the edges of the individual tiles are automatically beveled and no later sponging is necessary. The die is carefully placed over the sheet of clay and the three layers (die, clay, and plywood board) are turned over.

Fig. 9.8 The Starbuck-Goldner Studio produces flat tiles in almost any shape using a plaster die to stamp a sheet of clay. This is the die for the "Star and Petal" pattern.

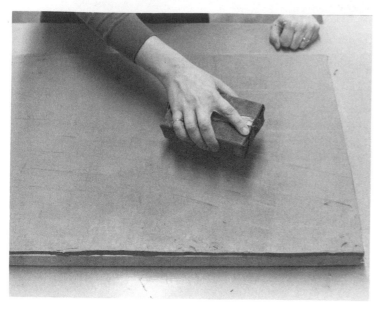

Fig. 9.9 The clay is pressed into the plaster die with the aid of a fabric-covered wood block.

The next step is to lift the board away from the sheet of clay so that final pressing into the die can be made. Figure 9.9 shows this final pressing being done with a piece of 2″ × 4″ covered with coarse

Fig. 9.10 After the die is lifted from the clay, a fettling knife is used to finish cutting apart the tiles. The tiles are left on the board to dry. The die is carefully made so the edges of the tiles are already beveled, and no sponging is needed.

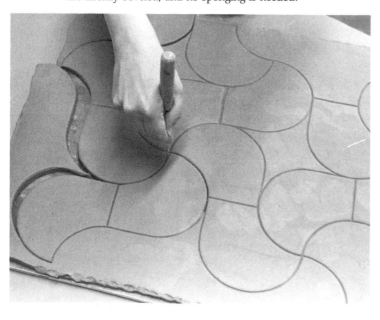

fabric such as canvas or denim. This pressing action does not consist of repeated poundings with the fabric-covered block. The clay must be brought in full contact with the surface of the die, but a simple once-over is all that is required to establish the die pattern on the sheet of clay. If too much pounding is done, the tile will be thinner than required. Little extra clay should be forced over the edges of the die during pressing.

The absorbent action of the plaster die on the clay makes the clay slightly stiff. Usually it takes about 15 minutes for the plaster to withdraw enough moisture from the clay so that the die and clay can be separated.

When the die is ready to be removed, the plywood board is placed on top of the clay again and the stack is flipped over so the die is on top and the board is on the bottom. The plaster die is lifted away from the clay on one edge. As the die is lifted, the sheet of clay falls away from the plaster surface. This step must be done with care so as not to distort the sheet of clay. The key to accomplishing this separation successfully is allowing enough time for the plaster to remove a certain amount of moisture from the clay. Obviously, the amount of moisture removed is greater as the time of contact is increased. Only experience will determine the amount of time required.

The sheet of clay is now ready to be separated into individual tiles. The die has imprinted the deeply beveled pattern onto the sheet. A fettling knife carefully cuts into the beveled outline (Figure 9.10), and the excess clay is removed from the board. The tiles are left on the board to dry slowly so that no warpage takes place. To take further precautions against warping, the tiles can be dried in layers, sandwiched between support boards, and turned over periodically during drying.

Figure 9.11 shows a completed section of the Star and Petal tiles on a wall. The design elements are clearly defined by color. The inherent interest of the interlocking pattern becomes even more intriguing as it is more carefully examined. This "mosaic" system is ideal for producing limited numbers of tile in unique shapes. The tiles are pressed to an almost finished state by the plaster die, the system is inexpensive, and it is simple.

Dick Hay, Brazil, Ind. "Janet," 36"h. Hay makes plaster molds from mannequins, human forms, and a variety of other objects. All the pieces are press molded. In taking molds from the human body, he uses Pam, the nonstick cooking spray, as a lubricant. "My work with the mannequins began by using the entire object as it was found. Now the central form is constructed in a Frankensteinian manner from a series of press molds, and then the addition of other object-imagery to develop the personality of the piece."

Dick Evans, Milwaukee, Wis. "Landscape Bowl," 12" dia. The bowl is built up from very thin pieces of porcelain placed onto the surface of a bisque-fired hump mold. The mold is thrown on the wheel, trimmed smooth, and fired. Rings marked on the mold guide the application of the layers of clay. The bowls are finished by throwing a foot directly on the piece.

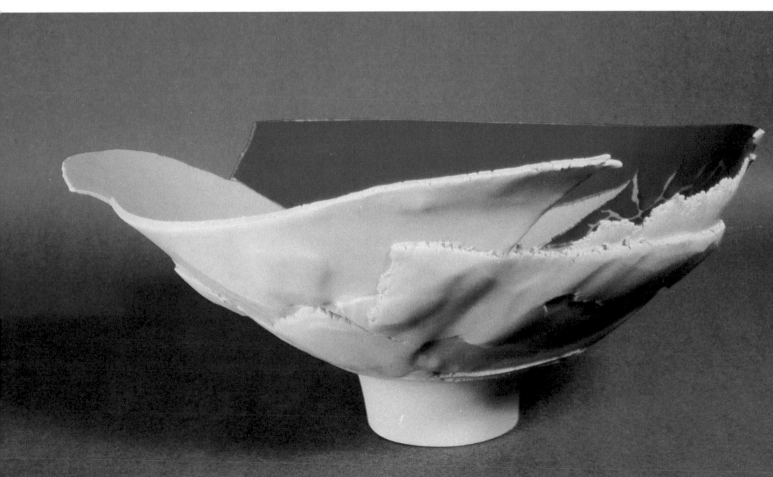

Louis Marak, Eureka, Ca. Top: "X-Pot," 10"x10"x17". The two pieces are made by press molding the major parts of the work and then assembling and adding by hand building.

Robert Shay, Columbus, Ohio. "True Yellow Cross." Hollowcast, approx. 40" h. To slip cast large forms such as these, Shay installs the mold in a steel cradle that is rotated to dump the slip. "Within each piece I try to create a relationship between sensibilities that are organic and geometric, geologic yet fragile, panoramic yet microscopic, and attitudes that are both spontaneous and ordered, demanding yet accessible, and subtle but energetic."

Robert Sedestrom, New Paltz, N.Y. "Cast Sculptural Form," 47"x20"x7". Sedestrom assembles a wide variety of precast forms to create cubistic sculptural molds. The assembled mold is designed to be clamped together with large furniture clamps. The piece here is vitreous china. Photo by Bob Barrett.

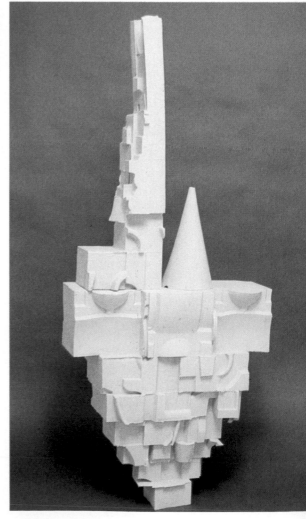

Victor Spinski, Newark, Del. "Trash Barrel with Spoons and Forks." The casting is done in plaster molds using a "Slip O Matic" machine that pumps the slip into and out of the mold. All the individual items in the trash barrel are slip cast separately. Most of Spinski's work is low fire. Courtesy of the Theo Portnoy Gallery, New York, N.Y.

Richard Shaw, San Francisco, Ca. "Book, Jar with Green Brush." The artist's life-like porcelain pieces indeed fool the eye. The components are all cast, assembled, and fired to maturity. Then overglaze decals are applied and fired. Courtesy of the Braunstein Gallery, San Francisco, Ca.

Fig. 9.11 Finished "Star and Petal" tiles from the Starbuck-Goldner Studio.

STAMP-MOLDED TILES

The third and last process presented here more closely resembles commercial tile production than do the first two approaches. Starbuck and Goldner call this the "stamp mold" process. The process uses a simple hand-operated lever press (Figure 9.12). A long lever actuates a vertical pipe. The vertical pipe has a flange screwed on the end, and a wooden plate is attached to the flange. This plate presses the die or mold into the clay. The press is made of scrap channel steel and pipe and can be made at reasonable cost by anyone who is interested enough to examine the drawing.

The press was constructed to make relief tiles that could not be made using either of the first two systems. Once again, Starbuck and Goldner have taken an age-old technique and adapted it to their production needs and studio facilities.

Figure 9.13 shows how slabs of clay are made for the stamping operation. The large pug of clay is sliced into thin slabs using a cut-off wire and two wood sticks to control the thickness. (The technique is identical to that used in 16th-century Italy as de-

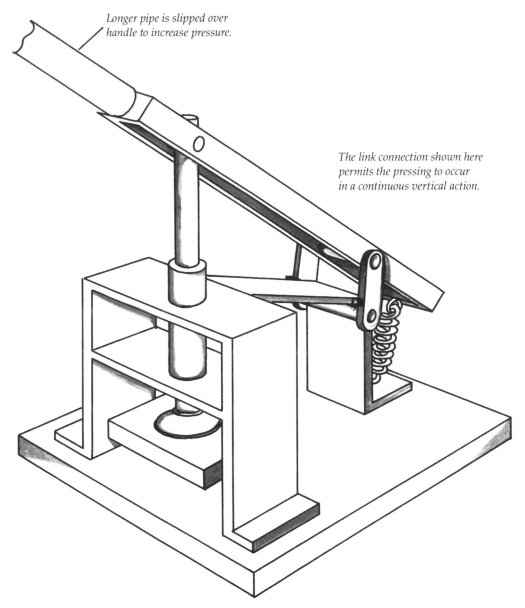

Longer pipe is slipped over handle to increase pressure.

The link connection shown here permits the pressing to occur in a continuous vertical action.

Fig. 9.12 A hand-operated lever press made of channel steel and pipe. The longer the handle, the greater the pressure that can be applied.

scribed by Piccolpasso.) The slab should be somewhat larger than the final tile so that there is enough clay to make a complete pressing of the design and outline of the tile.

In Figure 9.14 the plaster die for the tile is shown ready to be placed on top of the slab of clay. The clay rests on a heavy cloth carrier. Look carefully at the pattern on the die and notice that the pattern is positive, i.e., the design is in relief, not intaglio. Starbuck and Goldner use the raised, or positive, die to create a negative image on the end product. However, this negative pattern on the tile produces the effect of a positive design because the relief is high and the pattern strong (see Figure 9.17). Starbuck

Fig. 9.13 For the "stamp mold" process, slabs are cut from a large block of clay using a cut-off wire and two sticks of wood to control the thickness.

Fig. 9.14 The clay slab is placed on a heavy piece of fabric, which serves as a carrier. Note the positive design in the die, which will produce a negative design in the tile.

Fig. 9.15 The hand-operated lever press applies just enough force to press the clay into the features of the die.

Fig. 9.16 After the tile is pressed, the excess clay is trimmed away. The knife blade is pressed flat against the edge of the mold.

and Goldner, through their complete understanding of the molding process, have used negative stamped tiles to produce a pattern that seems positive.

The plaster die is placed on the slab of clay, and both are moved to the press. Figure 9.15 shows the tile in the press. The amount of pressure applied is only that adequate to force the clay into the features of the mold. Since each tile must be the same thickness, a stop on the press prevents it from pressing a tile too thin. Too much pressure might also break the plaster die.

After pressing, the die, with the tile attached to it, is removed from the press and the excess clay is trimmed away from the edges of the die (Figure

Fig. 9.17 The pressed tile can be removed from the die almost as soon as it is trimmed. While in the press, both the plaster mold and the carrier fabric absorb moisture from the clay.

Fig. 9.18 "Stamp molded" tiles by Starbuck-Goldner Studio. This is a very effective use of positive and negative shapes produced in a single mold and heightened by the glaze.

9.16). The blade of the trimming knife is pressed flat against the side of the mold to assure that the tile is cut correctly and that every tile is cut the same. The tile can be removed from the die almost as soon as the pressing and trimming procedure is completed. The die is simply lifted from the tile, and the tile is left on the piece of canvas to dry.

Since the tile edges are cut with a knife, it is a good idea to sponge the edges to smooth them. Then the tile is complete. Finished glazed tiles are shown in Figure 9.18.

Each tile production system used in the Starbuck-Goldner Studio has been well thought out to meet their design needs and production requirements. There is no attempt to make the tiles to the exacting standards of a large manufacture. Their designs are fresh and original, and their tiles are handmade—these are the features they capitalize on.

CHAPTER

10

Press Molding in 18th-Century America

This chapter represents something of a digression because it describes press molding as it was practiced in late 18th- and early 19th-century America. These techniques are not only interesting from an historical standpoint, but there is no reason the modernday mold maker cannot adopt them in his or her studio to produce pieces in small production runs.

Our subject is the press-molded pottery produced at the Old Salem Restoration at Winston-Salem, North Carolina. In the middle of the 18th century, a group of Moravians (a Protestant religious sect founded in Germany in 1722) moved from their settlement in Pennsylvania to start a new settlement in North Carolina. Old Salem is actually their second settlement in that state, and it is now the Old Salem Restoration of Winston-Salem.

The photographs accompanying this chapter show how the pottery shop in Old Salem made a press-molded salt shaker in the shape of a chicken. The year these chickens were first pressed was 1819, and two sizes were made, one selling for three pence and a larger one selling for five pence. (See John Bivins, Jr., *The Moravian Potters in North Carolina*, Chapel Hill, NC: The University of North Carolina Press, 1972.)

The potters of Old Salem produced many kinds of products in clay. They threw on the wheel most of their items such as crocks, bowls, pitchers, jugs, and churns. They press molded baking dishes of all shapes, salt shakers, and all sorts of small bottles and cruets in the shape of fish, squirrels, turtles, swans, owls, and other animals. In a type of screw press, they press molded pipes for smoking tobacco.

The technology used by the Old Salem potters came, of course, from Europe. They were familiar with such processes as salt glazing and producing white ware (in contrast to crudely made earthenware) as well as with the use of plaster for molds. There were even attempts to copy English Queensware and other forms that were common in England at that time.

The Moravians are a very orderly and hardworking people, and it was common to keep records of everyday happenings in the home, field, and workshop. These records make interesting reading today. For example, one member records sending one of the brothers to Philadelphia to purchase a barrel of plaster for making molds in the pottery.

The chicken form that is shown being pressed in these photographs is made using the traditional techniques that research has shown were used by the potters of Old Salem. It is made with red clay and it is given the brown glaze that was common to the pottery. Although this chicken is made into a salt shaker, it could just as well have been made into something else, such as a cruet for oil.

A wooden rolling pin is used to roll out clay on a piece of heavy fabric (Figure 10.1). If the pressing were larger, the fabric would be used to carry the batt of clay to the mold. However, because the mold is small, the batt of clay will be cut into an appropriate size for the pressing and then picked up without the fabric backing.

Historically, the presser did not use a rolling pin to roll the clay out into a thin section. Instead, he "batted" the clay with a "batter," which is shaped sort of like an old-fashioned iron. In this process, a cone of clay was placed on a "batting" stone (heavy flat table), and the batter batted the clay into a flat sheet. A long flat knife, called a pressing knife, was then used to press the batt of clay perfectly smooth. The pressing action is like using a spatula or trowel; it is very effective in revealing tiny pockets of air in the clay. The batt was then carried from the batting stone to the mold on the presserman's leather apron.

Although the potters of Old Salem might have batted instead of rolled the clay for pressing, the potters of today use a rolling pin. The batting procedure was probably more effective than rolling in conditioning the clay used at that time. Today, the clay receives much more conditioning prior to use, and rolling with a rolling pin is quite satisfactory.

After rolling, the potter cuts a piece of the rolled out clay and places it over the cavity of the press mold (Figure 10.2). More clay is cut than is necessary; after the pressing, the excess clay will be cut away.

Fig. 10.1 The potter uses a rolling pin to roll out a batt of clay. Traditionally, the clay was "batted" out with a batter, a tool shaped like a clothes iron. Courtesy of the Old Salem Restoration, Winston-Salem, NC

Fig. 10.2 The potter places a piece of the rolled-out clay on the mold. The square shape of this modern mold contrasts with the shape of the mold dating from 1819 (see Figure 10.11). The majority of plaster molds used in Old Salem indicate that a flexible cottle, probably leather, was used instead of flat mold boards. Courtesy of the Old Salem Restoration, Winston-Salem, NC

of a screw device. The pressure of the plunger forces the clay into every feature of the mold. The plunger is withdrawn, a small hole is drilled or punched in the bowl to receive the stem, and the pressed pipe is taken from the mold and put on a pin to dry.

Returning to the chicken press mold, after the mold is thoroughly pressed, the excess clay is trimmed away with a knife or cut-off tool so that the edge of the clay is level with the surface of the mold (Figure 10.5). Then the second half of the mold is pressed and trimmed.

Next, a comb-like tool is used to deeply score the clay edge to provide a better bonding surface when the two halves are put together. The comb-like tool seems to be a standard tool in potteries everywhere, but an actual comb with teeth broken out of it will accomplish the same thing. Scoring provides a better bonding surface because it increases the surface area of the edges to be bonded by perhaps 50%. When slip is applied to the surface, the increased area resulting from these deep scratches make the bonding of the two clays more effective.

Figure 10.6 shows slip being painted on the

Fig. 10.3 The fingers strongly press the clay into the cavity of the mold. The four clay pipes on the right, a staple item in the Old Salem pottery, were produced in a pipe press. Courtesy of the Old Salem Restoration, Winston-Salem, NC

Fig. 10.4 A pipe press typical of those used in Old Salem. The presses were made of metal or wood, and the mold was usually brass or pewter.

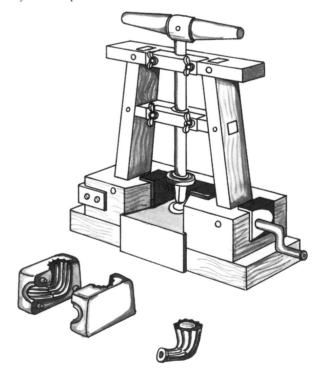

Figure 10.3 shows the pressing of the mold. The clay is pressed into the mold forcefully with the fingers. Although this process seems elementary, it takes a lot of skill to press the clay completely into a mold so that the clay takes on the complete image of the mold.

On the right in Figure 10.3 are some clay pipes with reed stems. Tobacco smoking was very popular, and clay pipes were a standard item of production in Old Salem. The pipes could be made in large quantities with a pipe press, which was a valued item in the inventories of the Old Salem potteries.

The pipe press consisted of a wood or metal frame that held a two-piece metal mold (either brass or pewter) and a plunger, shaped like the inside of the pipe, that was forced into the mold with great pressure (Figure 10.4). A small plug of clay is put into the cavity of the two-piece mold, the mold is locked together in position on the press, and the plunger is forced into the mold, usually by means

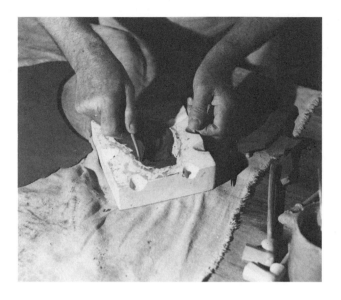

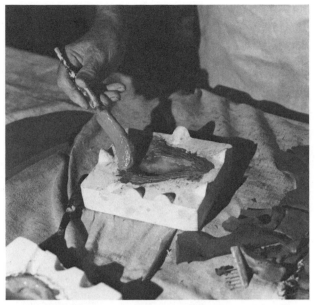

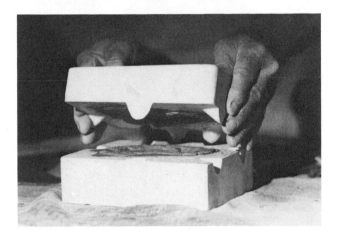

Fig. 10.5 After the mold is thoroughly pressed, the excess clay is trimmed away so the edge of the clay is flush with the surface of the mold. Courtesy of the Old Salem Restoration, Winston-Salem, NC

Fig. 10.6 Slip is applied to the textured edges of the clay. Courtesy of the Old Salem Restoration, Winston-Salem, NC

Fig. 10.7 The two halves of the mold are firmly pressed together. Courtesy of the Old Salem Restoration, Winston-Salem, NC

Fig. 10.8 The clay figure is released from the mold; excess clay at the seam has been squeezed into a thin layer between the halves of the mold. Courtesy of the Old Salem Restoration, Winston-Salem, NC

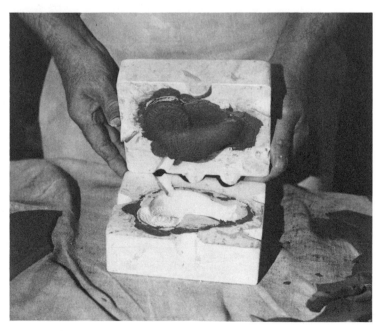

edges of the clay. In Figure 10.7 the two halves of the mold are being put together. If you look closely, you may be able to see that the edges of the pressing were not actually cut level with the surface of the mold and that the clay rises above the edge of the mold. This excess clay no doubt assures that the two halves of the pressing will bond satisfactorily, but if the molds are made accurately and care is taken with the pressing and cutting of the edge, there is no need for this excess clay. Of course, leaving the excess clay might be expedient in the rapid production of every-day items such as this salt shaker, and more care would be taken in the pressing of more formal items.

By pressing too much clay, the seam on the piece is made too large and the excess clay is forced between the halves of the mold, forming a thin layer of clay that must be trimmed away (see Figures 10.8

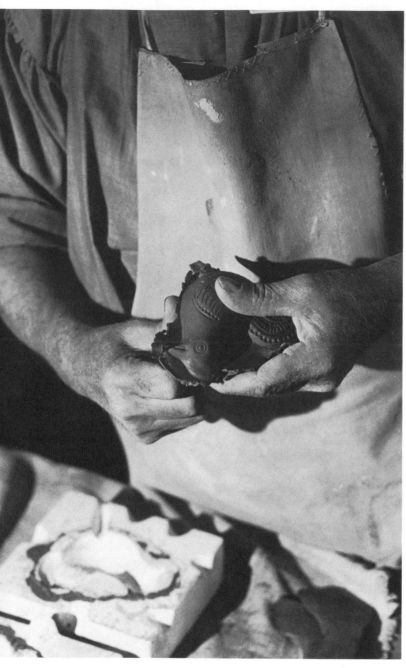

the pressing and permits the two halves of the mold to come together and form an accurate pressed piece. (A gutter is shown on a solid press mold in the Figure 7.14). A gutter is standard in a two-piece solid press mold, and the design of the gutter is crucial to the successful use of a Ram press.

After a very short time in the mold, the two halves can be separated and the pressed piece can be removed. Although the clay is still damp, the mold has absorbed enough moisture so that the clay chicken can be withdrawn from the mold without trouble. Figure 10.8 shows the clay figure and the excess clay that has been pressed into a thin layer between the halves of the mold.

In Figure 10.9, the flange of clay around the seam is being trimmed away. The trimming is called "fettling" and it is done with a fettling knife.

The clay figure is put aside to dry while the rest of the day's lot of chickens are pressed. If the potter had ten molds it would have been easy to make three or four "rounds" of the ten molds per day. By the time the last mold was pressed and assembled, the first pressed mold would be ready to open and remove the completed chicken. By the time the tenth mold was relieved of its chicken, the first

Fig. 10.10 The finished glazed salt shaker. Courtesy of the Old Salem Restoration, Winston-Salem, NC

Fig. 10.9 The clay figure is taken from the mold and the seam is trimmed with a fettling knife. Courtesy of the Old Salem Restoration, Winston-Salem, NC

and 10.9). If excess clay is deliberately used in the pressing and the two halves of the mold must come together completely, then a "gutter" is necessary. A gutter is simply a trough cut into the mold along the edge of the pressing; this holds the excess clay of

Fig. 10.11 An original plaster mold of the period, obviously made in a flexible cottle. Courtesy of the Old Salem Restoration, Winston-Salem, NC

mold would have dried out enough to begin the cycle again.

The chicken is not complete until it gets a base. The base is made in a simple one-piece press mold that contains the image of the chicken's feet. Texturing the joining surfaces, applying slip, and pressing the base and the chicken together completes the pressed chicken, feet and all.

To make the figurine into a salt shaker, a hole is cut in the base so the shaker can be filled, and a series of holes is cut under the neck so the salt can be shaken out. Now the piece is dried, glazed, and fired. The completed salt shaker has the brown glaze typical of the period (Figure 10.10).

The mold shown in Figure 10.11 is an actual mold of the period. These molds obviously were made in flexible cottles (probably leather), not in straight mold boards. Whether economy was a factor or not, using flexible cottles would have had the effect of saving on plaster.

In attempting to recreate the process of press molding as practiced by 18th-century American potters, one question remains: What did they use for models or blocks? Did the potter use an actual product to create new molds from, or did he have a block to cast the molds from? The word "block" as used in the 18th century meant the model or mold that

the working molds were made from, not the first mold from a model, as it means today.

There is no record of the potter using a case mold system as we know it today (where two cases are used to make the two halves of the mold by simply pouring plaster.) In England at that time, the procedure would have been to have a one-piece "block," from which the working molds were taken. This block, or master, was set aside and used repeatedly to make molds whenever necessary. There is no evidence that the potters of Old Salem had such "blocks" in their inventory, although they listed many kinds of molds and all sorts of other facts (such as amounts of clay and plaster on hand).

Molds such as the one in Figure 10.11 probably lasted at least 50 pressings before they had to be discarded and replaced. This is a guess based on experience of today. It is possible that the potters of Old Salem never wore out the molds because they didn't use them that often. If they did need replacing, they simply made a new item in clay and made a single mold from it.

If this chicken salt shaker were made today, how would it be made? Undoubtedly it would be slip cast, probably in a single two-piece mold mounted on a machine that holds a long row of identical molds. Two or three molds can be filled at a time through a hose. The entire line of molds are then dumped (emptied), by inverting the machine over a basin. The molds then go into a dryer, called a mangle, and, when ready, the chickens would be taken from the molds to be finished.

It is standard to have three turns of a mold per day, but in the case of this particular item, because it is small, more turns of the mold can be made. In mass production, the molds are left empty overnight to dry out before another cycle is begun the next day.

The potters of Old Salem "mass produced" things in their own way—in press molds and at the potters wheel. Clearly, their press molding techniques are as suitable today in the modern one-or two-person studio as they were then.

This chapter, the last in the series on press molding, introduces some basic factory procedures such as case making and jiggering. The idea is that these procedures are not limited to use in the factory, but that they can easily be translated into creative tools for the artist-potter.

The ancient practice of pressing plastic clay against the surface of a mold while it is turning rapidly on a wheel is the essence of our contemporary plastic clay production systems that produce most of the dinner-ware made today. While slip casting and other pressing systems produce ceramic products, the vast majority of items are produced with a spinning mold.

Teams of potters throwing as rapidly as they can simply cannot compete with one automatic jigger in producing items such as cups, saucers, bowls, covered casseroles, and plates. Automatic jiggering machines can produce hundreds of dozens of items per hour. On the other hand, machines cannot possibly impart to clay the personal quality that a skilled thrower is able to achieve. The subject of interest is not the contest of values between machine and individual production, but whether certain machine procedures can aid the clay artist in producing quality products while still maintaining an individual character.

This chapter shows two systems of production based on the spinning mold that are reasonable for the individual clay artists or the small pottery operation to consider.

The first procedure is a form of jiggering that relies on the hand as the jigger arm; there are no tools other than the hand, ribs, and sponge. The fingers force the clay against the turning mold. The second procedure introduces a jigger arm that is used with a jolly turned on the plaster wheel. The basic difference between the two procedures is simply one of economy.

However, the most important aspect of this chapter is not that the hand or a jigger arm is used to rapidly shape the clay. The important part is the system of making a two-piece case mold, which is necessary for any serious attempt at quantity production. So far in these chapters on press molding, the problem of quantity production has not been seriously addressed. It's true that the various types

Press Molding for Production

of press molds presented (the hump molds, Styrofoam molds, the Starbuck-Goldner tile molds) can produce hundreds of pressed items without concern over whether the mold wears out or not. However, hundreds of pressings from one hump mold or Styrofoam mold cannot seriously be considered quantity production. The hump mold and Styrofoam mold are well suited to limited production of simple forms with little or no detail in them.

HAND JIGGERING: THE CASE MOLD WITH BASE PLATE

This chapter introduces the jigger and jolly method of pressing clay against a mold surface. It also presents a system of making a wide variety of round items using a case mold and bottom plate (a two-piece case mold). The unique feature of the case mold with bottom plate is that the same mold can be adapted to make a variety of different designs by using dif-

Fig. 11.1 The plaster wheel head, jigger chuck, and working mold shown here are made as described in Figures 11.2–11.5. The mold tapers slightly more than the chuck so that the fit remains secure in spite of wear. The overhanging rim on the mold permits quick placement and removal from the chuck.

ferent plaster, clay, or rubber forms on the base plate. This system offers the potter a means for rapid reproduction of basically round items. The bottom plate also permits the design to be changed with very little effort. The pieces must be round because the system is based on a spinning mold. However, there is much latitude within that limitation. Six or eight-sided bowls, even sculptural, three-dimensional designs, can be easily produced using the concepts presented in this chapter.

For the purposes of this undertaking, the Randall-wheel-turned-plaster-wheel is made into a jolly wheel by making the gypsum-cement wheel head and jigger chuck shown in Figure 11.1. Figures 11.2–11.5 illustrate how the plaster wheel head is made, how the jigger chuck is made on the wheel head, and how a case mold is made for reproducing the working jigger molds.

In commercial operations that produce large volumes of jiggered products, a plaster wheel would not be used as a jolly or as a part of the jigger operation. A jigger and jolly would be used that could withstand the production of thousands of jiggered products. The jolly head would undoubtedly be made of metal and machined on a metal lathe to very close tolerances. However, the basic concepts involved in a large-volume set-up are the same as the system illustrated here. The main difference is in the studio setting and the use of a potters kick wheel to make the jigger set-up. Using the equipment and methods presented here, it is easily within the scope of the small throwing studio to jigger hundreds of items. Jiggering thousands of items is probably unrealistic because of the wear and tear on the machinery.

Making the Plaster Wheel Head and Jigger Chuck

The first step in setting up the jiggering system is to cast a gypsum-cement head for the plaster wheel (Figure 11.2). This head is formed by building up a base of plastic clay around the potters wheel head. A large aluminum cottle is placed around the potters wheel head to produce a casting of about 24" in diameter. The cottle is well set into the plastic clay base and secured with a band clamp and some heavy-

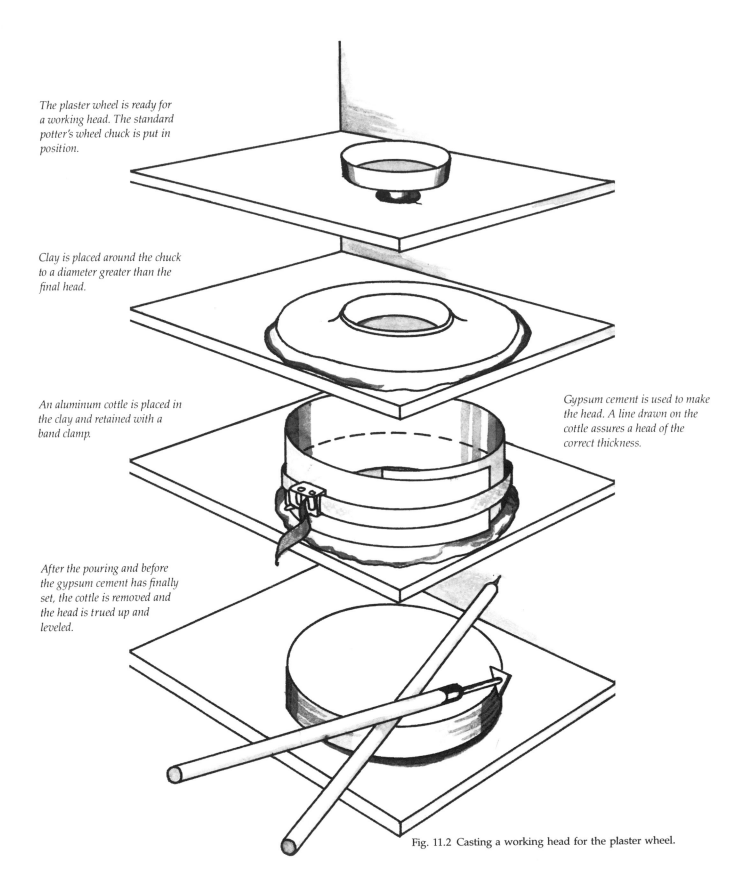

The plaster wheel is ready for a working head. The standard potter's wheel chuck is put in position.

Clay is placed around the chuck to a diameter greater than the final head.

An aluminum cottle is placed in the clay and retained with a band clamp.

After the pouring and before the gypsum cement has finally set, the cottle is removed and the head is trued up and leveled.

Gypsum cement is used to make the head. A line drawn on the cottle assures a head of the correct thickness.

Fig. 11.2 Casting a working head for the plaster wheel.

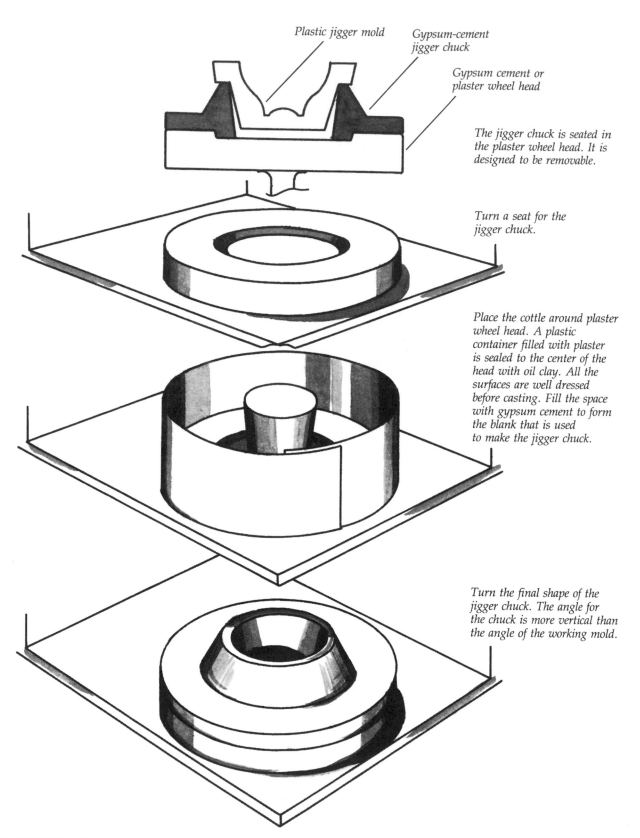

Plastic jigger mold

Gypsum-cement
jigger chuck

Gypsum cement or
plaster wheel head

The jigger chuck is seated in
the plaster wheel head. It is
designed to be removable.

Turn a seat for the
jigger chuck.

Place the cottle around plaster
wheel head. A plastic
container filled with plaster
is sealed to the center of the
head with oil clay. All the
surfaces are well dressed
before casting. Fill the space
with gypsum cement to form
the blank that is used
to make the jigger chuck.

Turn the final shape of the
jigger chuck. The angle for
the chuck is more vertical than
the angle of the working mold.

Fig. 11.3 Making the jigger chuck on a plaster wheel head.

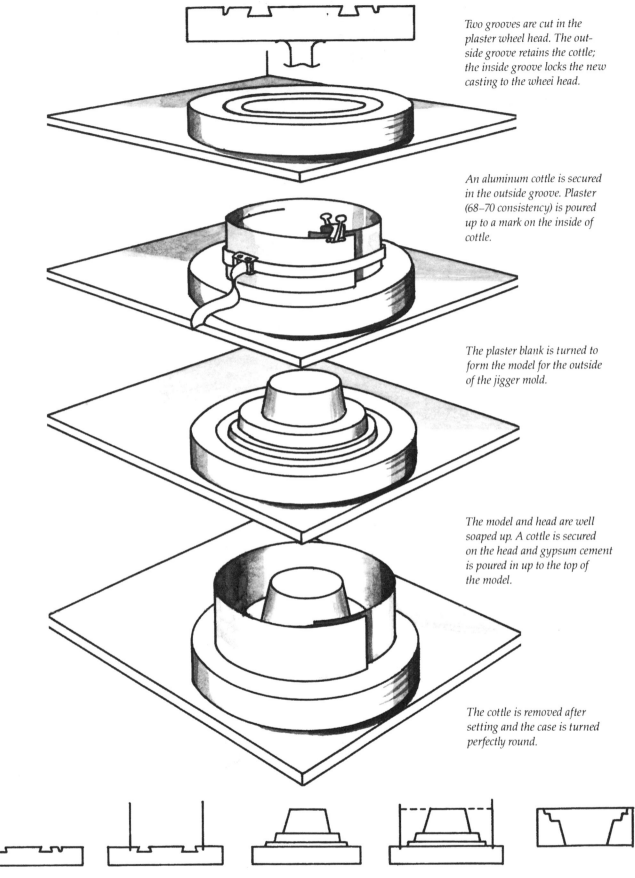

Two grooves are cut in the plaster wheel head. The outside groove retains the cottle; the inside groove locks the new casting to the wheel head.

An aluminum cottle is secured in the outside groove. Plaster (68–70 consistency) is poured up to a mark on the inside of cottle.

The plaster blank is turned to form the model for the outside of the jigger mold.

The model and head are well soaped up. A cottle is secured on the head and gypsum cement is poured in up to the top of the model.

The cottle is removed after setting and the case is turned perfectly round.

Fig. 11.4 Casting the outside piece of the case mold.

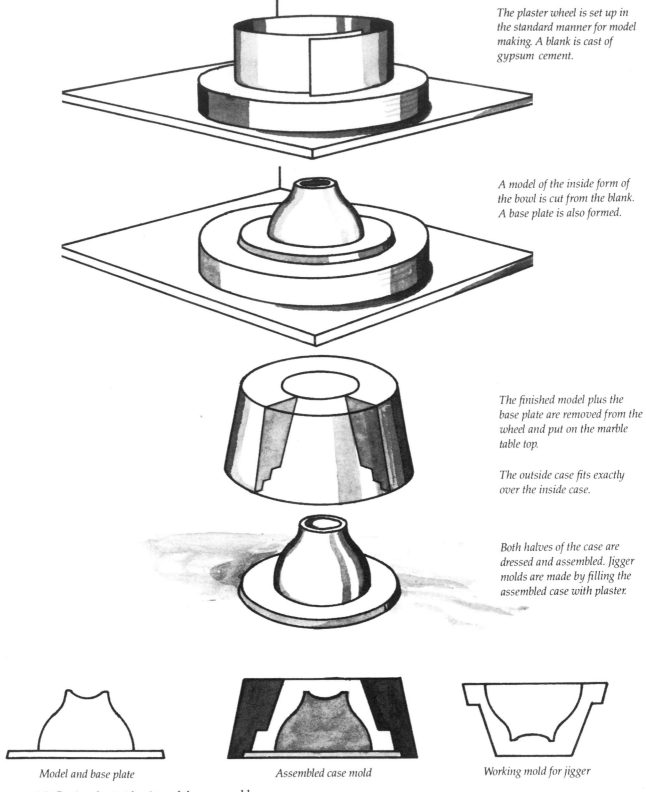

The plaster wheel is set up in the standard manner for model making. A blank is cast of gypsum cement.

A model of the inside form of the bowl is cut from the blank. A base plate is also formed.

The finished model plus the base plate are removed from the wheel and put on the marble table top.

The outside case fits exactly over the inside case.

Both halves of the case are dressed and assembled. Jigger molds are made by filling the assembled case with plaster.

Model and base plate

Assembled case mold

Working mold for jigger

Fig. 11.5 Casting the inside piece of the case mold.

duty board clips at the top edge. The surface of the metal wheel head and the inside surface of the aluminum cottle is then soaped up.

Gypsum-cement is used to make this plaster wheel head. The thickness of the head should be at least 3″, and maybe more if the diameter is much less than 24″. The cottle is a thin sheet of aluminum that can be purchased by the linear foot at any hardware store. Buy at least $6\frac{1}{2}'$ so that there can be an overlap of 6″ when the cottle is used to make a 24″-diameter casting. Store the aluminum rolled up so that when a cottle is needed for the plaster wheel it is a simple matter to form a basically round cottle of any diameter. The smaller the diameter, the more laps the cottle material will make.

After the wheel head is cast, a jigger chuck is cast on top of it, also of gypsum-cement (Figure 11.3). This jigger chuck is the piece that transforms the plaster wheel into a jigger wheel operation. It is the piece that holds the working molds in position during the jiggering operation. It is also the item that would be made of metal and mounted on a much heavier piece of equipment if large quantities of jiggered ware are contemplated.

Figure 11.3 includes a cross section of what the whole assembly (head, chuck, and mold) looks like. Notice that none of the banding of the cottle is shown, because it is assumed that the method of securing the cottle is well understood.

The hole in the jigger chuck is formed by a plastic container such as a cottage cheese container. This container must be weighted down with plaster or clay and it must be secured to the surface of the plaster wheel head with a ring of oil clay. The opening provided by this container will not necessarily be the required shape; the container simply provides a cavity in the casting that must be turned to the correct angle to receive the working jigger molds.

This jigger chuck must fit perfectly on the plaster wheel head. If there is any play between the chuck and the head, the whole jiggering operation will not be satisfactory.

Making the Case Mold

Figures 11.4 and 11.5 show how to make a case mold to reproduce the working molds. First, the finished jigger chuck is removed from the plaster wheel head. The plaster wheel head is prepared for making the case mold by turning the surface level and cutting two grooves into it. The outside groove will help retain the cottle in position; the inside groove will lock the new casting to the wheel head (see also Figure 12.4 and accompanying text).

A plaster blank is cast in the normal manner and the outside shape of the model for the working mold is turned with a base plate. The cottle is then placed in position around the model to permit casting one half of the case mold. Gypsum-cement is used to make the case mold. The result is a mold to form the outside shape of the working jigger mold. (This piece is shown on the top left in Figure 11.6.)

To make the second half of the case, the model of the outside shape of the jigger mold is removed from the plaster wheel head and, once more, the plaster wheel is prepared for model making by turning a cottle-retaining groove and a locking groove in the head. A casting is then made using gypsum-cement, and the shape of the inside of the jigger mold is turned out of this casting. Since the casting is gypsum-cement, which is harder to cut than plaster, the initial turning is done rapidly to get rid of the extra material before it sets up.

The model is the shape of the outside form of

Fig. 11.6 A two-piece case mold (darker plaster) is made to reproduce the working molds (light-colored plaster) necessary for production. Note that the bottom plate fits exactly inside the top part of the case.

Fig. 11.7 This case mold is designed so that various items can be made using the same case and flat base plate. A flat base plate permits an unlimited variety of clay, plaster, or rubber forms to be used on it to cast the molds. Here, a press-molded model for the lid of the bowl is positioned on the bottom plate in preparation for casting a production mold. The pressing is soft clay and adheres to the bottom plate easily.

Fig. 11.8 The bottom plate and the case mold are dressed with mold soap and assembled for casting.

Fig. 11.9 The lid is made by pressing clay into the mold. The excess clay on the edge is thrown to a finished form, including an inner rim for the lid. The bowl is made in the same way, pressing clay against the turning mold with the fingers. The combination of pressing and throwing allows a wide variety of forms to be made with a simple production system.

Fig. 11.10 The bowl, lid, and the molds in which they were made. The case mold for making the molds for both lid and bowl is in the background.

the hemispherical bowl that is to be jiggered. The model is completed with a base plate. Much care and precision must be employed to assure the proper fit of the diameter and edge angle of this base plate to the diameter and edge angle in the outside case mold that has already been completed.

The model with its base plate is removed from the wheel with a saw blade and placed on the marble table top. The outside case is placed over this model (which is actually the inside case mold). Working jigger molds, such as the one shown in Figure 11.6, are made by casting in this two-piece case mold. Figure 11.6 shows one half of the case mold; it shows also the working jigger mold for the bowl and the bottom rim of the other half of the case mold.

In any jiggering operation, the ability to reproduce molds in quantity by using a case mold is the key to quantity production. The system to reproduce the jigger mold for the small bowl is complete.

Varying the Designs
Using the Base Plate

The unique feature of this system of incorporating a base plate is presented in Figure 11.7. On the left is one half of the case that has been completed. In the center is a round base plate that fits into the rim of the case. This plate is made on the plaster wheel with a thin sheet of gypsum cement. It fits exactly into the rim of the case mold pictured. It must be emphasized that this plate is completely flat; that is, no model is attached to it. In the upper right of Figure 11.7 is a press mold of a domed, segmented design. This mold is thoroughly pressed with plastic clay to fill the mold completely. After a few minutes, the pressing is carefully withdrawn from the mold and placed in the exact center of the base plate. Figure 11.8 shows the outside piece of the case placed in position over the base plate that has the pressing secured to it. This is the completed case mold for the lid. Plaster is poured into the case up to the top of the opening.

Figure 11.9 shows this jigger mold being used on the jigger chuck. The rim for the piece is shaped with the fingers as in throwing. There is no jigger arm in use in this particular presentation; the inside of the piece is formed with the fingers. This system is a very good one for short runs of a particular design. It is appropriate for very sculptural pieces where the outside of the mold is formed with the outside case mold and the inside of the mold consists of a basically circular, sculpted form. Since the fingers do the forming, the fingers can compensate for the unevenness of the sculptural form and still make a rim in the round.

Figure 11.10 shows the two molds made from the one case mold, and the products from each mold. This system of making various sculptural forms from press molds as the source of the model is limited only by the imagination and ability of the artist. If many working molds will be needed, then the pressing of the sculptural form should not be made of plastic clay. However, it could easily be cast in flex-ible rubber that would assure a relatively permanent two-piece case mold for any particular sculptural form.

Renewing the Plaster Wheel Head

The repeated use of the plaster wheel in making the models and case molds has reduced the thickness of the head and the proper seating for the jigger chuck is lost. To restore the wheel head for further use, the surface of the plaster wheel is once again prepared for model making by cutting a locking groove into it. A cottle is placed around the outside edge of the wheel head, all surfaces are dressed, and a new surface is cast with gypsum-cement. This new head is then turned to fit the correct placement of the jigger chuck. As the plaster wheel is used in model and mold making, further renewal of the plaster wheel head will be necessary. The renewed head must always be locked into the surface of the old head.

Positive and Negative Molds

One other factor needs to be considered before introducing the jigger arm, and that is the relation of positive and negative forms. The bowl and lid molds in Figure 11.10 are clearly negative molds that produce positive forms. Although a negative form is produced when pressing the clay into the mold, it is in reality a bowl or a lid with a positive outside surface. Positive-to-negative and negative-to-positive has to be constantly considered in mold making. For example, if this system were used to make saucers, then the choice of which comes first (positive or negative) is up to the clay artist. If it is positive to negative, then the saucer would be designed to be made upside down with the mold creating the top surface of the saucer and the fingers creating the back or underside of the saucer. This is the standard procedure in factories: saucers and plates are made upside down, and the template or roller shapes the back or underside. On the other hand, the reverse procedure is worth considering because then the inside or eating surface of the saucer is open to hand manipulation or even decorating while on the chuck. Wonderful subtle spirals could be placed on the surface of the plate or saucer with the fingers, or strong underglaze decoration could be applied after the fingers and sponges have created the item.

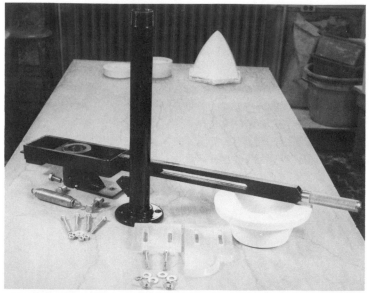

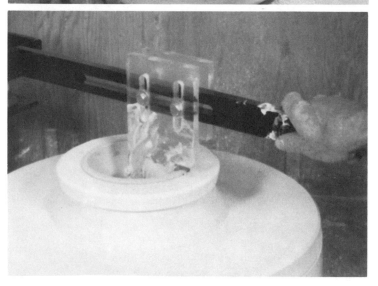

USING A JIGGER ARM

The obvious next step is the incorporation of a jigger arm into the set-up. The previous section introduced the hand-pressed jiggering procedure as well as the system to make molds for this type of jiggering method. The same molds are used with the jigger arm as were used with the hand-pressed jiggering.

A Studio-Made Jigger Arm

Figures 11.11 and 11.12 show a fine jigger arm made by Patrick McGuire of Champaign, Illinois. Figure 11.11 shows the unassembled jigger arm. All the adjustment bolts can be seen, as well as the Plexiglas profile plates used in this photo sequence. The jigger arm is designed to fit any potters wheel that has a sturdy table attached to it. It is adjustable vertically on the vertical pipe support and, of course, the profiles can be changed to fit the need. This jigger arm is made from pipe and rectangular steel stock, and it is very sturdy when it is bolted into position on the table of the wheel.

This particular jigger arm was made in a well-equipped machine shop. The supplies include a length of 3″ pipe, a 3″ flange, a length of steel bar stock $2\frac{1}{2}″ \times \frac{1}{2}″$, a few scrap pieces of $\frac{3}{8}″$-thick steel plate, a reclaimed knurled steel handle, a section of heavy steel pipe that fits over the 3″ pipe, a large spring, and various nuts and bolts. The tools used in con-

Fig. 11.11 This jigger is designed for use with converted potters wheels, such as the kick wheel converted to a plaster wheel in this text. The design is very strong and fits any type wheel that has a sturdy table mounted with the wheel. The profile plates are made of $\frac{1}{2}″$ Plexiglas.

Fig. 11.12 The jigger is assembled, bolted to the table of the wheel, and the height of the arm is adjusted to fit the profile plates. The spring is attached to elevate the arm, and the profile plate is attached to the jigger arm. Final adjustment of the profile plate is made after the mold is placed on the jolly head.

Fig. 11.13 To use the jigger, a ball of clay placed in the mold is opened up with the fingers in a manner similar to throwing on the potters wheel. Then the clay is sponged with water and the jigger is brought down into the opening. The profile plate forces the clay to the contours of the mold, and the excess clay sticks onto the profile plate. The profile plate for this particular design can work just as well turned around on the jigger so that shaping is done on the opposite (far) side of the mold.

struction were a power drill, a power hack saw, a tap and dye set, and a welding set up. The profile plates are made from $\frac{1}{2}$"-thick Plexiglas that is cut with a hand coping saw. The actual blade part is filed into the beveled contour with wood files and then polished with sandpaper and emery cloth.

The design of the profile plate is very similar to the profile plates that have been used for two centuries in the ceramic industry. Ordinarily this plate is made of steel and backed with wood. The wood provides the bevel that is necessary to move the clay correctly, and the steel provides the exact form of the piece being jiggered.

The $\frac{1}{2}$"-thick Plexiglas does a fine job of jiggering up to a point. That is, the Plexiglas will last long enough for small production runs, but it will not last for thousands of pieces made day after day. If the Plexiglas plates were backed with a steel plate, then any quantity of production is possible. When the profile wears to the extent that it does not produce the correct cross-section for the bowl, then the plate is removed, reshaped to the correct profile, and returned to the jigger arm for continued production.

*(**Note:** If you cannot build your own jigger arm, a few jigger set-ups are available commercially for converting a potters wheel to a jigger operation. For limited runs, they appear to be adequate, but they are not heavy duty enough to withstand the wear and tear that occurs in mass producing very large quantities of ware. A number of commercial pottery equipment manufacturers also handle used or recycled equipment. It may be possible to locate a commercial jigger arm or even a whole jigger and jolly machine through one of these companies. However, it may need to be converted to fit your particular needs, and it may not fit conveniently into a studio situation. Nevertheless, a heavy-duty used commercial jigger set-up would undoubtedly last forever.)*

Figure 11.12 shows the jigger assembled and bolted into position on the wheel head. The height of the arm is adjusted according to the size and shape of the profile plate. In this case, the profile forms the inside of the bowl in the mold. The mold shown here is the same mold used in the previous photo sequence for hand-pressed jiggering. The exact position for the profile is determined by placing the profile on the jigger arm and tightening the wing nuts slightly. By bringing the arm down over the bowl

Fig. 11.14 When the profile plate has finished shaping the inside surface of the bowl, the jigger arm is raised out of the way. The rim is trimmed with a potter's knife and sponged, and the mold is lifted out of the chuck and replaced with another.

mold, the profile enters the mold and can be adjusted to the correct position to enable the profile plate to "jigger" the bowl with the correct cross-section.

This profile is designed to rest on the edge of the mold—almost. The part of the plate that hits the top of the mold is adjusted so that when the arm comes down over the mold and the profile plate enters the mold, the profile will stop when it hits the mold. Then the adjusting bolt under the arm next to the support pipe is adjusted so that the plate stops short of the mold by about 2 mm (about the thickness of a potters knife blade or less). This prevents wear on the mold. The excess clay is removed with a potters knife after the jiggering operation.

This particular set-up for jiggering is done with the profile facing the operator; because the direction of the wheel is counterclockwise, this set-up is probably handled most efficiently by a left-handed operator. The left hand manipulates and sponges the clay while the right hand operates the jigger arm. By turning the profile plate around so that it works on the opposite side of the mold than is pictured here, the operation becomes right-handed. In fact, it is normal for the profile plate to operate on the side of the mold away from the operator.

A hand-operated jigger requires skill to operate. After everything is adjusted correctly, a ball of clay (using slightly more clay than is necessary to make the bowl) is thrown into the mold. This ball of clay is opened with the fingers of the left hand (in the left-handed set-up) as is done when opening a ball of clay in throwing. (This is the same procedure as is used in the hand-pressed jiggering operation, except that then the fingers formed the complete bowl without the use of the profile plate and jigger.) The opening of the ball of clay in the mold is done while the jolly head turns rapidly. As soon as the opening of the clay is completed, the clay is sponged with water and the jigger arm is brought down into the mold and the actual jiggering process begins. Figure 11.13 shows the profile arm contacting the clay in the mold and forcing it up the sides of the mold to form the bowl. The profile plate forces the clay against the contours of the mold, and any excess clay usually sticks to the surface of the profile plate.

This first jiggering action basically forms the piece. The jigger arm is raised and the excess clay is removed from the profile plate. The clay in the mold is sponged with water, and the jigger arm is again brought in contact with the clay. The second action of the jigger refines the bowl, and it is finished in a few seconds. The arm is raised out of the way, the rim of the bowl is trimmed with a potters knife, and the bowl is given a final sponging (Figure 11.14). Then the mold is removed from the chuck and a new mold takes its place.

The design of this bowl is very simple (it is nearly a hemisphere). This particular profile plate does, in fact, work in either position, that is, either on the far or near side of the mold. The height of the jigger arm is adjusted to the point that it is close to horizontal when the jigger is in the final stages of jiggering.

In designing profile plates for items that are more involved than this one, it is important to consider which side of the mold the jigger is going to work on. It is also important to consider the arc that the arm rotates on. The arm's rotation must permit the profile plate to hit the mold in the correct place to produce the desired item. There is great latitude for adjustments on this set-up, and products can be made in either negative or positive molds. This particular hemispherical bowl is made in a negative mold; a plate or a saucer would be made in a positive mold. The bowl is made with the jigger forming the inside of the bowl. Usually a plate or saucer is made with the profile plate forming the back of the piece and the mold forming the top surface of the piece.

The Double-Action Jigger

The next sequence of photographs shows, step by step, the production of a fritting crucible by jiggering. These photographs were taken at the University of Illinois Ceramic Engineering Department. This jigger is considerably different than the one discussed previously. It is especially designed to make deep vessels such as the frit crucibles. It is a double-action jigger. In the first action, the jigger arm and profile plate enter the mold, open up the clay, and begin to shape the clay against the wall of the mold. In the second action, the profile plate moves a certain distance toward the mold and forces the clay to climb the wall of the mold to complete the shaping.

A double-action jigger can make many types of vessels, such as crocks with shoulders (like old-fashioned bean jars) and deep or partially closed forms. Although the frit crucible that is shown in this series is open and does not have a shoulder on it, it is nevertheless necessary to use a double-action jigger to make the crucible. Deep pieces need a double-action jigger because the clay will not climb the wall of the mold in one action but will peel off the profile plate and fall back into the mold.

The profile plate is made of metal and wood. The metal is cut to the desired profile shape and mounted on a wood backing that reinforces the sheet metal profile and also forms the part that is bolted onto the jigger arm. On this machine, the speed of the head is controlled with a foot pedal.

Figure 11.15 shows the operator preparing to

Fig. 11.15 A double-action jigger, in which the profile plate is used in two positions: the first to push the clay against the wall of the mold and the second to force the clay up the wall of the mold to complete the jiggering operation. To begin making the deep frit crucibles, the operator takes a measured amount of clay, roughly shapes it into a tapered cylinder, and drops it into the mold.

drop a piece of clay into the mold. The clay is prepared in a de-airing pug mill, and the amount of clay for each piece is weighed to assure no wasted clay. The clay used in this type of jiggering is softer than most clay prepared for throwing on the potters wheel. The softer clay is more responsive to the rapid action of the jigger. When the arm of the jigger is lowered into the mold (Figure 11.16), the first action of the jigger is to force the clay to the walls of the mold. As the jigger continues to be lowered into the mold,

the profile plate continues to press the clay against the surface of the mold and force the clay up the sides. When the jigger has been lowered to the bottom of the crucible, the walls of the crucible are about half as high as the mold and about twice the final thickness. At this point the double action part of the jigger comes into play. By pushing the lever on the left-hand side of the jigger arm (Figure 11.17), the profile plate moves forward and presses the wall of clay towards the wall of the mold. This action forces

Fig. 11.16 The operator lowers the jigger arm into the turning mold with his right hand. The profile plate opens the clay and forces it about half way up the height of the mold.

Fig. 11.17 The second action of the double-action jigger now takes place. With the left hand, the operator moves the template forward, which forces the clay to climb the wall of the mold.

Fig. 11.18 The jiggering action is over. The jigger arm is withdrawn from the mold and pushed aside, and the operator cuts the excess clay from the rim of the crucible.

Fig. 11.19 The last operation is to sponge the rim of the crucible to round it off.

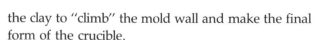

the clay to "climb" the mold wall and make the final form of the crucible.

If this double-action jigger were used to make items such as a large bean jar, then the second movement of the profile plate would produce the shoulder of the pot. This type of jigger could be used to make crocks of all sizes. The first-action would open the clay into the mold, and the second action would force the clay up the wall of the mold.

The last operations are to trim the excess clay from the rim, sponge the rim with a wet sponge, and remove the mold from the chuck (Figures 11.18–11.20). Figure 11.20 shows the molds drying on the drying rack. In the foreground are four unfired crucibles. The molds used to produce these crucibles are made from a case mold very similar to the case mold presented in Chapter 17.

The presentation is intended to show the pro-

Fig. 11.20 After the final sponging of the rim, the mold is lifted out of the chuck head and placed on the drying bench. This bench has steam pipes under the wire mesh to accelerate drying. The four crucibles in the foreground have been removed from the mold and are continuing to dry.

cess of jiggering forms different than a hemispheric bowl. The double action permits closed as well as open vessels to be made. The jiggger that is pictured here is actually a very dated piece of equipment. It is good for short production runs where the quantities needed are not great. If this machine were on a production schedule, it would require a team of operators instead of one person. Probably three people would operate the jigger: one to put the correct amount of clay in the mold, one to do the actual jiggering, and the third to take the mold from the chuck and put it in the drying area. The third person would also remove the dried crucibles from the molds, and the empty molds would be returned to the first operator to be prepared for the repeat cycle.

Figure 11.20 shows eighteen molds, which is a

Fig. 11.21 The Autoform roller jigger manufactured by the A. J. Wahl, Inc. This jigger is shown as a separate piece of equipment, but it is normally part of a much larger automated production system. Courtesy of A. J. Wahl, Inc., Brocton, New York

very small number for a jigger. If this jigger were in production with a skilled team of operators and with all the appropriate equipment (e.g., a pug mill and drier), normal production would be 500 pieces in 8 hours. Of course, the production quantity attainable depends upon how many molds are available and the length of time between jiggering until the same mold is returned to the jigger, ready for another cycle.

SUMMARY

This chapter introduces the use of a spinning mold for rapid production of pieces. The fact that the mold spins on a wheel does not limit the type of piece to simple round ones. Many variations are possible, and even very high relief pieces are possible using the hand-pressed jiggering system. Hand pressing could even be combined with a jigger arm and a profile plate to finish a rim.

The hand-operated jigger and profile plate is a very old-fashioned machine in the industry. Hand jiggering is now limited to perhaps the production of oval platters or limited-run items. The hand-operated jigger is an excellent machine for small production, which is why it is presented in this book. For producing quantities in a factory setting, all jiggering is done on semiautomatic or totally automatic machinery. The principle is the same, except the profile plate is replaced with a roller that rolls the clay into the mold instead of scraping with pressure as the profile plate does. The roller takes many interesting forms depending upon the item to be produced.

Figure 11.21 shows an Autoform® roller jigger made by A.J. Wahl, Inc. This machine is one of the simpler machines produced by this company. The mold is placed on the jolly head with a thin sheet of clay on it. The jolly spins at approximately 300 rpm (twice the speed of very rapidly turning potters wheel): the roller also spins at this speed or even a little faster. The roller is often heated so that the water content of the clay comes quickly to the surface of the hot spinning roller, serving as an excellent lubricant. This Autoform jigger would undoubtedly be part of a semiautomated system containing a pug mill, a transport system to move clay-covered molds to and from the jolly, a drier, and so on. The only action a human operator takes in this type of system is to supply clay to the pug mill and to remove the dried plates from the molds.

Wahl, Inc. produces a line of roller jiggers that use this same principle but are multi-headed, that is with multiple jolly heads and rollers. The production capabilities of such multi-headed machines is measured in hundred dozens.

This chapter has presented the jigger and a case mold system as a possibility for limited mass production for the clay artist. The next step towards expanded production would be to make the system more rapid by increasing the clay supply, the number of molds, and the size of the operating team. Or one could seriously look into the Ram process or perhaps a roller jigger to replace the profile plate jigger. The Ram press and the roller jigger are the obvious next step in quantity and quality production, though they are not seriously presented in this book because the capital outlay involved in setting up such a system is beyond the reach of most small studios.

Part III: Slip Casting

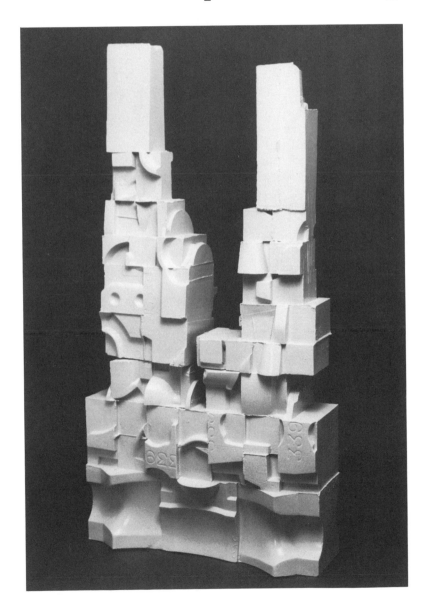

Robert Sedestrom, New Paltz, N.Y. "Cast Sculptural Form," 47″ × 20″ × 7″. Vitreous china, made from a wide variety of precast forms used to create cubistic sculptural molds. Photo by Bob Barrett.

147

Richard T. Notkin, Myrtle Point, Or. "Universal Trooths," slip-cast low-fired porcelain, redwood base, 9"x14"x7". "In my early slip casting days, all of my molds were made from found or store-bought objects. Soon my work demonstrated tremendous abilities as a mold maker, but said little about my abilities as a sculptor. Now I always create my own original prototypes, or models, from which I fabricate a mold. In this way, I feel that I retain artistic control (and artistic responsibility) for the final object. I remain the sculptor, and not just a borrower of someone else's three-dimensional design." (From "Reflections of a Former Slip Casting Addict")

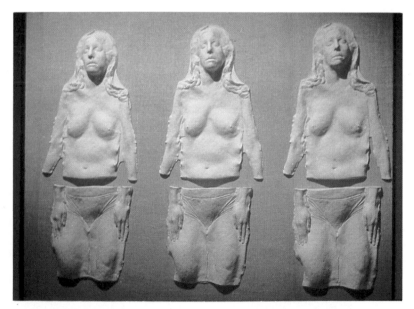

Charles Fager, Tampa, Fla. "Tiny Alice Triplets," 36"x60". Fager uses alginite (a molding material used by dentists) to make impressions from life models. It is capable of capturing incredible detail, limited only by what is chosen as a model. A plaster positive is then cast into the alginite impression and a mold is made from the plaster cast.

Marek Cecula, New York, N.Y. "Vase," 14"x14". The artist uses several slip casting methods. The porcelain vase was created in a mold made by assembling thick plaster pieces together to create unusual angles. The cavity of this assemblage is filled with slip. A preplanned plug is removed to dump the slip.

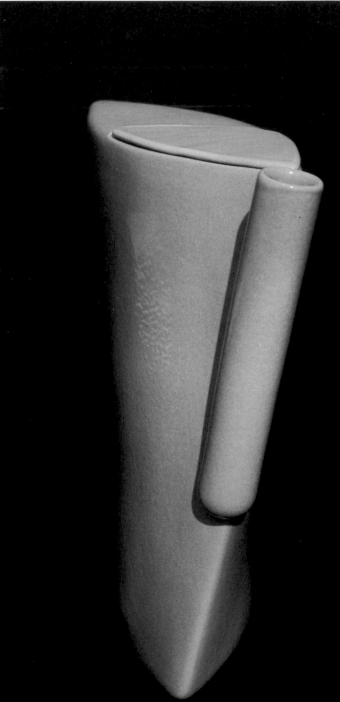

Joseph Detwiler, Fredericksburg, Va. Above: "Spiral Vases," 12½" h.; right: "Teapot," 10" h. Both porcelain. In "Spiral Vases" Detwiler has assembled a number of identical pieces in a spiraling fashion. The pink teapot is also based on a spiral motif.

Kevin Hluch, Frederick, Md. "White Shell Teapot," earthenware, 8" h. Hluch uses patterns of scallops, spirals, and flutes in his designs. Much variety is achieved by altering the form as it comes out of the mold, or by adding another cast form to it.

Mary Rush Shaw, Washington, D.C. "Covered Jar #2," low-fired clay, 4"x4"x4". Shaw, a professional mold maker and mold designer, also produces her own slip cast work. Her forms are often altered and rearranged objects such as automobiles, irons, ducks, etc. Her works are exciting individual statements that are quite original in their inspiration and execution.

Rick Pope, Boseman, Mont. "Cast and Thrown Teapot," salt-glazed porcelain, 12" h. Pope combines a cast form and other processes to make a pot that is much more than a simple slip-cast piece. A basic spherical slip casting is used for the foundation of his assembled pieces, to which he adds thrown parts such as feet and pulled handles.

INTRODUCTION

Slip casting is the process of pouring liquid clay into a plaster mold, waiting for the plaster to withdraw some moisture from the liquid clay, and then dumping the remaining liquid clay out of the mold. The layer of thickened slip left on the interior surface of the mold is the "slip casting," or "slip-cast piece." After the extra slip is dumped out, the plaster continues to absorb water from the slip casting until the clay image is firm. The casting is then removed from the plaster mold. After trimming and sponging, the slip cast piece is dried and completed in a normal ceramic firing and glazing process.

Today, slip casting is a large industry; it ranges from the slip casting of sanitary fixtures in modern, semiautomated factories to the hobbyist pouring molds in a basement studio. The process is the same whether the casting consumes many gallons of slip or only a few spoonfuls.

Pouring liquid clay into plaster molds is a simple technique in practice, but why and how slip casting works is more complicated. There are many technical papers available that explain this process, especially the theory of deflocculation.

Throughout history, water-clay mixtures have been used for everything from patching mud and thatch houses to attaching a handle onto a clay cup. In most clay-working civilizations, even plastic clay was prepared by mixing the clay ingredients into a liquid to achieve a thorough mix and then letting the clay dry to a plastic state.

The problem with using any clay-water mixture, however, is that the mixture must be constantly stirred to keep the clay suspended. The fact that clay and water tend to separate, with the clay sinking to the bottom and the water rising to the top, prevented successful casting of molds with liquid clay until satisfactory deflocculants were discovered in the 19th century.

The use of fired clay molds was another inhibition to successful slip casting. Slip casting can be done in fired clay molds, but the process is so slow that it is not appropriate for quantity production. By the middle of the 18th century, plaster had become the standard mold-making material in potteries, and the use of plaster molds eventually proved to be one half of the solution to the slip-casting riddle.

CHAPTER

Setting Up the Plaster Wheel

Although various systems were used to slip cast non-deflocculated slip in plaster molds, slip casting never competed with press molding for production requirements. All this changed in the 19th century when the chemistry of clay and glazes was beginning to be understood. Soon practical deflocculants were developed that enabled liquid clay to be successfully used for slip casting in plaster molds. With the discovery of how to suspend clay in water by deflocculation, the demise of the press molding for production was just a matter of time.

Slip casting and jiggering have some common features. Both methods depend upon plaster molds to produce a large number of clay products. In both systems, case molds are used to create new production molds when the old ones wear out. However, the basic structure of a mold for slip casting is much different than a mold for a jigger. Slip casting is usually used to make such items as coffee pots, pitchers, cookie jars, and three-dimensional sculpture; a jigger is commonly used to make more open forms such as plates, bowls, cups, saucers, and casseroles. In jiggering, a plaster mold forms one side of the piece, and the profile plate on the jigger arm shapes the other side. Slip casting, on the other hand, is done in hollow molds. The molds have a spare that holds extra slip to keep the mold filled; the spare also serves as the opening for the entry and exit of the slip. Slip casting molds are usually negative molds that, when cast, produce positive forms. The jigger mold can be either positive or negative.

Part III of this book centers around the use of slip and a particular system to make molds for slip casting. In Part II, many mold systems were presented. In Part III, only one mold system is presented over the course of several chapters. The mold system presented in Part III is an accepted procedure used in commercial potteries throughout the world. It starts with a design of a product and ends with the case molds for quantity production. This system is as close to that practiced in a large pottery as it is possible to get in a studio setting. The molds and cases made can be transferred to a porcelain factory, and the item put into production.

The plaster wheel plays a central role in mold making. It is used to produce the model and the mold of the model. The next section describes how to make the heavy plaster head in preparation for making the model and mold. (This procedure was also described in Chapter 11, but it bears repetition here.)

CASTING A NEW PLASTER HEAD

The accompanying photographs illustrate how the plaster wheel is set up for making models and molds on the wheel. The head of a plaster wheel is a very thick, heavy plaster disk, sometimes as big as 12″ thick and 18″ in diameter. The plaster head shown in Chapter 2 on the making of a plaster wheel is not quite as big as this. These photographs show a plaster head about 3″ thick being cast upon a base plaster head that is already 3″ thick. The total thickness of 6″ is more than satisfactory for studio use.

The first step is to prepare the surface of the head to receive the new layer of plaster. Using a triangular-headed turning tool, a series of $\frac{1}{2}$″-deep grooves are cut into the surface of the head. These grooves will anchor the new layer of plaster to the plaster wheel head. These grooves can be undercut so that the new layer of plaster is actually locked into place.

After the anchoring grooves have been cut in the plaster head, the surface of the plaster is well dressed with mold soap. This is most important because if it is not done there will be a very hard layer of plaster at the joint between the two layers, and this will cause trouble if the top layer needs to be removed. To dress the plaster, soap and rinse it three times, and test with a drop of water as described on page 66.

Next, an aluminum cottle is put around the plaster head and secured with a band clamp (Figure 12.1). At the top of the cottle, the overlapping layers of aluminum are secured with a small C clamp. Aluminum works very well for a cottle this size because it is sturdy and cleans up easily. Roofing paper is used in many mold shops for flexible cottle material, but for large, round molds, aluminum is preferable to roofing paper. Only one layer of aluminum is necessary, whereas two or more layers of roofing paper would be required for a large cottle.

After the cottle is in place, a small coil of oil clay is wedged into the seam between the plaster head and the inside surface of the aluminum cottle. This actually is not needed, because the roundness of the wheel head and the close contact of the aluminum cottle form a very good seal. However, the oil clay provides security against a possible leak. The inside surface of the aluminum can be treated with mold soap or a light spray of WD40, well rubbed in; this helps in cleaning up the cottle after use.

Given the diameter of the wheel head and the desired thickness of the new plaster layer, the plaster batch calculator is used to determine a correct amount of plaster to prepare. (For this purpose, a standard consistency of 68 to 70 is appropriate.) The plaster is poured carefully into the cottle.

So that the initial cutting can be done rapidly on soft plaster, the cottle is removed as soon as the plaster begins to get hard (no heat is yet being generated). This point is sometimes difficult to determine, especially for a beginner in mold making. One clue that is helpful in determining when to remove the cottle is to press a finger on the surface of the plaster after the plaster passes from the liquid stage to the plastic stage. At first, the pressure of the finger brings water to the surface, but soon the pressure produces no water and the plaster begins to resist the pressure completely. This is the moment that the cottle is removed.

In the initial cutting, the plaster head is cut to be perfectly round and level. Figure 12.2 shows the start of the cutting, using a large cutting tool. At this point there are no shavings of plaster on the wheel table. Now consider Figure 12.3 and note the pile of plaster shavings. Most of these shavings are a result of the initial cutting with the cutting tool shown in Figure 12.2. This represents less than 1 minute's work. In less than a minute, the new plaster wheel head is made accurately round and level. All this is done while the plaster is in the plastic stage so it can be worked very rapidly.

Figure 12.3 shows the final leveling of the new plaster wheel head. The tool being used is a long-handled triangular turning tool. Compare the position of the hand holding the short tool in Figure 12.2 with the position of the hands in Figure 12.3. The long handle of the tool is anchored to the turner's hip, while the belly stick and the left hand anchor the cutting blade.

Fig. 12.1 After turning a series of locking grooves in the plaster head and dressing the surface with mold soap, an aluminum cottle is secured around the head with a band clamp and C clamp.

Fig. 12.2 As soon as the new layer of plaster begins to harden, the cottle is removed, the new head is quickly turned to exact roundness, and the top surface is cut smooth. This takes less than a minute's time because the plaster is still quite soft. Note the position of the large cutting tool anchored securely on the belly stick.

Fig. 12.3 A final leveling of the new plaster wheel head is done with a triangular-shaped blade. Most of the movement of the cutting tool against the plaster is accomplished with the legs, not the hands. The tool is anchored to the belly stick with the hands (a long-handled tool will also be secured under one arm). The legs move the tool smoothly and accurately, and the belly stick is repositioned in the back board frequently.

It is impossible to show exactly the movement of the legs when plaster is turned using the belly stick, but the legs are the source of movement, not the hands. The hands are anchored firmly to the turning tool and the belly stick; in using a long-handled tool, the right hand holds the handle securely against the right hip, or the handle may be tucked under the right arm for more security.

Actually, the working position for turning plaster using a belly stick is based on three points: right foot, left foot, and the point of the belly stick that is driven into the back board. This belly stick point is a pivot point. The legs provide mobility for the tool. The movement is made mainly by bending the knees or by moving smoothly with the hips and knees. With a little practice, the method of using a belly stick and the legs for support in cutting plaster can be mastered.

MAKING THE PLASTER BLANK FOR THE MODEL

In preparation for model making, two grooves are cut in the plaster head (Figure 12.4). The deeper, inner groove is to lock the plaster blank for the model to the plaster head. By giving this groove a slight

undercut and making it about an inch wide, it will do an excellent job of holding the plaster blank to the plaster head without any other support. (Some workers use nails to lock plaster blanks to the plaster wheel head, but I do not recommend this.) After the blank of plaster is turned into a model, the model will simply be cut off and the plaster head will be ready for a new blank of plaster.

The narrow outer groove serves to help hold the cottle in place. Although the cottle can be positioned reasonably securely on the plaster wheel head without this groove, the groove helps hold the cottle in a fairly accurate round form, and therefore less cutting is required to make the plaster blank perfectly round. This groove also aids in sealing the cottle to the plaster head to prevent any leaks when the cottle is filled with plaster. It only takes one accident with a leaking cottle or mold set-up to prove that extra precaution in securing cottles and mold boards is worth the effort. This groove is especially important when a tall or high cottle is used, because the larger amount of plaster exerts considerable pressure and mandates strong, leak-proof procedures. It is not standard to use a groove to retain the cottle in a round position or to undercut the locking groove, but these two procedures are sound practice.

After the grooves are cut, the surface of the plaster head is thoroughly dressed with the mold

Fig. 12.4 In preparation for model making, two grooves are cut into the plaster head. The deep inner groove will lock the plaster blank for the model in place, and the outer groove helps position the cottle.

soap in preparation for pouring the plaster blank onto the plaster head.

The cottle set-up shown in Figure 12.5 is standard for making a blank of plaster to be used in turning a model. Four C clamps are used on the aluminum cottle for two reasons. The first and main reason is that the clamps add weight to the cottle and will counteract any tendency for the cottle to float or to rise when the plaster fills the cottle. It is very important to eliminate any possibility of this happening. The second reason is that the clamps secure the overlapping cottle material. If the overlap is loose, plaster has a tendency to fill in the gap between the overlapping material. Not only is this plaster wasted, but it is a mess to have to unwind the cottle and find a thin layer of plaster on both sides of the cottle material.

After the cottle is fixed in place with a furniture band clamp and the C clamps, the seam at the base is sealed with a coil of oil clay. Then the correct amount of plaster to make the blank for the model is carefully poured into the cottle. In pouring large amounts of plaster (over 25 or 30 pounds), it is important that the whole procedure be done correctly. The cottle pictured in Figure 12.5 is rather tall, and if plaster were poured directly into the cottle, the plaster would hit the bottom and splash upon the sides of the cottle, which might trap air. Always pour plaster over something or against something. As discussed in Chapter 3, a stick of wood or a broom handle placed in the mold set-up will help the plaster flow smoothly into the cottle. If the plaster is poured against the wood or broom handle, it will not splash around inside the cottle.

Some mold makers use their hands as a baffle for large pours of plaster. This only works if there are two people doing the job, one pouring and one with a hand in the cottle or mold form guiding the

Fig. 12.5 After the plaster head is dressed with mold soap, the aluminum cottle is placed into the outer groove. It is secured with clamps and oil clay, and plaster is carefully poured in to form the blank for the model.

flow of the plaster. Another accepted practice is to put a hand deep into the plaster after the pouring is completed and carefully stir the plaster with upward movements of the hand. The idea is to bring to the surface any air bubbles that may be trapped in the pour. This is a rapid procedure, and it needs to be considered only in pouring large amounts of plaster.

As soon as the plaster begins to set, the cottle is removed and the blank cylinder of still-soft plaster is ready for model making, which is covered in the next chapter.

13

Making a Model and Mold of a Non-Round Form

The photographs in Chapters 12 and 13 illustrate a single continuous procedure in mold making. The procedure is covered in two chapters instead of one because the first part of the procedure (presented in Chapter 12) is the standard method to start any model on the plaster wheel. The second part (presented in this chapter) covers how to turn a model and change it from a round form to a four-sided, spiraling form.

This chapter also shows the standard system to find a half-line on a model, and, more important, it introduces the contoured separation plane as a way to divide non-round forms in mold making. This system results in a mold that is self-locking and that requires no natches. It also assures that there are no acute angles in the mold that would break off during repeated use.

Almost any form under consideration can take advantage of the system presented in this chapter to produce a superior mold for slip casting. Once the point is reached where a spare is made on the model (Figure 13.8), the shape of the model is really immaterial as far as applying the procedure goes. No matter how many pieces the mold has to have, this system for finding a separation line, determining the various pieces necessary, and developing a no-natch contoured separation plane is valid.

TURNING THE MODEL

Figure 13.1 shows the soft plaster being rapidly removed from the plaster blank for the model. The tool being used is a small, heavy-duty loop tool, and this size tool can remove all the plaster necessary to form a crude model in just a minute or two. The plaster must be in the plastic stage. When the tool is placed against the turning wheel, the plaster is carved so rapidly that the excess shavings seem to shoot off the turning blank, filling the work table in a moment's time. The plaster is removed so fast that the scraps of damp plaster have to be removed continuously from the space around the plaster head.

As the plaster hardens, a long-handled turning tool is used to make the final rough shape. Various turning tools and ribs are used to refine the model to its finished turned form (Figure 13.2). Note the concave top, which adds greater interest to the form.

Figure 13.2 also illustrates the use of a shrink ruler to determine the exact size of the final product. As the ruler shows, the final product will be $7\frac{1}{2}''$ high, based on a predetermined shrinkage of $12\frac{1}{2}\%$ for the clay body. This shrink calculation and the $12\frac{1}{2}\%$ ruler are easily made using the shrink calculator accompanying this text.

MODIFYING AND FINISHING THE MODEL

The final model is planned as a non-round, four-sided spiral shape. However, it is based on equal spaces to make the four sides. Figure 13.3 shows how to begin dividing the model into equal vertical segments. This method is used either to find separation lines for a mold or, as here, to divide the model equally to guide further alterations. A circle is drawn on the surface of the plaster head with an indelible pencil. The circle has a larger diameter than the model. This circle will serve as the basis for altering the model into four sides. This is a standard procedure whether or not the model is round or irregular; this circle is the beginning of the orientation of the mold. The circle is divided into halves using a divider, and the half points are marked with the indelible pencil. Then equidistant points are marked on the circle from each half point. It is important that these points are far enough away from the half point so that when the divider is used against the model, as in Figure 13.4, the arcs that are made from each point clearly cross. Note the distance from the half mark to the points where the divider is placed to make the half-line crosses.

Dividing the model is shown in Figure 13.4. This is a standard procedure to determine the half-line on a model, and it works on any form when the half-line is a flat plane. On very complicated models (such as a very large model for a piece of sculpture or a tall, elaborate lamp base) some shops use a light to throw a shadow onto the model, and the half-line

Fig. 13.1 The rough shaping of the model is done with a small, heavy-duty loop tool while the plaster is still in a plastic state. The basic shape is cut in a very few minutes. As the plaster hardens, long-handled tools are used to do the final cutting.

Fig. 13.2 The final turned form is shown here. Note the concave top. The shrink ruler shows that this piece, at $12\frac{1}{2}\%$ shrinkage, will be $7\frac{1}{2}''$ high when it is a finished product.

is marked along the line indicated by the shadow. Either system can be used when there is no undercuts on the model and when the separation line indicates that the mold will withdraw from the model without a problem.

Figure 13.5 shows how the crosses made with the divider are connected to form the half-line. This procedure is repeated on the opposite side and across the top of the model. A half-line is also indicated on the plaster wheel head. It is important that the flexible ruler used to connect the crosses is used in the manner shown in Figure 13.5. If the model is small or complicated, then a small portion of the ruler is used to connect only two crosses at a time. The line that is established by this system should be straight and not wavy when viewed from a short distance. With this particular model it is possible to check the smoothness and accuracy of the line against a shadow thrown on the model from the light that is fastened to the edge of the plaster wheel table.

The next step is to establish lines on the model to guide the transformation of the round form into a spiraling, four-sided form. This is done with a compass holding an indelible pencil. The model is divided into eight equal vertical parts and into eight horizontal spaces that are not necessarily equal. The horizontal lines on the model are reference lines that guide the drawing of the spirals that make the four sides of the model. Figure 13.6 shows the compass making a guide point on the horizontal line, using the vertical line as the point of reference. In this

Fig. 13.3 To find a half-line on a model or to divide a model into equal vertical parts, the first step is to draw a large circle on the wheel head. Then divide the circle in half with the dividers and, on the circle, mark two points equidistant from one half mark and two points equidistant from the other half mark.

Fig. 13.4 Using these two points on the circle, arcs are lightly drawn on the model and an indelible pencil is used to mark the cross points. This process is repeated, using various-length arcs from the points, to establish an exact half-line.

Fig. 13.5 The crosses are connected using a flexible plastic ruler and indelible pencil. The ruler is placed carefully against the crosses at the bottom of the model; then it is bent around the surface and placed next to the cross marks at the top. The half-line is then drawn on the model and on the wheel head as well.

manner, four equal spiraling sides are indicated on the model.

A Sureform blade is used to remove the plaster from the model to form the four spiraling sides (Figure 13.7). (The blade is used without the handle because the handle prevents the shaved plaster from easily falling away. The plaster is damp at this stage, and if the blade were used with the handle, it can quickly clog up with damp plaster that soon hardens and is impossible to remove.) The half-round Sureform tool is best to use because it is stiff. If the flat Sureform is used, it should be held with both hands to assure a smooth flat cut. (Note how the flat Sureform blade is used in Figure 5.11 where it bends easily to a contour.)

The Sureform blade works quickly to remove the plaster almost up to the line that indicates the edge of the side. The side, or facet, is then refined into a flat spiraling plane, using a heavy power hacksaw blade, first on the toothed side and then with the sharpened back.

The model is finished and dressed with mold soap. Then a dry cloth is used to burnish the surface to a dull shine.

MAKING THE SPARE

All molds for slip casting need a spare of some sort. In simple terms, a spare is an extra space that holds a reservoir of slip that keeps the mold filled while the plaster extracts water from the slip. Even in a simple one-piece mold for a tumbler, extra height is allowed in the mold to assure that the tumbler will be the correct size. Approximately ½" extra height is sufficient to assure enough slip is in the mold. A spare line cut into the top part of the mold acts as the cut-off line when the tumbler is taken from the mold.

In more complicated slip castings, the mold has two spares, one at the top and one at the bottom of the piece. This type of mold is thoroughly discussed in Chapter 14. For the four-sided spiral piece in Figure 13.8, the spare serves two functions: the first is to serve as the reservoir for the slip, and the second is to form the recessed part of the piece. To make

Fig. 13.6 The model is divided into eight equal vertical sections and eight horizontal sections. These lines are reference lines for drawing the spiral edges of the altered model. A compass and indelible pencil are used to mark guide points for the spiral design that forms the four sides of the model.

Fig. 13.7 A half-round Sureform blade is used to remove the plaster and form the spiraling planes.

Fig. 13.8 All slip casting molds need a spare. It provides the opening for slip to enter and exit the mold and it acts as a reservoir of slip necessary to keep the mold filled as the plaster absorbs water from the slip. In this case it will also shape the concave top of the piece. Here a cut-off plastic cup, secured with oil clay, serves as the inside cottle for the spare.

Fig. 13.9 A small strip of roofing paper serves as the outside cottle for the spare. The cottle is secured with oil clay, a clothespin, and a C clamp. The plaster is poured into the space between the plastic cup and the roofing paper cottle.

the spare, a plastic coffee cup is cut to about ⅔ of its original size, placed on the top center of the mold, and secured to the plaster with oil clay inside the cup. This will form the opening for the slip. A cottle of roofing paper is then put around the shoulder of the piece and secured with oil clay (Figure 13.9). A clothes pin holds the roofing paper together, and the C clamp is put on the top edge to add weight to the cottle so that it does not move when the plaster is poured. The diameter of the cottle is larger than necessary for the finished spare so that the final shape of the spare can be refined after the plaster is set.

Plaster is carefully poured into the space between the coffee cup and the roofing paper cottle. The mold has been dressed so this new pouring of plaster will not stick to the model. After the plaster has set, the roofing paper cottle is removed. Because it is a small piece, the spare is turned to the correct

shape (Figure 13.10) when the plaster is hard. After turning, the spare is tapped with a rubber mallet to loosen it; it is lifted from the model, and the coffee cup cottle is removed.

The shape of this spare is typical of that used in the ceramic industry for quality work. The protruding ring around the spare forms an excellent locking mechanism to hold the spare in position in the mold (see Figures 13.16 and 13.17). It is also round; as the mold wears slightly, this type of spare will turn easily in the mold. Since the spare is not locked into one position, it wears slowly and its performance is unaffected.

This spare is the third piece of the three-piece mold. A form like this could be made in a two-piece mold (i.e., no separate spare would be cast), but the concave top necessitates a three-piece mold. (This principle is illustrated in Figure 13.11.) If the top were simply cut off flat, a two-piece mold is in order. The spare and vessel would be turned from a single plaster blank, and the spare would be a straight, solid cylinder rising from the top of the form to the height of the mold. Undoubtedly, if cost were a crucial concern, then this particular item would be converted to a two-piece mold. A three-piece mold requires three case molds instead of two, and a three-part mold is more time-consuming to use than a two-part mold. But where quality and attention to detail are important, then the concave top justifies itself by producing a much more interesting form than one that is simply cut off flat.

Cost is not the central concern of this book, whereas mold-making skills are. The process of making a separate spare like the one shown here is a skill every mold maker should have.

After the spare is made, the model is cut from the plaster wheel with a hacksaw blade, and the bottom is carefully leveled with a Sureform blade and ribs. The finished model is moved from the plaster wheel to the marble-topped work table where the rest of the three-piece mold is made.

FINDING A SEPARATION LINE FOR A NON-ROUND FORM

Establishing the proper and workable separation line for non-round forms is a critical aspect of mold making. The method shown here for finding a separation line is much different than the common practice of resting a complicated form on its side in a bed of clay and attempting to find a separation line by only looking at one side of the model. Of course, this latter method can be used, and it is practiced in mold shops throughout the world. However, it is hoped that the system presented here for finding a separation line on a non-round form will be given serious consideration. It is an easy method to use, and it is far superior to resting a model on its side and trying to orient the model to the shape of the mold while trying to determine the separating line when only seeing half of the model. Although the illustrated project is a rather simple spiraling four-sided form, the method works just as well on a very complicated piece of sculpture.

Fig. 13.10 The outside cottle is removed after the plaster has set, and the plaster is turned to the correct shape. The shape of this spare forms an excellent locking design and is typical of those used in the ceramic industry. After turning, the spare is removed from the model and the inside cottle is removed.

The procedure is as follows:

1 The spare and the model are glued together with Duco Cement. The top surface of the spare will be the top of the proposed mold, because that is where the slip enters the mold and is emptied out.

2 Two perpendicular axis lines are drawn on the base plate, dividing the plate exactly in half in two directions. Then the dimensions of the mold are established on the base plate, as shown in Figure 13.12. The square is 3" wider and longer than the maximum dimension of the model. That is, it is $1\frac{1}{2}$" larger than the model on all sides. A circle in the center indicates the size of the spare. All lines are drawn with an indelible pencil. Then the base plate is thoroughly dressed with mold soap.

3 The model and spare are placed upside down on the circle in the center of the base plate. This automatically establishes the top surface of the mold.

4 A large carpenter's square is aligned with one corner of the square drawn on the base plate. A

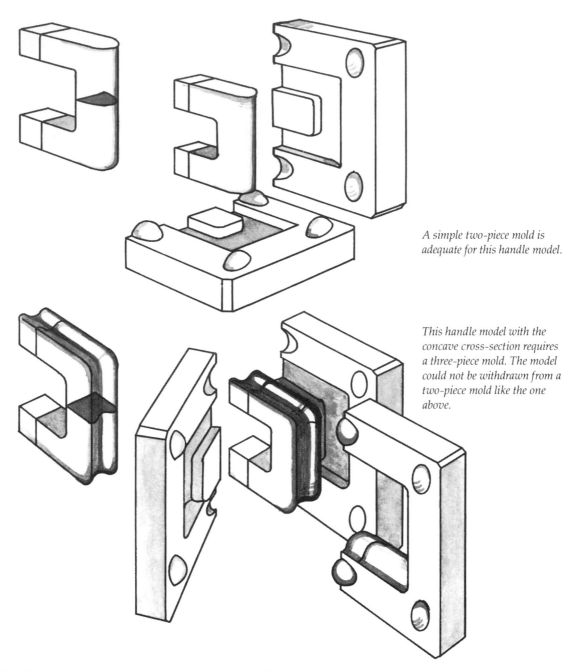

A simple two-piece mold is adequate for this handle model.

This handle model with the concave cross-section requires a three-piece mold. The model could not be withdrawn from a two-piece mold like the one above.

Fig. 13.11 Determining the need for a two- or three-piece mold.

smaller carpenter's square is placed on the edge of the large square (Figures 13.13 and 13.14). This smaller square will be used to determine the proper points for a separation line.

5 The model and attached spare is rotated to a point that seems suitable for a separating line in ref-

erence to a half-line (axis line) on the base plate. This point is checked for any withdrawal problems (undercuts or shallow angles) by placing the small square against the model. *The angle that appears between the square and the model will determine if the model will withdraw from the mold with ease or not.* If the angle is very small, then the model is rotated a few degrees to

Fig. 13.12 The base plate system of orientation for the mold is used, as was done in Chapter 7. The calipers indicate the size of the mold, and the circle is the size of the spare.

Fig. 13.13 Two carpenter's squares are positioned as shown, and the model is rotated until a point is reached where the smaller square, when held up to the model, indicates that a two-piece mold will separate easily at that point because there are no undercuts or extremely shallow angles. The square also indicates the direction of withdrawal of the mold. A series of "successful" points are connected to make the separation line.

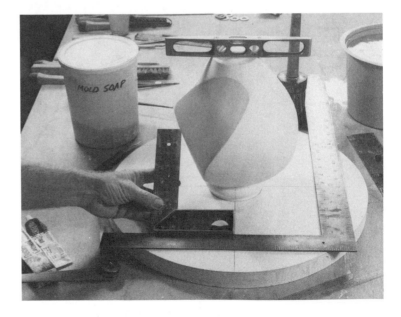

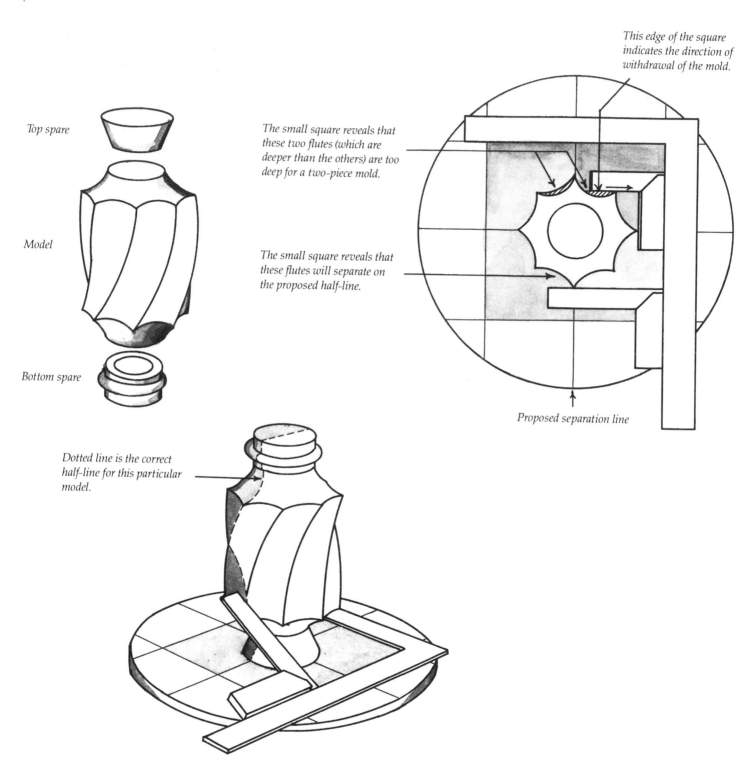

Top spare

Model

Bottom spare

This edge of the square indicates the direction of withdrawal of the mold.

The small square reveals that these two flutes (which are deeper than the others) are too deep for a two-piece mold.

The small square reveals that these flutes will separate on the proposed half-line.

Proposed separation line

Dotted line is the correct half-line for this particular model.

Fig. 13.14 Determining the correct separation line.

increase the angle and find a more satisfactory separation point. A series of successful points are determined in this way, and they are connected with indelible pencil to form the separation line.

By using the small square to check the separation line for the ability of the two pieces to separate and for the model not to be "hung up" in the mold, a satisfactory mold can be made. Perhaps the method seems complicated at first, but in reality it is much less complicated than trying to establish a suitable orientation of a model and mold while the model is on its side. In this system, the whole model can be seen in relation to the mold separation line, and it can be easily checked for any withdrawal problems and corrected if necessary. This system is especially appropriate for establishing the separation lines for multi-piece molds. Using this system, it is easy to see the various pieces that need to be made and establish the line for proper withdrawal of the pieces.

The final mold is made directly on the base plate by building up one side of the mold with water-based clay and placing the mold boards according to the lines on the base plate. The next section presents a unique no-natch system of locking the mold pieces together.

THE NO-NATCH
CONTOURED SEPARATION PLANE

Whenever a model demands a separation line that is not a straight half-line, such as the spiraling four-sided form in this presentation, the separation line can be used to form a contoured plane that not only provides the correct separation but also is self-locking, so there is no need for natches.

To assure that this contoured plane is illustrated clearly, the model and spare have been placed on their side so that the planes can be easily seen in the accompanying photographs. Figure 13.15 shows the model on its side in the correct position as determined by the lines on the base plate. The separation line is easily seen on the model and spare. Because the model was placed on its side, the planned dimension line for the base of the mold had to be extended, but the rest of the dimension lines were correct.

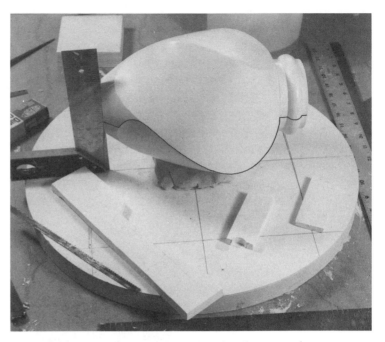

Fig. 13.15 The model is carefully placed on the plate to match the mold dimension lines. To permit better photography of the contoured separation plane, the model was placed on its side, instead of upright as originally planned. Consequently the line for the bottom of the mold had to be extended. Three control plates, made from thin sheets of plaster, will be used in casting to assure that the top and bottom of the separation plane are perfectly flat.

Three plaster control plates are made with thin plaster pieces. They are shown in Figure 13.15 and their use is evident in Figure 13.16. The use of these plates during casting will assure that the top and bottom of the separation plane are straight and that they follow the half-line on the model exactly. Anytime an area of a mold must be straight and level, it is far more satisfactory to use something straight and level to cast against than to try to make a straight and level area with moist clay.

Figures 13.16 and 13.17 show how the contoured plane is built up out of moist clay to follow exactly the edge of the separation line. It is important to note the angle of the separation plane at the surface of the model. The angle is never a sharp one, and it changes as the line changes, ensuring that both sides of the future mold have strong edges. The continuous contouring of the plane provides the locking system for the mold.

Anytime the separation of a mold does not fol-

Fig. 13.16 The contoured separation plane is built up from water-based clay, and it follows the exact edge of the separation line. The plane is carefully modeled to meet the model at an angle such that there will be no thin, fragile edges in the mold. Plaster control plates guarantee that areas of the mold will be flat and level where required.

Fig. 13.17 The contoured separation plane on the other side of the model. The most important aspects of this system are that there are no thin edges to the mold that might break off during use and that no other locking, or keying, of the mold is necessary.

Fig. 13.18 The first half of the casting with the model and spare in place.

Fig. 13.19 All three pieces of the completed mold are self-locking, and there are no thin edges to break off.

low a flat plane, two factors are essential for the success of the mold:

1 The separation line, or lines, must produce a mold that separates from the model easily.
2 The separation line must not produce sections of mold with acute-angled or thin edges that are easily broken off, thus marring or destroying the mold.

Determining an appropriate separation line and using the contoured separation plane will guarantee good separation of the mold and no thin or "feather" edges on the mold to break off. The contoured separation plane is also self-locking and automatically eliminates the necessity for natches in the mold (which sometimes break off in use).

After both contoured separation planes are modeled in plastic clay and the top and bottom plates are in correct position, the final casting of the mold is routine. The model, spare, and the top and bottom plaster control plates are dressed with mold soap. Mold boards are correctly placed along the lines indicated on the base plate, and all seams between the mold boards and the clay and plaster set-up are sealed before casting.

The first half of the mold with the model and spare in place is shown in Figure 13.18 and the completed mold is shown in Figure 13.19. After casting, the mold is separated and the spare is pried from the model with a knife. Since this spare forms part of the mold, it is returned to its position in the mold, the mold is clamped together, and the edges are beveled. (If the spare simply forms the opening in the mold, it is retained on the model for future use.)

Two furniture clamps are placed on the mold and tightened to assure that the mold will not warp in drying (Figure 13.20). Warpage in molds is likely to happen if the molds are subjected to rapid drying techniques, such as very hot air passing over the mold. Direct heat from an oven or kiln is also bad for the mold because of the danger of the mold getting too hot. It is much better to dry the mold slowly, unless there is a controlled drying method available. Figure 13.20 shows the finished mold under clamps for an initial dry period of 24 hours. After 24 hours,

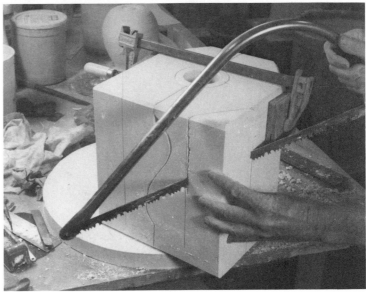

Fig. 13.20 The finished mold is clamped together for the first 24 hours of drying. A mold this size can take as long as two weeks to dry in a temperate climate, but moving air and *moderate* heat will shorten the drying time considerably.

Fig. 13.21 This mold is too heavy to be used constantly. By cutting off the corners, a savings of 25% is made in the weight and there is less variation in the thickness of the mold.

the clamps can be removed and retaining straps applied for continued drying.

A mold this heavy, with the standard minimum thickness of 1½" at any area, is satisfactory for limited studio use (that is, for a few individual castings). But for production runs that use the mold to the limit of its capability, the mold is too heavy. The corners of the mold are removed (Figure 13.21) to save weight (about 25%) and to equalize the thickness of the mold from the thinnest to the thicker areas. This equalization aids in the efficiency of the mold.

The methods presented in this chapter for determining the separation line(s) on non-round forms and for creating a mold with a contoured separation plane is applicable to very complicated forms (such as a sculptured head or animal) as well as to the simpler four-sided spiral form used in this demonstration. The contoured separation plane is appropriate for any separation line that does not form a flat plane. It is easy to use and eliminates the need for natches.

Chapters 14 through 18 actually present one continuous procedure to bring a design prototype (a coffee pot) from the model stage through to the case molds, which are then used to reproduce the working molds for production. The reason for presenting this process in five separate chapters is that it is easier to digest a large amount of information when it is served in smaller batches. The material is presented as follows:

Chapter 14: The Presentation Model
Chapter 15: Mold Making on the Plaster Wheel
Chapter 16: Molding the Handle, Spout, and Lid
Chapter 17: Case Mold for the Pot Form
Chapter 18: Case Molds for the Handle, Spout, and Lid

The choice of a coffee pot for this presentation is not accidental. A formal porcelain coffee pot is an ideal product for demonstrating many mold-making techniques for production. The design requires numerous molds to produce it. It involves making case molds of gypsum-cement and flexible rubber compounds, and, finally, it involves the assembling of the various cast parts into a completed pot.

The techniques presented in these chapters are just as applicable to the modeling, molding, and assembling of an intricate human or animal figurine with arms, legs, and head for which molds must be made (and then one has to make "molds of the molds" for production). In fact, these techniques apply to any slip-cast ceramic product that needs numerous molds to reproduce the end product.

Figure 14.1 shows the pieces made from the molds produced in these chapters. They are formal coffee pots that involve assembling the various parts to make the final piece. With the exception of the inset lid and the concavity of the back of the handle, this piece could be made with a two-piece mold. Of course, it would not be as elegant in design, but it could be done. However, the inset lid and the concave part of the handle add to the design interest and permit us to explore more complex mold-making techniques.

The Presentation Model: A Coffee Pot

Fig. 14.1 The end product of the mold-making techniques presented in Chapters 14–18. A rather formal coffee pot made for production in porcelain, this project represents the multitude of procedures necessary to bring a design from the model through to the case molds. The two pieces shown here are in the greenware stage.

TURNING THE BLANK FOR THE BODY

There is no need to repeat the setting up of a plaster wheel for model making, which was described in Chapter 12. Figure 14.2 shows the soft plaster blank being rapidly turned to rough out a shape for the model. The cottle has been removed when the plaster is in the plastic stage, and the photo accurately shows how rapidly plaster can be removed at this stage. Some old-time plaster turners might disapprove of turning "plastic" plaster because of the danger of removing the cottle too soon, resulting in a pile of spreading plaster. However, if the plaster is watched carefully and tested for firmness, there is no danger of this. The time saved by roughing out the model while it is in the plastic stage is considerable, compared to turning fully-set plaster. Actually, letting the plaster blank cure for 24 hours will help equalize any unevenness of the set, so there seems to be good reason for taking advantage of the best features of both practices. In a production shop, it would be possible to rough out the model while the plaster is still plastic, and then let the rough model set for twenty four hours to allow the plaster to cure before the final shaping is done.

Figure 14.3 shows the finished roughed out model, which was completed in less than 5 minutes. From this point on, the turning action is very carefully controlled. Long-handled tools remove a little plaster at a time, and the shape is constantly checked against the design requirements with calipers. The model is carefully checked against the required size for the finished product, by using a shrink ruler. (Sometimes experienced model and mold makers take a small cloth bag, fill it with six or eight cups of sand, moisten the sand with water, and then pat the bag into a very rough shape of the proposed piece. This is to assure that the model is large enough to make a six- or eight-cup coffee pot; otherwise, the size of the piece is based on a knowledgeable guess, judging from the size of other coffee pots available.)

Fig. 14.2 The plaster blank for the model is quickly cut with a large loop tool made from a hacksaw blade. By turning the plaster when it is still soft, a particular design can be roughed out within a few minutes. Note the position of the turning tool: it is held in both hands and anchored on the belly stick.

Fig. 14.3 The rough plaster model takes less than 5 minutes to turn. It is now ready for finishing with long-handled tools. The plaster is completely set; it is hard, but still damp.

Fig. 14.4 This part of the coffee pot is complete, including the top and bottom spares, which are turned and finished right on the model in order to save time. In a true presentation model, which is made to look exactly like the finished product, the spares would not be included in the turning of the model, but would be turned separately. The handle and spout are carved from the two pieces of plaster shown. Half-lines on the plaster blanks guide the carving and placement on the body.

THE HANDLE, SPOUT,
AND COMPLETED MODEL

The model shown in the accompanying photographs is actually not a presentation model because this model has the top spare and bottom spare turned on the model. This practice saves time in making the four-piece mold. To make this model into a presentation model, the model is carefully and exactly finished as if it were made of white porcelain. The handle, spout, and lid are carved and turned to the exact requirements, then they are glued on the model with Duco Cement. The completed model is dried thoroughly and sometimes sprayed with a clear lacquer. From a few feet away the model will appear to be a finished, glazed coffee pot. The model is then used for presentation purposes with sales people, management, clients, or whoever needs to see a prototype. This way there has been no commitment of time to mold making, casting, firing, etc. It is possible to use this model just as if it were the real thing, and to carefully slide any decals being considered for surface deco-

Fig. 14.5 The spout and handle models are completed according to the required design and joined to the body with Duco Cement. The model is then finished with fine sandpaper and steel wool, and tiny holes in the plaster are filled with wax or oil clay.

Fig. 14.6 Detail of the handle. Notice the design element at the shoulder of the handle which complements the design of the spout seen in Figure 14.5.

ration right onto the smooth lacquered surface. To save modeling and mold-making time, a presentation model is often made with the shrink-plus factor included in its size; upon approval of the model, it can actually be used to make the block molds that lead up to the working molds.

Figure 14.4 shows the completed model with the top and bottom spare turned with the model. Two pieces of plaster are used to carve the handle and the spout. Sureform blades are used for the rough carving, and various knives are used to finish the shapes. Prior to carving, a center line (or half-line) is drawn on the plaster pieces; if it is carved away during the shaping of the piece, it is carefully and accurately renewed with an indelible pencil. The half-line goes all around the model; when the handle and spout models are placed on the body model, the half-lines on the spout and handle models match the half-line on the body of the coffee pot.

The joints between the body and spout and handle are carefully done so that when glued to the body, the coffee pot has a finished, "real" appearance. The completed model is then carefully cleaned up with fine sandpaper and steel wool, and tiny holes in the plaster are filled with wax or oil clay.

Figures 14.5 and 14.6 show the completed model and a detail of the handle. Even with the spares attached to the body of the piece, this model could serve as a presentation model to determine the merit of the design before expensive mold making is undertaken for production. The exact size of the finished product can be made in plaster much easier than a finished clay model, and the plaster can be finished to appear to be a glazed, porcelain piece.

15

Mold Making
on the Plaster Wheel

Any shape that can be modeled on a plaster wheel can also be molded on the plaster wheel. The mold-making system that is presented in this chapter is most appropriate for forms that need a top spare and a bottom spare. In the case of this coffee pot body, the top spare provides the necessary mold to form the recessed top rim, and the bottom spare provides the mold to form the foot.

This system also provides a built-in base plate in the form of the plaster wheel head itself. The surface of the plaster wheel head is the surface for the bottom of the proposed mold, and all the orientation of the mold is planned on this wheel head surface.

USING THE WHEEL
HEAD AS THE BASE PLATE

Figure 15.1 shows the half-line established on the model, with the larger circle serving as the orientation for the half-line. The half-line is plotted with a large divider, as shown previously in Figures 13.3 and 13.4. If a large divider is not available, then a potter's caliper can be used (by taping an indelible pencil on one arm and filing a point on the other). If a potter's caliper is used as a divider, the pivot joint must be capable of being tightened enough to permit repeated identical measurements without the arms moving.

The inside circle shown in Figure 15.1 is the circle established as the minimum thickness for the mold. This line is about 3″ larger in diameter than the widest part of the coffee pot body. This measurement provides a $1\frac{1}{2}$″ thickness for the mold on each side of the model.

Next, a square is drawn, based on the location of the half-line on the diameter of the smaller circle. This square indicates the exact location for the mold boards. The two parallel lines on each side show the thickness of the mold boards.

The orientation of the mold is now established. The model and the plaster wheel head are dressed with mold soap. The dressing seals the indelible pencil lines on the plaster so that they can be referred to constantly during the mold-making process.

Fig. 15.1 The handle model and spout model are removed, and the half-line is established on the coffee pot body. The wheel head is prepared as the base plate for the mold. The outside circle orients the half-line. The inside circle is the limiting line for the mold. The square is the proposed size of the mold. The double line indicates the placement for the mold boards.

Fig. 15.2 A profile of the model is cut from a thin plaster sheet with a bandsaw blade. The outside dimensions of the sheet are dictated by the size of the mold. To avoid breaking the plaster, it is supported on two 2 × 4's placed over a trash barrel.

Fig. 15.3 The profile is placed on the half-line of the model and wheel head. The profile is slightly larger than the model so that a seal of oil clay can be placed in the space. It is easier to fill this space (about $\frac{1}{2}$") than to cut the profile exactly to the shape of the model.

MAKING THE WASTE MOLD

The separation line for the mold is the vertical half-line on the model. A template is cut from a thin sheet of plaster according to the shape of the half-line on the model (Figure 15.2). To do this, the sheet of plaster is put behind the model and a rough sketch is made on the plaster sheet, indicating the shape of the model. The profile of the model is cut out with a piece of bandsaw blade, in the manner shown in Figure 15.2. The profile is cut slightly larger than the shape of the model. Notice that the profile sheet has a center line and the outside dimensions of the sheet match exactly the size necessary as plotted on the wheel head (Figure 15.3).

Figure 15.3 shows how the profile is placed on the model and wheel head. The space between the profile and the model will be filled with oil clay to form the seal between the profile and the model (Figure 15.4). Notice how closely the outside dimen-

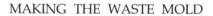

Fig. 15.4 The space between the profile and the model is filled with oil clay. The profile is held in position by a large lump of oil clay on the back of the profile and by a smaller profile plate at the base. This smaller profile is cut to fit the shape of the mold and is held in place with plaster.

Fig. 15.5 This "back" side of the profile is not dressed with mold soap, but the model, wheel head, and front side of the profile are. A small amount of plaster is applied with a brush and spatula to secure the profile in position for casting the first half of the mold. Notice that the small base profile plate is aligned correctly with the mold lines on the wheel head.

sions of the profile sheet follow the indicated size of the mold on the wheel head. The height of the top end of the profile doesn't matter, except that it must be higher than the top of the mold.

A second profile sheet is cut to conform roughly to the base of the model. It is placed flat on the wheel head and is used to help secure the bottom of the vertical (first) profile. One corner of this profile sheet is barely visible behind the vertical profile in Figure 15.4, and more of it can be seen in Figure 15.5. Its outside dimensions are cut to the limit lines of the mold.

The "back" surface of the profile is *not* dressed with mold soap, nor is the small base profile. However, the model, the wheel head, and the "front" side of the profile are dressed. A small batch of plaster is brushed on the base profile at the joint where the base profile meets the vertical profile. This se-

cures both profiles in position while the oil clay seal is applied from the front side of the profile. As is evident in Figure 15.4, this seal is very carefully modeled to fill the space and to be on the same plane as the vertical profile. In other words, the oil clay seal completes the profile up to the surface of the mold.

Figure 15.5 shows the profile secured in the correct position with plaster brushed onto the profile and the model. A small batch of plaster is mixed in a bowl, and before the plaster is at the "marking" stage, the plaster is brushed on as shown. The plaster only serves to secure the profile in place. There is no need to cover the model with a large amount of plaster, unless the mold is a very big one and large amounts of plaster are needed to pour one side of the mold. Under those circumstances, the profile plate needs to be extra secure to withstand the pressure of the plaster when the first half of the mold is poured. Another small profile might be necessary, placed at the top of the model.

This part of mold making is sometimes called making a "waste mold" because this part is discarded when the second half of the mold is poured.

SETTING UP THE MOLD BOARDS

Figure 15.6 shows dressing the model, profile, and wheel head. The importance of thorough dressing cannot be overemphasized, because it is the one area that seems to cause all the trouble for mold makers. If a mold is not dressed properly, the next casting will simply stick to the first cast, and it is a considerable (if not impossible) task to part the two castings. (Dressing is described on page 66.)

The dressed mold boards are now placed on each side of the profile on the guidelines on the wheel head and secured at the top with a furniture clamp (Figure 15.7). The bottom clamp shown in the figure is securing the third mold board to the base profile and the two side mold boards. In Figure 15.7, notice that the right mold board extends beyond the limit line for the mold, and the left mold board is right on line. This is to permit the fourth mold board to be placed in the correct position shown in Figure 15.8.

(*Note: mold boards are always kept in a dressed state. After the mold boards are used and cleaned up, they are dressed again; and they are dressed once again when they are being set-up for a mold.*)

In setting up mold boards, it is important that the security of the set-up be given extra attention. Don't be careless, or you will have plaster exploding from the set-up when it is poured. The nails shown in Figure 15.8 are for security. A furniture clamp

Fig. 15.6 In dressing the model, profile, and wheel head, a good lather is worked up and then rinsed away. This process is repeated three times. A dry cloth polishes the surfaces to a dull shine.

Fig. 15.7 Two dressed mold boards are placed according to the lines on the wheel head and secured with a clamp. A third mold board is placed at the back of the mold and secured with another clamp.

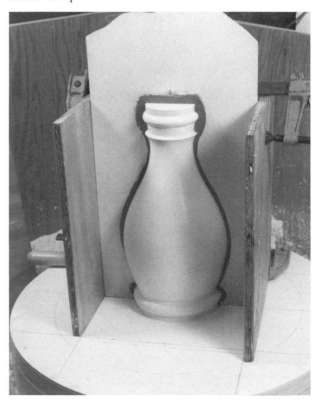

could be used just as well, but finishing nails are often used to secure mold boards even though clamps are used, too. The nails are driven half their length into the plaster wheel head, on both sides of the mold board. The nails are easily removed with pliers after the pour, and they are then sprayed with WD40 to prevent rusting.

After nailing, the tops of the boards are clamped and the set-up is ready to pour.

The set-up is complete. All the seams are secured with oil clay. To do this, long thin coils of oil clay are placed along the seam, and a wooden tool is run along the seam, forming the oil clay into a narrow fillet. Oil clay is preferred to water clay because it is easier to handle and it is waterproof. After the pour, the oil clay is easily removed and formed into a ball ready for reuse.

After the pour is completed, the mold boards are removed, cleaned, and dressed, and set aside for the second half of the mold. The waste mold (containing the profile plates) is separated from the model (Figure 15.9).

CUTTING NATCHES AND POURING THE SECOND HALF OF THE MOLD

A natch bit is shown in Figure 15.10. This bit is easily made from a stainless steel spoon simply by flattening the spoon and removing part of the handle. It would be easy to make several natch bits of different sizes; three sizes would probably be adequate. The type of natch knives shown in Chapter 2 could be replaced by these natch bits made out of spoons.

Fig. 15.8 The fourth mold board is set in place along the line indicated on the wheel head. Because of the height of the mold, finishing nails are driven into the wheel head along both sides of the mold boards to help secure the boards against the pressure of the poured plaster.

Fig. 15.9 After the pour is completed, the mold boards are removed, cleaned, and dressed, and the waste mold is separated from the model.

They cut perfectly shaped natches and are easier to use than natch knives, which require some practice to get good results. (Natches that are a full half-sphere are actually too deep, and the positive ones have a tendency to break off. However, natches that are too shallow will not form a satisfactory lock.)

Once again, the mold is dressed (Figure 15.11), and the boards are set up for casting the second half of the mold. The mold is almost complete in Figure 15.12. Both halves are cast and the mold is taken apart. The separation of the halves of the mold is no problem if the mold has been dressed thoroughly and if there are no undercuts to hold the mold to the model. In this case, there is no problem what-soever, and the mold is separated from the model by a soft rap with a rubber mallet to break the surface tension.

THE TOP AND BOTTOM SPARES

Figure 15.12 shows the two-piece mold with the spares on the model. Figure 15.13 shows the turned alter-ation of the top spare in order to make a space for the "real" top spare to be cast in. This tapered cyl-inder represents the mold for the opening where the slip enters and exits the mold. It must be tapered so that the casting of the spare will contract with the casting of the coffee pot body. The spare is removed from the body of the coffee pot after it has been taken from the mold in the form of a completed casting. The rest of the original spare is trimmed out of the coffee pot at the correct place on the recessed rim of the pot.

The advantage of this system is that the com-pleted spare is made from the model and no addi-

Fig. 15.10 A natch bit and brace make perfect hemispherical natches. The bits are made from flattened stainless steel spoons, with enough handle left to form a shank for the brace.

Fig. 15.11 The negative natches are completed, and the model and the first half of the mold are prepared for the second half pouring.

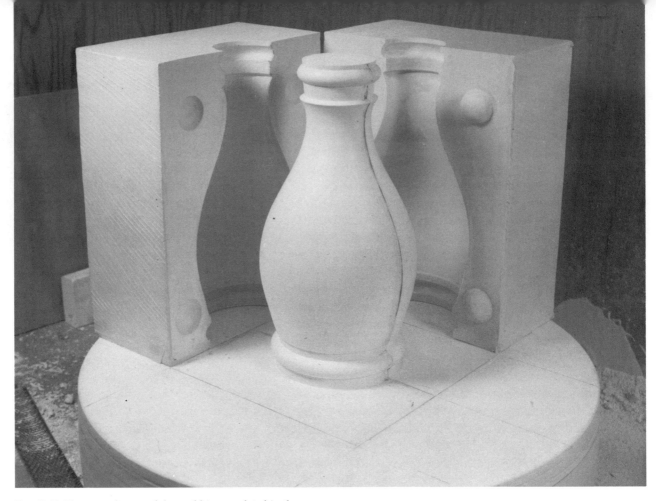

Fig. 15.12 The second pour of the mold is completed in the standard manner. After the plaster is set, the mold can be taken apart and checked for any air pockets that might occur on the inner surface of the mold.

Fig. 15.13 This photograph illustrates one of the numerous reasons for using the model on the plaster wheel for mold making. The top spare has been turned to the shape of the opening for the slip. The top spare is completed by casting in the space left between the two-piece mold and this tapered cylinder. The taper of the cylinder permits the spare to withdraw from the rest of the casting when the mold is slip cast.

tional castings need to be done other than filling the space where the spare is with plaster.

The bottom spare is the next problem to tackle, and it is already solved because the outside shape and bottom surface of the spare is defined by the two halves of the mold.

To form a foot for the coffee pot, the model is cut off the wheel head at the base of the spare, leaving the wheel head surface flat. The model is now inverted on the wheel (Figure 15.14) and secured with a large amount of water-based clay. (Water-based clay is preferred for fastening down models to plaster wheel heads.) Enough clay must be used to securely retain the model in exact position for the turning of the foot rim. The foot rim is turned at the

Fig. 15.14 The next step is to remove the bottom spare from the model. The model is inverted with the top spare in place, secured with water-based clay, and the bottom spare is turned away, forming the foot.

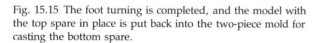

Fig. 15.15 The foot turning is completed, and the model with the top spare in place is put back into the two-piece mold for casting the bottom spare.

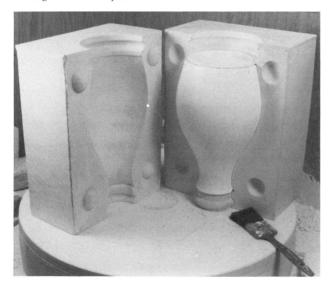

Fig. 15.16 The two-piece mold is reassembled with the model in place, and the bottom spare is cast.

same time the bottom spare is removed. In other words, the bottom spare is turned off the model, and the bottom foot rim is turned on the bottom of the model.

The model with the top spare is put back into the mold (Figure 15.15) and the foot and the surfaces forming the spare are dressed. No mold soap touches the inside of the mold at any time. One can see in Figure 15.16 the bottom spare being cast. Clamps are used to make sure that the molds are held tightly together.

A small cottle of oil clay is put on the opening for the bottom spare. All surfaces that need dressing in order to become water resistant are dressed. No soap of any kind is put on the inside or working surfaces of the mold. The cottle provides extra space for plaster and assures that the bottom spare is cast well. The excess plaster is removed while in the plastic stage.

Finally, the corners are trimmed off the mold as shown in Figure 13.21.

Lynn Turner, Berkeley, Ca. "Tea Service." A first-rate mold maker, Turner uses natural forms such as bananas, cantaloupe, gourds, corn, and bamboo as models for her molds. She then uses the slip castings as a basis for her fantasy world of imaginative tea sets and espresso services.

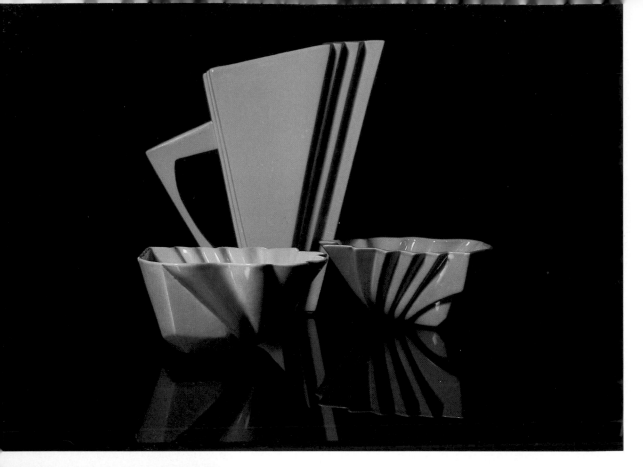

Charles Nalle, Wilmington, Del. Above: "Parvenu Pitcher and Cups"; left: "Model for 'Parvenu' Pitcher." Nalle designs and produces a line of cast porcelain pieces that include the pitcher and cups pictured here. The model is made of Hydrastone, a gypsum-cement product that is harder and more durable than plaster. Note the spare system used on the model.

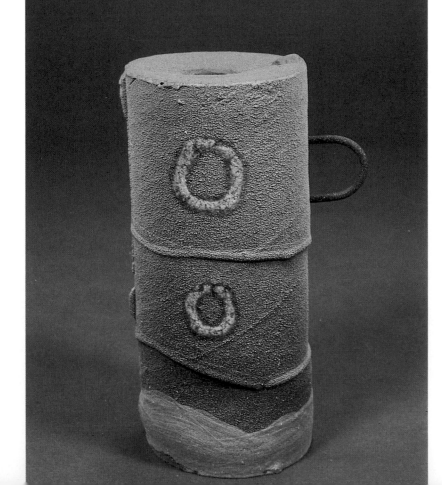

Charles Olson, Whitewater, Wis. "Cup, Altered," 7½"x3". Olson uses slip castings as forms to alter with surface treatments. The cup is slip cast porcelain that is fired to a high temperature with a sandpaper-like glaze. The cup is then fired with low-fire colored glazes to obtain the final effect. Olson uses this same technique on bowls and alters the interior to resemble the lunar surface.

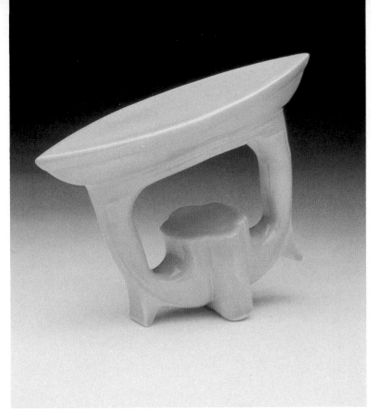

Karen T. Massaro, Santa Cruz, Ca. "Double Iron,"
8¹/₂"x4⁷/₈"x4". Massaro has done considerable work with slip
casting forms that include an iron series, represented here. The
Double Iron is in vitreous china.

Dorothy Hafner, New York, N.Y. "Asterisks" coffee/dessert
set. Hafner produces a line of porcelain dinnerware that
includes both press molding and slip casting. The plates, saucers, and platters are pressed. The bowls, cups, teapots, and
coffee pots are cast. Under the name "Art for Dining in Porcelain," Hafner offers unique designs, contemporary in both
form and decoration.

Jeffery Chapp, West Lafayette, Ind. "Begging Bowl,"
4"x10"x6". Chapp has developed a highly finished
style that combines cast forms and multifiring of
low-temperature glazes. His comments about a
recent exhibit of his work reflect the thoughts of
many artists today: "I am working on only a very
few number of pieces, working them over and over
again, seeking the 'right one' that will best express
the aesthetic sense I am looking for. The 'right one'
may never exist as an object, but it will always exist
in my mind; and is, therefore, the carrot in front of
me, keeping me searching."

Michel Conroy, San Marcos, Tex. "Vessel, Image
Series," 8"x11". Conroy's molding technique is
neither slip casting nor press molding. It is perhaps
most closely akin to slumping layered glass plate
into a mold to make a bowl. Using a bisque-fired
clay mold, Conroy builds up layers of glaze materials in the mold and fires the mold and glazes until the
glaze materials almost melt. Most of the pieces
require several firings to achieve the desired result.
Apparently, there is no problem of stress cracks
because of the slow-cooling kiln.

The molding procedures presented in this chapter are appropriate for any form that separates on a flat plane and that can be cast in a two- or three-piece mold. Handles and spouts are the specific examples used because they are part of the mold making process for the demonstration coffee pot. The spout is divided into halves by a flat plane; the handle is basically the same, except for the third mold piece necessary to establish the concave features of the back of the handle.

The lid is presented as an example of making a round mold on the plaster wheel and employing a "ring lock" system of keying the molds together.

There is very little new or unusual about the system presented here, except, perhaps, the incorporation of plastic natches in the molds (which is also presented in Chapter 7.)

Figure 16.1 shows most of the tools and other items needed to make these molds. The tools are standard, but note especially the thick plaster base plate on which the spout mold will be made and the thin plaster rectangle which will form the profile for the spout. This plaster rectangle is made to be the exact dimensions of the proposed mold, based on a 1″ thickness at the thinnest part. A surface gauge and torpedo level (not shown in the photograph) are used to confirm that the table and profile sheet are perfectly level.

16

Molding the Handle, Spout, and Lid

THE SPOUT MOLD

First, the models of the spout and handle are removed from the coffee pot, and the half-lines are renewed with indelible pencil. The base plate is prepared for the spout mold by finding the center of the piece of plaster with diagonal lines drawn from the corners. Then the size of the mold is plotted on the plaster. The lines are drawn with indelible pencil, and the finished base plate is dressed with mold soap.

The profile is cut with knives and a piece of bandsaw blade to the shape of the spout. Figure 16.2 shows the back of the profile, with oil clay being used to hold the spout in place. The gap between the spout and profile is filled with clay and finished smoothly on the front surface. Since no plaster is

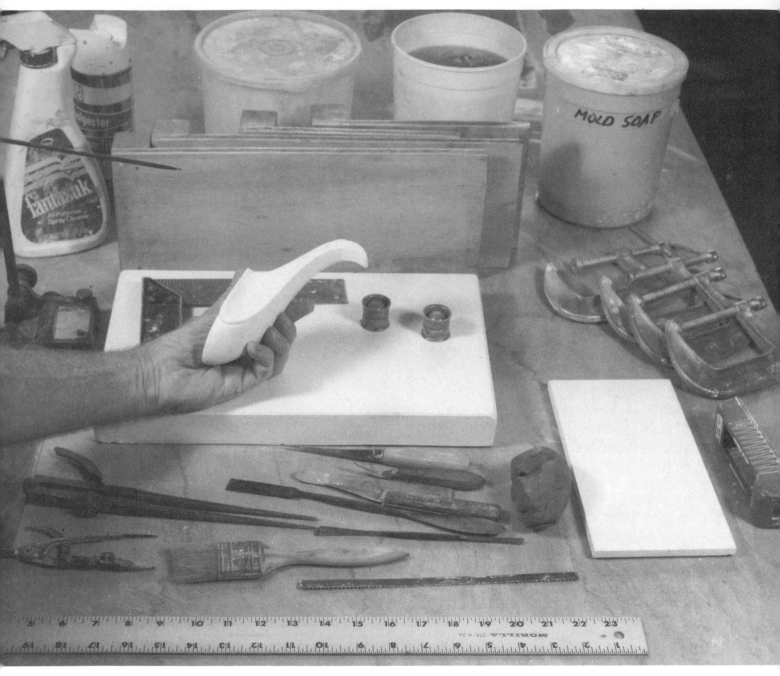

Fig. 16.1 Tools for making the mold for the spout include base plate, plastic natches, and profile sheet.

required to hold the spout in the profile, the profile is not actually made into a waste mold; the oil clay is enough to hold the spout in place. On a model of this scale, the plaster application is unnecessary.

The main difference between this approach and the approach of the previous chapter is that the spare is not part of the model. The spare will be made with oil clay according to the position of the spout in the profile. Since the spout model and the handle model are made to fit on the coffee pot body for evaluation purposes, they do not have spares attached to them. The spares will be made with oil clay and applied to only one side of the mold at a time.

The location of the spares is clearly seen in Figure 16.3. The large spare is made as large as possible and still conform to the needs of the spout. This spare is large to make it easy to pour slip into and out of the mold. The smaller spare serves mainly as a vent to insure that the slip does not trap air when it is poured. Sometimes molds of this type do not employ a secondary spare of this size, and one must resort to making two or three air vents in the form of small grooves in the surface of the mold from the model to the outside. These vents sometimes become clogged with slip and fail to function. A "vent" spare of the size indicated in Figure 16.3 works well, the only drawback being that slightly more slip is used to cast the piece.

After the spares are applied to the surface of the profile, the profile (with the spout and spares in place) is put on the base plate in the correct position for casting. The profile is supported by three small blocks of plaster, and it is carefully leveled with a level and surface gauge.

The profile, model and spare, and all four mold boards are dressed with mold soap. Before the mold boards are finally put in place for the casting, the plastic natches are put in position on the profile. The female natch, or negative natch, is the one that is placed on the profile. It is held in position with a little ball of oil clay.

The needed thickness of the casting is marked on the wall of the mold board. All the seams are

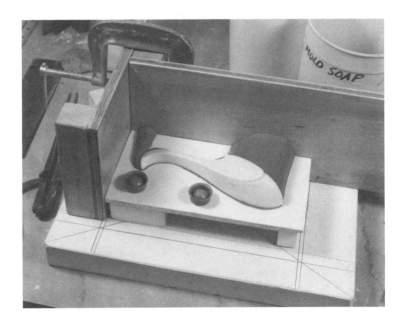

Fig. 16.2 After the base plate is prepared with guidelines to orient the mold, the profile sheet is cut to receive the spout model. Oil clay holds the model exactly on the half-line.

Fig. 16.3 Two spares are built up with oil clay. The large one is for entry and exit of the slip; the secondary spare is an air vent. The profile is supported on three blocks of plaster and carefully leveled. The correct height of the poured plaster is marked on the mold board. Female plastic natches are held in place with oil clay.

Fig. 16.4 After the first half of the mold is cast, the profile plate is removed and the spout and mold are prepared for the second casting, including spares and male natches.

filled with small coils of oil clay to assure no leakage of plaster.

The mark indicated on the mold board actually indicates the thickness of the whole mold. When the profile is setup to receive the first half pouring, the height of the profile is exactly half the planned thickness of the mold. It is adjusted to this correct height by oil clay placed on the blocks of plaster under the profile. Although the profile does not necessarily have to be the height of one side of the mold, this procedure makes it easier to assure that both halves of the mold are the same thickness.

The first half of the mold is cast. The mold boards are carefully removed and cleaned, the profile is removed, and the spout and first mold half are reversed on the base plate.

Two new spares are made for the second half of the mold. As seen in Figure 16.4, these spares match the first ones exactly. Once again, the mold surface and model are dressed with mold soap. The male (positive) natches are placed on the female natches and secured with oil clay. The mold boards are returned to the mold and secured with the C clamps. The seams are sealed with coils of oil clay and the second half of the mold is cast.

After the second half of the mold is poured, and when the plaster is set and has started to cool to room temperature, the mold is removed from the mold boards. The model is removed, the spares are removed, and the edges of the mold are beveled. The mold is then put away to dry.

A mold of this small size needs no clamping or strapping to prevent warpage during drying. However, the drying process is allowed to occur naturally. If heat is considered to help dry the molds, it should never be applied without the accompaniment of moving air. Do not put molds in an oven, even on low heat. Low heat in a kitchen oven may be hot enough to burn the molds and make them worthless.

THE HANDLE MOLD

Figure 16.5 shows the completed mold for the handle. It is made the same way as the spout mold, except that it is a three-piece mold instead of a two-piece mold. Because of the design, a third piece is

Fig. 16.5 The handle mold is made in the same way as the spout mold, except a third piece is required for the concave back of the handle. This mold is for a solid casting; the mold will not be dumped.

necessary to form the concave part of the handle. The procedure for making a three-piece mold is exactly the same as for a two-piece mold, except that there is a third preparation of the set-up and a third pouring of plaster. In this particular case, the third piece was filled in with oil clay in a manner similar to the oil clay spares used on the spout. Then, after the first two pieces of the mold are cast, the third oil clay piece is removed and a third preparation routine is done, ending with the third piece being cast between the two halves of the mold. The handle mold is for a solid casting; the mold will not be "dumped," and a solid cast handle will be made.

Making multi-piece molds (more than two pieces, not counting the spares) is not difficult once the fundamental procedure is understood. It is important that the correct procedures, (i.e., those learned for two-piece molds) be applied to every step; if they are, a superior mold will result.

In unusual mold-making problems, such things as casting two pieces of the mold at the same time are common. For example, two pieces of a four-piece mold could be cast at once. These two pieces would not be in contact with each other, and they could be separated with oil clay cottles or even with plaster profiles. After the first two pieces are cast, the cottle or profile is removed, and the next two pieces are cast in the proper spaces. This may seem complicated, but it isn't. It is simply a matter of sustaining the same procedures for each step; each step is often a repetition of the previous step. Once a routine is worked out that is logical, efficient, and (most important) produces molds of superior quality, then this particular routine should be used all the time.

In a two-piece mold, the natches are usually carved hemispherical shapes, or plastic natches can be used. The natches are often shaped according to what has been successful in a particular situation in the past and is used repeatedly in molds of all type. For instance, the natch system used in the mold for the chicken salt shaker in Chapter 10 is based on forming the locking shapes on the edge of the mold. This design is satisfactory for small molds. However, on larger molds, these kind of natches are more subject to wear and tear. Larger molds need hemisphere natches on straight, flat planes.

The locking system for holding molds of three or more pieces together is similar to the locking system for two-piece molds. The common hemispherical natch is put on each side of the third piece, and it locks into position between the other pieces of the mold.

The locking system for the third piece of this handle mold is slightly different, however. It is specifically made so that after the two main pieces of the mold are separated in preparation for removing the handle casting, the third piece can slide out without altering the casting. This is easily seen in Figure 16.5. If this piece of the handle mold had a hemispherical natch, then it would need to be lifted, rather than slid, from the mold, and that would distort the casting.

THE LID MOLD

One more item for the coffee pot is left to be cast—the lid (shown in Figure 16.6). Careful measuring is done to determine the size of the opening on the coffee pot and the diameter of the flange on the lid (the part that goes into the coffee pot). This model is turned on the plaster wheel in the same manner as was the coffee pot body model. The spare

Fig. 16.6 The lid model with spare is turned on the plaster wheel. In preparation for casting the top half of the mold, the dressed model is placed in a hole turned in the wheel head, oil clay is packed around the model up to the rim, and a roofing paper cottle is put in place.

is turned with the lid (in Figure 16.6 it looks like a narrow, tapered extension of the flange). After the lid model is completed, it is cut off the wheel and put aside.

The mold for the lid is made on the wheel. The process begins with placing the dressed lid model in a recessed opening that has been turned on the plaster wheel head. This opening, which can be seen in Figure 16-6, fits exactly the diameter of the spare on the model. The lid model is placed in the hole on the wheel head, and oil clay is built up around the model to the rim of the lid. The oil clay is carefully leveled and trimmed round. A roofing paper cottle is put around the oil clay and secured with a clothespin. The top part of the lid mold is then cast.

Figure 16.7 shows the finished lid mold. The first casting produces the top of the mold, which is shown on the right in the photograph. To cast the second piece, the dressed mold is placed in the center on the wheel head, secured with oil clay, and a groove

Fig. 16.7 The completed mold for the lid. A groove cut into the first casting (right) forms a "ring natch" when the second piece (left) is cast.

is cut into the mold to serve as the keying system. This type of locking system is sometimes called a "ring natch." The dressed model is placed in the first part of the mold, and the casting procedure is repeated.

The difference between the mold-making procedure for the lid and the one for the handle and spout is that the whole mold is made on the plaster wheel. The keying system is a ring instead of a series of hemispheres.

The way molds can be made on the wheel is shown in the lid mold-making procedure. It is very easy to make a mold from a turned model without even removing the model from the wheel. The way to do this is to cast the first half of the mold directly after the model is completed. This casting produces the bottom half of the mold. A keying groove is cut in this casting, and the second half of the mold is cast. After the second casting, which completes the mold of the lid, the mold and model are cut off the wheel. This procedure is very simple, and it can be used for any model that can be separated with a horizontal separation plane.

CASTING AND ASSEMBLING THE COFFEE POT

The four molds required to cast the coffee pot are now completed. Figure 16.8 shows the molds ready to be slip cast. The weight of the coffee pot body mold has been reduced by about 25% by cutting the corners off the mold. The molds are dried slowly and are then ready for slip casting.

To slip cast the molds, they are held tightly together with elastic bands and Velcro fastening bands and filled to the top with slip. A porcelain slip was used here. The slip is left in the molds for about 20 minutes, and then the molds are dumped, or emptied, back into the slip container. (In the case of the handle mold, the slip is not dumped; it is left in the mold to create a solid handle.) After dumping, the molds are allowed to sit for about 2 hours, and then the molds are carefully separated (Figure 16.9).

Slip casting is a relatively simple process, but there are some basic rules to follow to achieve a quality product from the mold. These rules are guide-

Fig. 16.8 The complete set of molds for slip casting a coffee pot.

Fig. 16.9 After casting, the molds are allowed to sit for about 2 hours, and then they are carefully separated. The seam marks are noticeable on the coffee pot body, and the shrinkage of the casting is seen on the spout mold.

lines rather than fixed standards. Experience in slip casting many molds will indicate which of the rules to short cut.

1 Always use thoroughly prepared deflocculated slip. There must be no lumps in the slip whatsoever,

and the slip should pour easily. As a rough indication of the proper condition of the slip, it should "web" between the spread fingers after dipping one's hands in the slip.

2 The molds must be dried adequately in order for the process to work. A common production rou-

Fig. 16.10 The assembled coffee pot.

4 When dumping the mold, the slip should be poured out continously to prevent any excess build up of the slip. The mold is put on a rack to dry upside down while the slip continues to drain out.

5 After the mold has dried the slip casting, the spare may be cut away from the piece. (This is not done on the coffee pot example because the casting is thin to take advantage of the porcelain qualities. To remove the spare at this time might distort the piece.)

Experience in casting will undoubtedly raise other factors to take into consideration, such as the most appropriate time to assemble various pieces of several castings, or perhaps an unusual system to dump the mold and still retain enough slip in the mold to fill a handle space.

Figure 16.10 shows the assembled coffee pot. The spares have been removed and returned to the reclaim barrel, and each piece is fettled to remove any seam line. The various pieces are assembled with slip.

When assembling the final product, the correct location of the handle and spout must be scrupulously maintained. Always examine an assembled piece from several sides and angles to assure the correct relationship of these pieces to the body. If changes need to be made, make them carefully and once again examine the piece from all sides.

The processes involved in making this piece are standard. The processes may be standard, but the design of the piece itself can be almost anything. It is a fact that a mold can be made for almost anything imaginable. It may take many molds, and each mold may have numerous parts, but it can be cast.

There are many possible systems for mold making for slip casting. Each system is developed to solve one particular problem. The system presented here is a basic approach to modeling and slip casting that is used in many factories around the world. It should not be seen as a fixed procedure, but it should be studied and used as a foundation and starting point for producing slip cast products.

tine is for the molds to be cast three times per 8-hour-shift. They are dried overnight, and the cycle is repeated again the next day.

3 Once you begin pouring the slip into the mold, do not stop until the mold is filled. If by chance the pouring is interrupted, a line called a "veil" will appear on the surface of the casting. If the casting is a quality piece of thin transparent porcelain, then the cast should be returned to the reclaim barrel. If it is thicker casting, the veil can be ribbed away. It cannot be very successfully sponged away.

Simply put, a case mold is a mold from which to make other molds. The fact that plaster molds wear out with use to the point that they can no longer accurately reproduce the design requires a system to replace the worn molds. The case mold is used to cast new molds, and it usually is accompanied by its own plaster mold boards, called "rails." The rails are placed around the case, and plaster is poured into the cavity to create the mold. Although the case and rail system is not needed in a small shop where the quantity of production rarely wears out the molds, it is a necessity for volume production.

The case mold is cast many times, and, therefore, it comes under very hard usage. Regular plaster molds with a standard consistency of 65 to 75 would not hold up under such use. Therefore, gypsum-cement is the usual material for case molds and rails. Where the amount of detail in the mold is great, rubber compounds are used for the case molds instead of gypsum-cement.

For reproducing extremely fine detail in case molds (in such items as intricate tea cup handles, for example) sometimes a metal compound that can be cast at very low temperatures is used. The detail capabilities of metal case molds are extremely fine. The metal is capable of being sprayed while molten, and the result is an ultra-smooth surface for the case mold.

In this chapter a case mold and rails are made for the body of the coffee pot. They are made from gypsum-cement, which is the standard material used for this purpose. Rubber is sometimes used for case molds of this size, but rubber is usually reserved for more detailed items (such as the handle, spout, and lid.) In the next chapter, case molds of the handle, spout, and lid are made with rubber compounds.

CHAPTER

17

Case Molds for the Coffee Pot Body

MAKING THE
GYPSUM-CEMENT CASES

Figure 17.1 shows a case for one half of the coffee pot body. The mold on the left in Figure 17.1 is referred to as the block mold. It is not used as a working mold. It is the first mold made from the model, and it is set aside to be used only for recasting of the model or making the case, as is shown here.

To make this case, the block mold is set-up with mold boards all around. The inside surface of the mold is dressed with mold soap, and the seams on the mold boards are sealed with small coils of oil clay. The casting is made using gypsum-cement with a consistency less than 50.

The case mold is cast very thick. The base of the case mold in Figure 17.1 is $1\frac{1}{2}''$ thick. In some professional shops this type of case mold would have an additional shelf or base piece on it besides the thick base shown in this photograph. This additional shelf serves to hold the rails for the case, and the whole unit consists of the heavy case and two rails resting on a shelf made on the case. This design feature has the advantage that it can be used on an uneven work table surface. The case and rails presented in this chapter need a flat, smooth table top to be used properly.

Using the proper mixing technique for gypsum-cement is important. The normal 2-minute slaking period for plaster must be increased to maybe 3 or 4 minutes, and the power mixing time must be increased to 4 to 6 minutes. Mixing gypsum-cement feels much different than mixing plaster. Plaster is smooth and creamy during mixing. Gypsum-cement feels almost oily, and it has an oily appearance during mixing. In mixing gypsum-cement, the consistency should be between 50 and 25. These consistencies produce a very hard, durable material.

The most common failing of beginners in mixing gypsum-cement is that they do not mix long enough or thoroughly enough. Gypsum-cement needs thorough power mixing. The actual time necessary for the mixing may vary, but a reasonable guess would be to double the mixing time of plaster.

USING THE CASES WITH WOODEN MOLD BOARDS

Figure 17.2 shows one of the cases that are needed to reproduce working molds for the coffee pot body. This photograph shows a possible way to use the cases with wooden mold boards if not many molds are required. (Actually, four cases are required for the working molds, not two, because the top and

Fig. 17.1 The gypsum-cement case mold (right) for making working molds for one half of the coffee pot body. The mold on the left is the block mold (first mold from the model). It is used only to make the case mold; it is not used as a working mold.

Fig. 17.2 The case can be used as is with plywood mold boards to reproduce working molds. This method is completely satisfactory for limited production needs.

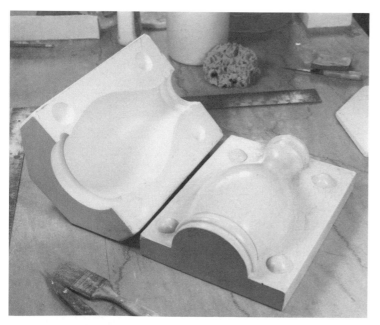

bottom spares require a case for each. Making the cases for the spares is not presented in an effort to keep this presentation to a reasonable length. They are made in the same way as the lid cases, described in the next chapter, or as a two-piece case with a vertical separation.)

To use the case as it is shown in Figure 17.2 to produce a working mold, the case is simply set-up with mold boards around it, dressed properly, and cast with plaster up to a line indicating the desired thickness of the working mold. Using this method produces a mold with three outside walls instead of the five outside walls of the block mold. This is satisfactory if only short runs are required of the mold. (The completed mold is four-sided, rather than eight-sided.)

MAKING RAILS FOR THE CASE

If high production is contemplated where many molds will be used over a long period of time, then proper rails for the case need to be made. The rails are L-shaped molds that form the outside shape of the

Fig. 17.3 A rail system is needed to shape the outside of the mold if it is not square or to protect the case if many molds will be cast from it. To form the first of the two required rails, the block mold is placed on the case and mold boards are set up to make the L-shaped rail, which will be cast here on the right side of the mold and case. All the planning for the rail mold is done on a base plate.

Fig. 17.4 This is the final set-up for casting the first L-shaped rail. Plaster blocks help make the final shape, and the rail is cast over a wire mesh and steel rod armature.

working mold. Two L-shaped rails fit together to surround the case (see Figure 17.6).

Figure 17.3 shows how to start making one of the two rails needed for this mold. A base plate is used to make the rail on, and the final size of the rail is drawn on the base plate with indelible pencil. Mold boards are set up to form an L-shaped space around two sides of the mold and case. The final set-up is shown in Figure 17.4, where small blocks and strips of plaster are used to help make the required L shape of the rail. The rail is cast over a wire and steel armature. This strong reinforcement is necessary; otherwise the rail might break under hard use. The wire mesh and threaded steel shaft are fastened together with wire.

Figures 17.3, 17.4, and 17.5 need to be studied carefully to understand how the L-shaped rail is made. Figure 17.5 may be a good place to start because this picture shows what the rail looks like after it is cast. It is a heavy casting that will not move easily when used to cast working molds. Note that there are no natches or locking mechanism used other than an exact fit. This feature will provide a positive seal for the rails, yet it will be able to absorb any expansion of the plaster when a working mold is cast.

The second rail is cast using the same proce-

Fig. 17.5 After the gypsum-cement is set, the mold boards are removed, and the rail looks like this.

Fig. 17.7 The two cases for the coffee pot body with the two rails just completed. In production, each case needs to have a rail system of its own.

Fig. 17.6 The second of the two rails is cast using the same procedure. The finished product, two rails and the case mold, are shown here. No positive locking system is used to hold the rails in place. They fit perfectly together with the case and will absorb any expansion of the plaster when the working molds are cast.

dure. The end result is shown in Figure 17.6, which shows the two rails in place around the case.

This form of case and rails make a mold that has the five outside walls exactly as does the block in Figure 17.1. For high volume, this type of case and rail is worth the effort to produce, because there is a 25% savings in plaster and an improvement in mold performance due to the reduced variation in the thickness of the mold.

The three pieces (case and rails) shown in Figure 17.6 are quite heavy. They must be used on a level table because the rails sit on the table at the sides of the case. In most situations this is perfectly satisfactory. An "improvement" would be to cast the case with an added shelf to hold the rails.

Figure 17.7 shows both case molds and two rails. Although these rails will work with both cases, each case should have its own rails so that the coffee pot cases can be cast together. One batch of plaster should be used for the working molds, casting all the cases—body (four cases), handle, spout, and lid —at the same time with the same plaster.

PRODUCTION QUANTITIES

In practice, this coffee pot mold can produce 3 complete coffee pots per 8-hour shift. For instance, if there are 10 complete molds in the coffee pot mold line (that is, 40 molds to produce the whole coffee pot), then 30 complete coffee pots can be made per 8-hour shift. Of course, these figures assume all the other aspects of production are going on at the same time, including assembling the coffee pot. In large production, the parts of the coffee pot would be moved to a separate assembly room. If this mold were used in a high-quality porcelain production situation, it would be common for one trained person to do the casting and assembling of a few items. One trained person would be responsible for the quality of the casting and assembling of the product.

Everything being equal, the production of 30 coffee pots per 8-hour shift is within reason.

The next consideration is how many units can be cast from a mold before the mold must be replaced. Generally, 50 units could be cast before the mold is discarded. (In this particular case, more than 50 coffee pots could probably be cast.) Hence, using the above figures as a guide for mold replacement needs, approximately every 3 weeks all 10 "mold units" (4 molds per coffee pot) would need to be replaced. If the needs were greater, and the numbers of molds doubled, then every 3 weeks this "line" would need more than 80 molds to keep production going.

Quality cases are essential to produce quality molds, and rails are essential for high-volume usage of the cases.

CHAPTER

18

Case Molds for the Handle, Spout, and Lid

Making the cases for the handle, spout, and lid of the coffee pot presents an opportunity to use rubber molding materials. This chapter shows how to make two case molds (handle and lid); since the third case mold (spout) is made in exactly the same way as the handle case, it is not shown. The case molds for the handle were made using PURE-CMC PL 4042 from the Perma-Flex Mold Co. and gypsum-cement. The lid case was made using PMC-724 from Smooth-On Inc. Another successful synthetic molding compound is ADRUBRTV-7/79/7180 from Adhesive Products Corp. (See Sources of Supplies.)

These synthetic molding compounds require no heat to become hard and rubber-like. (CMC stands for Cold Molding Compound, and RTV stands for Room Temperature Vulcanizing.)

THE HANDLE AND SPOUT CASES

The Rubber Cases for a Three-Piece Mold

Figure 18.1 shows the two halves of the handle mold dressed and placed on the marble top with a Plexiglas divider between them. This divider is about 1 inch higher than the surface of the molds and serves as the divider for the case. Before the two halves of the mold were set up this way, the three-part handle mold was very accurately squared up. Although the mold-making process provides relatively square molds, the squaring up for making a case needs to be as exact as possible. The case must produce molds that fit together accurately. Molds need to be the same thickness on each side as well as be level on the casting table. In the squaring up process, less than $\frac{1}{8}''$ was removed from one corner of the mold, but that $\frac{1}{8}''$ would have made the case mold $\frac{1}{8}''$ off, and every mold made with the case would have been off that amount.

As shown in Figure 18.1, mold boards are placed around the edges of the two molds. The Plexiglas divider is exactly as long as the molds and, therefore, it touches the mold boards.

The product used in this case is PURE-CMC PL 4042 from Perma-Flex. This compound is a two-part compound, and it is mixed according to the directions on the container. In mixing plaster, there

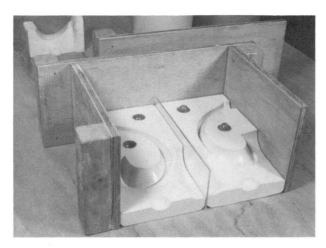

Fig. 18.1 Two molds from the three-piece handle mold are being prepared to cast with a synthetic molding compound. The Plexiglas separator permits cases for the two halves of the handle to be made with one pour of plaster.

Fig. 18.2 The rubber compound is poured, and after the required curing time, the molds and mold boards are separated. This rubber case is made thick enough to be used without the additional support of a rail system. It is cast using PURE-CMC 7/79/7180 from the Perma-Flex Mold Company.

Fig. 18.3 When only a few molds will be cast, a simple "railless" mold board set-up like this is quite satisfactory. The Plexiglas divider indicates the exact height of the plaster.

can be some variation in mixing procedures and the end product will still be satisfactory for use. In mixing CMC or RTV compounds, it is imperative that the mixing be done according to the manufacturer's directions. A mistake in plaster mixing can result in a mold that may not perform well; a mistake in mixing rubber compounds results in a sticky, never-drying mess that takes forever to clean up with paint thinner or other solvent. In mixing rubber compounds, never take experience or memory for granted; read the directions before the containers are even opened.

After completing the mold set-up to receive the rubber compound (including extra care given to placing the oil clay coils used to seal the seams), the rubber is mixed and poured. A large enough quantity of the compound is prepared to assure the case will be thick enough to be stable; therefore, the base of the case is cast about $1\frac{1}{2}''$ thick. This thickness produces a very stable case that can be used without additional support.

After the proper curing time indicated by the manufacturer, the case mold and mold boards are separated (Figure 18.2). After further curing, the rubber case is ready to use.

For limited production requirements when only a few molds are needed, the set-up shown in Figure 18.3 is satisfactory. A set of mold boards is arranged in the standard manner around the rubber case. After

Fig. 18.4 Rail reinforcements for the rubber case are appropriate for large-volume mold requirements. Rails protect the rubber case and hold it exactly in place.

the rubber case and the mold boards are dressed, plaster is prepared and poured into the set-up.

The Plexiglas divider is the depth indicator for the plaster. If the plaster is poured beyond the height of the Plexiglas, then the molds will have to be broken apart. The height of the Plexiglas is the exact height for the correct thickness of the molds.

The Rails

Making rails is somewhat more involved than normal mold making, but rails are often necessary for quantity production with less stable cases. The rail shown in Figure 18.4 not only provides support and shape for the outside edges of the case, it also supports the back of the case. Although this particular rubber case is thick enough to be self-supporting, this kind of rail is very useful for rubber cases that are more delicate.

To make the rails, the first step is to return the molds to the rubber case and invert the case onto the marble table top. Set the mold boards up to cast an L-shaped rail and a bottom, all in one piece. This cast is made with gypsum-cement. Repeat the process to make the L-shaped rail for the other two sides of the case.

Making the type of two-piece rail pictured in Figure 18.4 is similar to making the rails for the coffee pot body, except that the first casting includes a bot-

tom for the rubber case as well as the two sides. This bottom serves as protection and carrier for the rubber case. The rubber case fits very snugly in this type of rail. In Figure 18.4 note that the Plexiglas divider comes to the top edge of the rail and that there is no keying system to hold the two pieces together. The two pieces of the rail fit together exactly.

To use this type of case and rail, the two pieces of the rail are held together with an elastic band; and the whole unit is thoroughly dressed before plaster is poured. Actually, the weight of the rails and the way they fit together make the elastic band unnecessary.

The case for the spout is made the same way that this two-piece case for the handle is made.

The Third Piece of the Case

The third piece of the three-piece handle mold is different in shape and requires another approach to make a case mold for it. The procedure uses the base plate technique to establish the correct dimension for the case. Figure 18.5 shows the base plate with the dimension lines on it. It also shows the third mold piece in correct position on the base plate and the mold boards ready to be clamped together.

Fig. 18.5 In making a case for the third piece of the handle mold, a base plate is used to plan the desired thickness of the rubber walls so they will be sturdy and not distort during use. The model is set up on the base plate, and mold boards are positioned and clamped in place. Before casting, all parts are dressed with mold soap.

The important dimension in this type of case is the thickness of the rubber sides (this is easier to see in Figure 18.7). The sides must be thick because they are self-supporting and they must not distort in use; they need to be stable, yet pliable. The thickness of these edges is roughly $\frac{3}{4}''$.

After thoroughly dressing the mold set-up, the rubber case is cast using Perma-Flex's PL 4042. This material is pliable, yet very strong. It is stable in case molds of this small size; yet the release of a casting from this case requires only a slight pulling apart of the case; then the cast piece is easily separated from the case.

In case molds of this small size with thick, self-supporting walls (Figure 18.6), there is no need for a protective rail system, unless the case will come under hard or careless use. It takes little effort to make an addition to the case if it needs additional support and protection.

Two small pieces of plaster are used as the end pieces for this case mold (Figure 18.7). The top edges of the plaster end pieces are exactly level with the top edges of the rubber case. The end pieces are slightly wider than the rubber case so that the retaining band does not touch the rubber surface of

Fig. 18.7 Two end boards for the case mold are made from plaster. The top surfaces are exactly flush with the rubber case, but they are wider than the rubber so that the retaining band does not distort the rubber.

Fig. 18.6 This rubber case is small and thick enough to make a rail system unnecessary. This photograph also shows the locking system for keying this piece to the other two pieces of the handle mold. This piece can be withdrawn easily from the mold without distorting the handle casting.

the case. The end pieces are also marked to indicate which piece is used for the top and which for the bottom of the case. Note that even in small mold pieces (such as these two ends of the case), the outside edges are bevelled to prevent chipping during use. The inside edges are not bevelled. If the inside edges were bevelled, the mold that is cast in this case would not fit correctly between the other two mold pieces. An extra step would be required to trim off two extra flanges of plaster that would be on the mold.

Figure 18.8 shows the case mold filled with plaster. As the plaster enters the plastic stage, a metal scraper is used to remove a small amount of excess plaster. The scraping is done without any pressure whatsoever so as not to distort the casting.

Always prepare more plaster than necessary for small castings. It is much easier to maintain consistent quality in the plaster if larger batches of plaster are mixed. Even in small castings, such as this part of the handle mold, it is important to maintain quality. Any extra plaster is used to make mold boards and sheets to be cut into profiles.

Fig. 18.8 The case mold is filled with plaster, and the excess is gently scraped away while still wet.

Fig. 18.9 The complete three-piece working mold (foreground) is made with the case molds. The finished mold is put together and dried thoroughly before using. In the left background is the original block mold, which will now be put in storage.

In the case of this three-piece mold, it is always good practice to cast all three pieces at the same time. Even better would be to cast all the cases necessary to produce the complete coffee pot mold at one time. This, hopefully, assures that the plaster is the same quality for all parts of the multi-piece mold.

Figure 18.9 shows the completed handle mold. These molds match the original mold exactly.

Rubber case molds should be prepared for mold making in the same way as models are. The case is thoroughly dressed with mold soap, making sure that no soap residue is left on the surface. If one of the excellent mold release products is used instead of mold soap, then the manufacture's directions should be followed to the letter.

Professional mold shops are always supplied with a compressed air hose that is used constantly to clean the cases and to aid in separating the cast mold from the case. The air hose is placed on the seam between the case and the cast mold, and the jet of air lifts the casting away from the case. Of course, a rubber case is easily distorted slightly and the mold piece pops out of the rubber case.

THE LID CASES

The lid offers an opportunity to combine gypsum-cement and rubber in a case that is very simple to make. The gypsum-cement half of the case forms an effective support for the rubber half.

The Gypsum-Cement "Ring" Cases

Figure 18.10 shows the set-up for tapering the sides of the lid mold. The mold is placed in a turned hole in the plaster wheel. Oil clay is used to fasten one half of the mold to the wheel. The second half, the top half, is put in position on the bottom half. A small ring of oil clay inside the mold holds the top of the mold for the turning procedure. Tapering the sides of the mold has two benefits. It is somewhat more economical in terms of the amount of plaster required and, more, it makes for a simpler, easier-to-use case mold. The taper is shown completed in Figure 18.11.

The next step is to make the gypsum-cement part of the case mold. This is done by assembling the lid mold on the plaster wheel in the position shown in Figure 18.10. After dressing properly, the roofing paper cottle is placed around the ring of oil clay ring and secured with a clothespin. Gypsum-cement is then poured into the cavity up to the height of the mold, making a case mold in the shape of a ring.

The whole process of tapering the lid mold and casting the two gypsum-cement cases is done in one operation on the plaster wheel. Having this horizontal separating line between the two pieces of the mold makes working on the plaster wheel very convenient. In fact, every step in making the lid for the coffee pot can be made on a plaster wheel.

In this case-making procedure on the plaster wheel, the actual size of the model, mold, and case is immaterial. The important point is that the whole process—model, mold, and case—is made directly on the plaster wheel.

Figure 18.11 shows the completed ring cases for the lid mold and the tapered lid mold in the center. If the lid mold had straight sides, then making a case mold for the outside surfaces would require a two-piece mold. That would mean that the cases for a small lid like this would be three pieces each, for a total of six pieces to make a small mold for the lid. With the change from straight to tapered sides, the cases are made of four pieces, a one-third savings in time. A two-piece mold is more economical than a three-piece mold, in every way. It takes less time to make and it takes less time to assemble and use. And, in this example, the quality of the product has not been sacrificed.

The Rubber Parts of the Lid Case

Making the rubber parts of the lid case is next. Figure 18.12 shows the two ring cases with their respective parts of the mold in place. A cottle for each ring is made from a plastic container. The plastic cottle is tightly wedged around the ring cases after they are dressed with mold soap. The cottles form a tight seal on the ring case because the plastic container is tapered. These plastic containers make excellent cottles for round molds.

The next step is to pour the rubber compound into the plastic cottle to form the second part of the case (Figure 18.13). Smooth-On's PMC-724 was used, which produces a white case mold that is excellent for making molds for porcelain. These cases need

Fig. 18.10 The lid mold is tapered by turning the top and bottom parts of the mold on the wheel. This tapered form is more economical and will make it easier to withdraw the mold from the case after casting.

Fig. 18.11 The "ring" case mold on the left is for the top piece of the lid mold; the ring case mold on the right is for the bottom piece. These two ring cases are made of gypsum-cement and form the outside surfaces of the two-piece lid mold shown in the center of the photograph. Two more case molds are needed in order to reproduce the molds for the lid.

Fig. 18.12 To cast the other two case molds, the two molds for the lid are placed in their respective ring cases and dressed with mold soap. Cottles are made from small plastic containers that fit securely around the rings; no oil clay to seal the seams is necessary.

Fig. 18.13 PMC-724, a rubber compound from Smooth-On, Inc., is used for these rubber cases. PMC-724 is a two-part compound that is easy to mix, and it produces a high-quality off-white flexible mold.

Fig. 18.14 The two parts of the lid mold (center) and the four case molds needed to reproduce them. The cases are gypsum-cement "rings" and rubber castings.

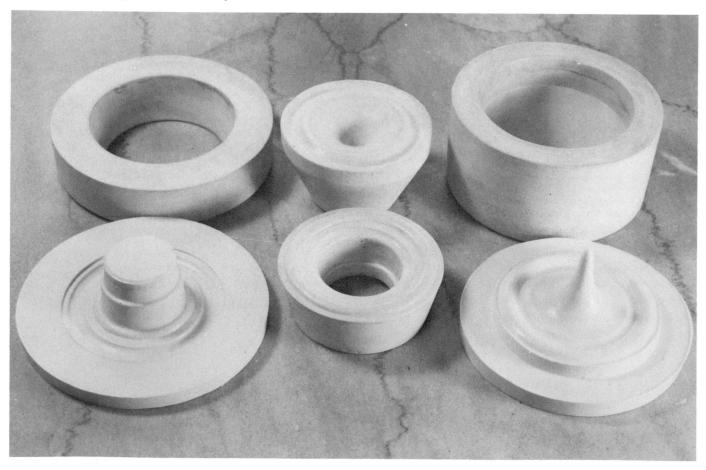

Fig. 18.15 The ring case molds are in place over the rubber parts, and the cases are ready for casting the working molds. The gypsum-cement ring supplies the support necessary to assure a quality mold is produced. No other support is needed.

not be as thick as the rubber case for the coffee pot handle. This is because the other half of these cases are rings of gypsum-cement that will hold the rubber half securely in position. Therefore, the thickness of the rubber bases is not as important as it would be if the rubber had to be self-supporting.

It would be possible to make the rings out of rubber, too. Actually, this would not be a bad choice for a mold of this size. However, larger molds need the stability that gypsum-cement provides. It is also possible to make rubber compounds harder or softer for molds with particular requirements. It would be possible in this case to make the ring mold of a harder mixture of rubber and the bottom half of a standard mixture of rubber.

After the rubber compound has been poured, the molds are left to cure for the time specified by the manufacturer. Any thin flanges of rubber that result from the casting can be cut away with a sharp scissors.

Figures 18.14 and 18.15 show the four pieces of the case molds used to make the two halves of the lid mold. Figure 18.14 shows the case pieces separated, and Figure 18.15 shows how they look when the two pieces of the cases are put together, ready to be filled with plaster to produce the two-piece lid mold shown in the center of the photograph.

It can be easily seen that the gypsum-cement ring sits exactly in the correct position on the rubber part of the case. Plaster is poured into these cases almost to the top of the gypsum-cement ring. The rubber center of the mold on the left should not be covered with plaster, as this is the opening for the slip in the mold.

This chapter has demonstrated the use of gypsum-cement and rubber for case molds. However, other materials are used for case molds as well as these two products. For example, large cases such as those for sanitary fixtures are made of fiberglass and epoxy; they are much lighter than large cases made of gypsum-cement.

CHAPTER

19

Solving Mold Separation Problems

The subject of this chapter is how to solve the problem of separating two halves of a mold that seem to be inseparable. Even in professional mold shops with experienced personnel, there are times when a mold will not separate from the model or a multi-piece mold cannot be separated using normal procedures.

The normal procedure is to jar the problem pieces with a rubber mallet, but not hit the mold hard enough to actually harm the mold or the model. Usually, this procedure will start the separating process, and the two pieces of the mold can be eased apart. There are times, however, when this doesn't work.

CAUSES OF SEPARATION PROBLEMS

There are two main causes of separation problems. The first and most common is that the quantity of separator used, or the technique used to apply the separator, isn't adequate to seal the surface from a second pouring of plaster. Even the use of traditional mold soap is no guarantee that the soap will function. For example, if the soap mixture is too thin, it will be easily absorbed by the mold and will not function as a barrier to the new casting. The new casting attaches itself to the mold surface and trouble sets in.

If the model is made of wood, there is a greater chance that it did not receive sufficient sealer; as a result, the wooden mold might absorb some of the moisture from the mold and swell somewhat. This problem is avoided by using some of the wood sealers available in hardware or paint stores. Proper sealing of a wood model, coupled with extra care given to applying the mold soap or release compound, should make wooden models just as satisfactory as plaster models.

It is standard practice to apply three coats of the mold soap mixture with a thorough rinse after each application. Under normal conditions three applications are enough. Even if six applications are made, there are times when the mold simply will not part. Some of the newer mold dressing materials seem to produce a surface that is absolutely water resistant. Even so, there are times when mold pieces seem to resist all effort to part them.

The second cause of separation problems is faulty

design. In making a mold from a model, it is easy to see undercuts that are obviously not going to withdraw from a mold. It is less easy to see other sources of withdrawal problems. This aspect of the design is discussed in Chapter 13. The idea presented in Figure 13.12 is that if the model can be seen all around, the angle of withdrawal can be accurately examined, and the separation line selected accordingly, then no withdrawal problems will occur. This is a very simplistic viewpoint, and, in theory, this method solves all of the design problems affecting the ability of a mold to come apart. However, in mold making there inevitably comes a time when a withdrawal problem arises.

Even if all the variables that cause separation problems are eliminated by careful procedures and careful delineation of a separation line, there is always a problem with molds that have "deep draw" characteristics. Say you must make a one-piece mold for a tall, slightly tapered cylinder. In theory, and on visual inspection, the long, tapered cylinder should separate from the mold without a problem. However, when the mold is made, it refuses to withdraw from the model. This is typical of the problem of deep draw. The angle appears to be enough to permit easy release, but it doesn't happen, and the mold seems to tightly grip the model (Figure 19.1).

Another common design fault is making a two-piece mold when a three-piece mold is required. The decision to make the mold in two pieces is based on the careful and accurate placement of the separation line to establish the two halves of the mold. The decision is based on the determination that the mold will indeed separate, no matter how deep the draw. The two-piece mold is skillfully cast, and the mold refuses to be separated by normal malleting or pulling apart!

In solving mold separation problems, we are concerned here with "after the fact" and not "before." Presumably the design and casting procedures have been applied correctly and the mold should part. Remember: no attempt should be made to separate a mold until the plaster has completely set-up.

APPLYING COMPRESSED AIR

Figure 19.2 shows the tools necessary to force a mold apart. The idea behind any forcing action is to make the mold separate without injuring the mold or the model. Most of the tools are wedges of various kinds. The use of compressed air forced into the seam to help break the bond that is holding the mold together is illustrated in Figures 19.3 and 19.4. Using the oil clay seal is much more effective than simply putting the air nozzle against the seam and applying air pressure. This latter method allows too much air to escape, with the result that very little air is forced into the seam.

To apply compressed air, first cut small wedge-shaped openings at each corner of the seam. Form the oil clay over the seam in a cone-like shape, remove the clay, and push a hole through it. Put the clay back in place and enlarge the hole so it is big enough for the nozzle. As shown in Figure 19.4, the oil clay is held firmly in place with one hand and the air hose is applied with the other. Use short blasts of air, and apply the process to each corner of the mold. The results seem to justify the oil clay procedure.

This same procedure is used in separating a one-piece mold from a model with a deep draw problem. In this case, the seam is not a seam between two halves of a mold; it is a circular seam around the edges of the model. The mold is put on its side and a small hole approximately $\frac{3}{16}''$ in diameter is drilled into the bottom of the mold. If the model is also made of plaster, the hole can be drilled right into the model. If the model is not plaster (perhaps it is a turned wooden model), then the hole can stop when the drill hits the model. Using oil clay to form a seal around the air hose nozzle, high-pressure air is directed into the hole. Short blasts of the highest air pressure available seems to be more effective than a continuous application of air at a lower pressure.

By using air pressure to separate molds, there is no danger in harming or breaking the mold. However, compressed air is not always available, and the obvious alternative is to attempt to wedge the molds apart.

WEDGING

Prying molds apart must be done in a manner that avoids serious injury to the mold. Figure 19.5 shows the first step in wedging molds apart. At the corners of the mold, a thin wedge shape is cut into the mold at the seam. By removing this little wedge of plaster,

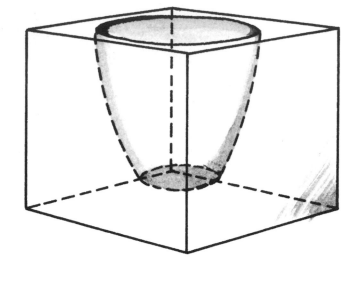

Wide angle of taper; slight expansion of plaster does not prevent the release of the model from the mold.

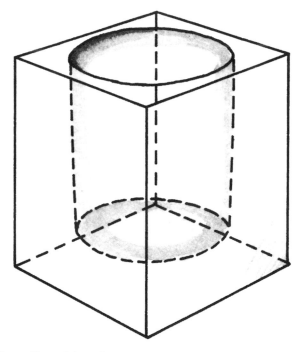

Narrow angle of taper; slight expansion of plaster causes the one-piece mold to grip the model. Release may be difficult or impossible.

Fig. 19.1 The problem of deep draw.

the prying action can start between the halves of the mold instead of at the corner; that is, more pressure can be applied to the mold itself. If the corner of a mold is forced by this type of action, it will often break off, and nothing is accomplished. Then knife blades are hammered into the corners. Figure 19.5 shows two corners being given this treatment. This type of wedging action can be applied to both sides or even all four corners of the mold at the same time.

This type of prying action usually is enough to start the separation process. If not, the knife blade is withdrawn, two metal ribs are placed in the seam, the knife blade is put between the ribs, and the wedging action is continued. The metal ribs are essential

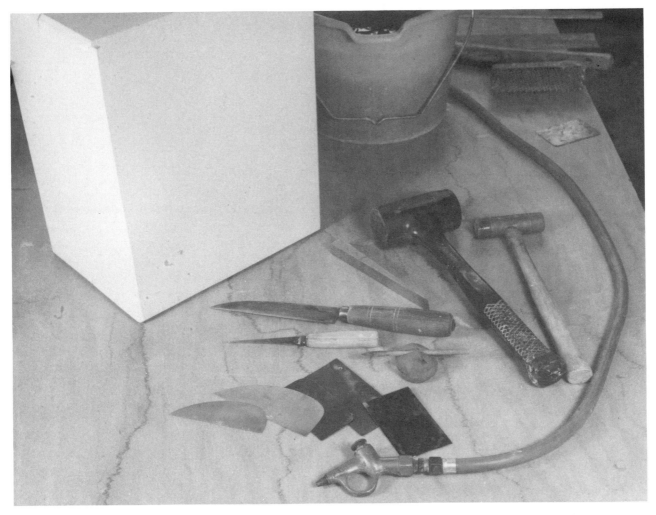

Fig. 19.2 The tools to separate molds that do not come apart include various wedges and a high-pressure air hose.

—they prevent the mold from breaking away at the pressure point.

If all of this prying from the corners of the mold fails, then the next step is to wedge the center of the mold. Figure 19.6 shows this additional wedging action being applied with metal ribs and a small steel

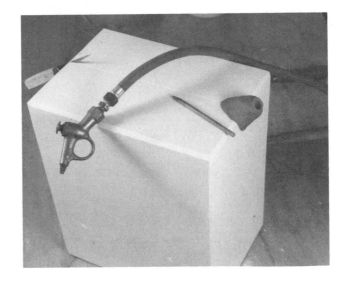

Fig. 19.3 Applying high-pressure air. At each corner of the seam a little wedge of plaster is removed with a sharp knife. A thin sharp knife is wedged into one corner of the mold with the nylon-headed hammer. Oil clay is pressed firmly against the other corner. Then it is removed and a hole is punched through. The clay is pressed into position again, and the hole is made big enough for the hose nozzle.

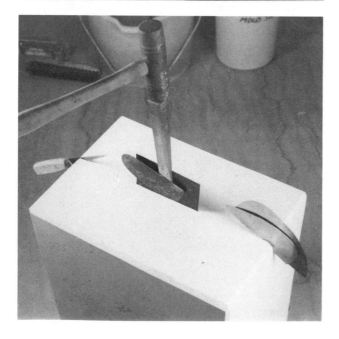

wedge. (This small steel wedge was made precisely for this purpose.)

If all of the above methods fail, then the attack is repeated, but this time the pressure is applied to one side only in an attempt to "rock" the seam open. When the wedging knife blade is hammered into place, it is immediately withdrawn; the action is repeated on the other side. The theory is that if equal pressure does not work successfully, then perhaps a rocking pressure might work.

Sometimes sustained pressure is more effective than a continued hammering of knife blades and wedges into the mold. Wedging action is applied using ribs, knives, and wedges, and the mold is set aside to dry, in front of a fan, if possible. This method is effective in another way, too: the mold maker involved in this frustrating operation is removed from the "scene of the crime" and, hopefully, a lowering of temper will take place.

PLASTER EXPANSION

Plaster expands slightly as it hardens. When there are no deep draw problems, this expansion does not interfere with molds separating from models or molds separating between halves. But whenever there is a severe deep draw, or whenever the angle of separation from the model is very small, then the expansion of the plaster upon setting must be considered, because it will likely interfere with separation. Whenever there is a question whether the mold will separate, then the mold should not be made at that particular separation line. Hence, the mold should

Fig. 19.4 One hand holds the oil clay firmly against the mold. The other hand inserts the nozzle into the hole and holds it directly on the small cut-out wedge on the seam. Short blasts of air are applied.

Fig. 19.5 In prying the mold apart without compressed air, small wedges of plaster are cut from the corners of the seam and sharp knives are hammered in. All four corners can be wedged at once, using four knife blades.

Fig. 19.6 The wedging action can be increased by combining metal ribs and a metal wedge placed in the middle of the mold. The metal ribs keep the mold from breaking at the pressure point.

be made in three parts instead of two. A decision to go to a three-piece mold instead of a two-piece mold would undoubtedly solve all the problems of separation, and none of the foregoing procedures would be necessary.

There are times, however, when an exact knowledge of just how much the plaster expands would be valuable information. This is even more important when making gypsum-cement molds on a Ram press. Of course, reference can often be made to the manufacturer's specification of the materials under consideration, but if the specifications are not available, then something else needs to be considered.

A simple procedure to test the expansion of various plasters and gypsum-cements is to take a straight-sided can (like a coffee can) and, using tin snips, make a cut down the side of the can to about 3" from the bottom. Reshape the can so that the edges of the cut are together and the can is round again. A can is cut for each plaster to be tested, and a batch of each plaster is mixed. One should make sure that the method of preparing the plaster or gypsum-cement is exactly the method that will be used for the molding project under consideration.

Each cut can is filled with a different mixture, and the mixtures are set aside to set up properly. In a few minutes, a comparison of the different expansions of the products tested can be seen at the cut in the can, and the product that has the lowest expansion rate can be chosen for projects where expansion might be a factor.

Various other ways to separate molds are practiced in some mold shops. Such methods as soaking one part of the mold, or heating one part of the mold, or even attempting to separate it with a hydraulic jack, all seem to be more trouble than worthwhile.

This chapter is the last one on mold making, and I hope it is the least read chapter in this book.

CHAPTER

20

Casting Slip and Deflocculation

The intent of this chapter is three-fold: first, to explain the phenomena of deflocculation for clay-water mixtures in words that are not too technical; second, to present methods of correctly deflocculating a slip; and third, to discuss the control of deflocculated casting slip.

UNDERSTANDING DEFLOCCULATION

An introduction to deflocculation is best accomplished by defining the various words associated with the phenomenon. One of the best sources of technical information on ceramics is *The Potter's Dictionary of Materials and Techniques*, by Frank Hamer (New York: Watson-Guptill, 1975). Hamer's dictionary is excellent, and almost any subject concerned with ceramics is covered in an understandable way. This dictionary should be the ceramist's first source of reference for technical information.

Six terms that need to be understood are deflocculation, flocculation, fluidity, specific gravity, thixotropy, and viscosity. Hamer is quoted briefly below on each of these topics; refer to his dictionary for further discussion:

Deflocculation. *The action of dispersing fine clay particles in a slip so that the slip becomes more fluid. Slips used in casting are deflocculated, and, thereby, have a higher density; that is, they contain a high proportion of clay while remaining fluid enough to be poured.*

Deflocculation is achieved by adding to the suspension water suitable, soluable alkalies called deflocculants. These exchange their ions (charged atoms) with those of the clay particles so that the clay particles are all of a similar powerful electrostatic charge. In this state they repel one another and are unable to aggregate. No matter how closely they are packed together they prefer to slide past one another and avoid contact. This repulsion acts as a lubricant.

Thus a slip can be created which contains a large proportion of clay and only a small proportion of water. A pound of plastic clay can be converted into a fluid slip with less than a tenth of a pint of water plus suitable deflocculants. Without the deflocculants it would require a half a pint of water to reach the same fluidity.

Flocculation. *The act of altering the physical properties of fine clay particles in suspension so that they no longer repel one another but aggregate together into large particles called flocs, and settle by gravity.*

Fluidity. *The property of a liquid to be able to flow or move freely without the hindrance of friction. The friction involved is between two adjacent particles or molecules within the liquid. The term is used to describe slip, e.g., deflocculated casting slips that pour freely; and to describe glazes which melt to very runny glasses. The opposite to fluidity is viscosity.*

Specific Gravity S.G. *Specific gravity is expressed as a number for each substance. It is best considered as the number of times by which a substance is heavier than the same amount of water. For example, the specific gravity of china clay is 2.5, which means that it is two-and-a-half times as heavy as water. It will therefore sink in water.*

Viscosity. *The stiffness of a liquid created by friction amongst its particles and molecules. The term viscosity can be applied to clay slips and glaze slops, and also to molten glazes. Viscous slips are thick and pour with difficulty.*

Thixotropy. *The property of slips to change fluidity by being left undisturbed; the slip at rest becomes more viscous. Also the property of plastic clays to resist initial pressure.*

All clay suspensions have this property which is the result of the establishment of mutual attraction bonds between the particles. Thixotropy begins to build up as soon as the slip comes to rest. It usually passes unnoticed but some slips and glaze slops containing clays show pronounced thixotropy if left undisturbed for a few days. On first restirring one is tempted to add more water but a thorough stirring returns the slip to its original fluidity and no extra water is required.

These six terms all relate to deflocculation—that is, adding soluble alkalis to a clay-water mixture so that the mixture will stay in suspension. By adding certain soluble alkalis to a mixture of clay and water, the amount of water necessary to make the mixture fluid is sharply reduced. This is a deflocculated slip.

GENERAL GUIDELINES FOR MIXING CASTING SLIPS

The following guidelines are standard rules of thumb to go by in making up casting slip recipes:

1 The ratio of clay to other dry ingredients should be 50% clay material and 50% non-plastic material. (This not a set rule, but only a guide to producing a satisfactory casting slip.) The ratio of dry ingredients to water can range from 25% to 45% water by weight.

2 The clay part of a casting body should always consist of more than one type of clay. In factory situations, the ingredients in a clay body are never limited to just a few basic ingredients from one company or locality. The clay body is always compounded of a number of ball clays and kaolins for white ware bodies. For non-white ware, the mixture of the clays is approached the same way.

3 The standard deflocculation agent is a 3:1 mixture of sodium silicate (N Brand) and soda ash. Darvan No. 7, a commercial deflocculant produced by R.T. Vanderbilt, Inc. (30 Winfield Street, Norwalk, CT 06855) is an excellent deflocculant; it takes the place of the combined sodium silicate and soda ash. Soda ash (sodium carbonate) is a white powder, and it has to be used very sparingly in the deflocculation process. Too much soda ash produces a casting that seems never to get hard. Sodium silicate (N brand) is a clear, syrupy liquid. The common name for it is "water glass," for the simple reason that if it is left open to the air, it will turn to a hard glass-like material in a short time and then it is useless. Because of this action, sodium silicate is often used to mend cracks in fired ware. (Use a mixture of approximately 30% sodium silicate and 50% finely ground fired clay of the same clay body that is going to be mended. Thin the mixture with water and force it into the crack. Repeat until there is an excess of the mixture on the surface of the cracked piece. Let the mixture harden and then scrape off the excess. The piece should be refired, but it can be glazed with success without refiring the repair. Of course, this is not an absolute solution to "fixing" cracks.)

A generally accepted ratio of three parts sodium silicate to one part soda ash serves as a starting point

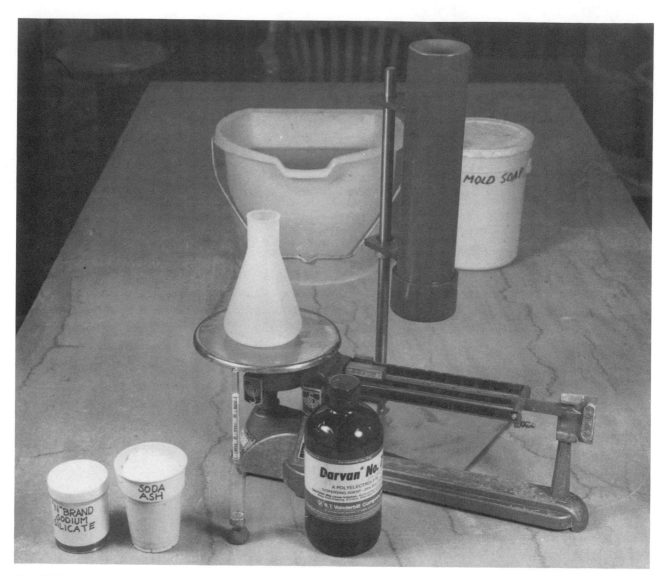

Fig. 20.1 In the foreground are the standard deflocculants: sodium silicate and soda ash, used in combination, and Darvan No. 7, a commercial deflocculant. The Ohaus triple beam balance is essential for weighing ingredients and controlling specific gravity. A hydrometer and viscometer are also useful.

for mixing the deflocculants. Also, as a general rule, 0.05% soda ash and 0.15% sodium silicate are considered the amount necessary to add to a casting clay body to deflocculate it.

The soda ash and sodium silicate are always carefully and accurately weighed before adding to a clay-water mixture. They usually are dissolved in hot water before they are introduced into the mixture, and the amount of hot water is counted as part of the water weight of the deflocculated slip.

Darvan No. 7 is used alone as a deflocculant with a typical addition of 0.8% being sufficient to deflocculate most casting body formulations.

4 Barium carbonate is often added to casting slip formulas to counter excess sulfates that are naturally found in the clays. Excess insoluble barium sulfate compounds in the clays results in the body scumming on the surface. R.T. Vanderbilt suggests that 0.05% barium carbonate be added to the casting mixture to counter any sulfate reactions that the casting slip may have.

5 In preparing a casting slip, always use a power mixer. The power mixer should be the kind that is attached to the edge of the mixing container, like a large, heavy-duty plastic trash container. The mixer should be able to run at a constant speed for relatively long periods of time.

The variable drill used to mix plaster would not be a satisfactory slip mixer because it is portable and it would be rather difficult to attach to the edge of a mixing container. However, the plaster mixing blade made from three layers of $\frac{1}{8}$" rubber would be excellent for mixing slip.

The Mixing Equipment Company (221 Rochester St., Avon, NY 14414) offers a complete line of mixing equipment. One of their Lightnin mixers made to clamp on the edge of large metal containers, used with their A 310 impeller, would be an excellent choice for mixing slip.

Another choice for a slip mixer would be one of the complete mixing systems made by Lehman Manufacturing Company, under the name of "Slip-o-Matic." Figure 20.2 pictures their model M30 that is able to mix 30 gallons of slip, pump the mixed slip into the mold, and then pump the slip out of the mold. Using this piece of equipment, large molds need never be dumped. Slip should always be kept tightly covered to prevent the surface of the slip from oxidizing.

6 The most important piece of equipment necessary to prepare and continuously control a casting slip is an accurate scale. The ideal scale is a triple beam balance (Figure 20.1). Ohaus is the standard in beam balances. An adequate triple beam balance can be purchased through ceramic supply houses for under $100. Perhaps this price seems high for a device to weigh slip; however, the purchase of an accurate balance will more than pay for itself in a short time through successful deflocculation of slip batches, time after time. One wrong batch of slip where considerable time must be spent correcting a miscalculation or where the batch must be discarded altogether is worth the purchase of a beam balance.

7 The triple beam balance will provide the means to accurately weigh the amount of deflocculant that

Fig. 20.2 The Model M30 "Slip-O-Matic" produced by Lehman Manufacturing Co. This particular model is capable of mixing slip, stirring it in a closed 30-gallon container, pumping it into casting molds, and pumping it out of the molds.

is added to the casting slip batch. It will also provide a very accurate reading for specific gravity. Specific gravity is the weight of a specified amount of slip compared to the weight of the same amount of water. By establishing a standard weight for a specified volume of successfully deflocculated slip, it is easy to continuously run spot checks on new slip batches by accurately weighing the slip on a triple beam balance, using the same volume as specified by the successful standard.

A hydrometer is sometimes used to test for specific gravity. This device consists of a thermometer-like glass tube with an enlarged base and a scale on the side of the tube. The hydrometer will sink to a certain point in a fluid and stop. The hydrometer is then withdrawn, and the scale is read like a thermometer. The problem with using a hydrometer is that it is very difficult to interpret the correct reading on the scale of the instrument. There seems to be too much variation possible in the way the hydrometer is used and read. Accurately weighing a batch of slip on a triple beam balance seems much more reliable. A hydrometer can undoubtedly be used successfully if the possible variations are controlled, however. One person, with an established routine for mixing casting slip and testing the slip with a hydrometer, will no doubt be able to set standards that can be interpreted correctly by the hydrometer. The important thing is to set a standard procedure for using and reading the hydrometer and use that procedure every time.

In factory situations, the standard and simplest way to spot-check slip is to weigh a certain quantity of slip. The exact weight of the test is compared to the weight of the standard and corrections are made. The key to success is once again quality control. The control of a casting slip is important because it may mean success or failure in the cast product.

Testing the weight of a deflocculated slip will determine its specific gravity, and hence determine the proportion of water to clay. Slip is heavier than water. Therefore, if the test sample is heavier than the standard, it has too much clay. If it is lighter, there is too much water. Accurate weight measurements are important because the weight will indicate the correct proportion of clay and water in a deflocculated slip. A non-deflocculated slip will require much more water to become liquid; thus a gallon of non-deflocculated slip weighs less than a gallon of deflocculated slip because it has more water than clay. A deflocculated slip requires much less water to become liquid; therefore, it will weigh more than a non-deflocculated slip.

8 Old timers in a slip casting factory could move their hands back and forth in a batch of slip, and then, by watching the slip run off their fingers, they could accurately determine the condition of the slip. Unfortunately, not everyone has the expertise or the ability to determine the quality of slip by "feeling" it. Specific gravity, or the proportion of water to dry materials is determined by accurate weighing. Viscosity, or the ability of the slip to pour, is another important factor. The opposite of viscosity is fluidity. A slip cannot be too fluid because the excess amount of water will cause trouble in casting. Neither can the slip be too viscous or thick. The slip must have a low enough viscosity so the slip can pour yet it cannot have high fluidity. A simple test for viscosity is to see if the slip will "web" between the fingers when the hand is withdrawn from the slip. This sort of system is fine for someone with 30 years of experience in mixing slip and pouring molds; however, it simply is not enough to indicate proper viscosity for the average person.

The Lehman Manufacturing Company makes a very simple viscometer that anyone can use with success. It is shown in Figure 20.4. Viscosity can be measured by timing how long it takes a certain amount of slip to pass through a small hole. The device shown in Figure 20.4 consist of a plastic tube with a closed bottom mounted on a stand. The bottom of the tube has a small hole in it that controls the speed of a liquid passing through the tube. This is a very simple device for comparing the viscosity of one batch of slip to another.

The successful preparation of a casting slip is dependent upon three control factors: (1) the amount of deflocculant, (2) the specific gravity, and (3) the viscosity. All of these factors are easy to control if reasonable care is exercised and a few simple devices are used correctly.

Today there are endless numbers of formulas available for casting slips. This book makes no attempt to be an authoritative source for successful slip casting recipes. The slip that is used in Part III was made by deflocculating a commercial porcelain clay body with Darvan No. 7. The clay body is #130 porcelain from Standard Ceramic Supply Company, Pittsburgh, PA. The slip was made by powdering dry scrap porcelain and then adding water to it until about 37% water by weight was reached. Darvan No. 7 was added, drop by drop, until the slip suddenly turned very pourable. Specific gravity and viscosity tests were run to establish a standard to be used for comparison when making new slip.

The above method served its purpose for slip casting the molds in Part III. The slip works beautifully, it drains well from the mold, and it makes a very good casting, but the amount of slip involved is less than 3 gallons. If 30 gallons of slip is required, then greater control is necessary to assure quality slip.

In summary, a casting slip should have the following characteristics:

1 It should have approximately 50% clay ingredients. Always use more than one kind of clay.
2 The water content can range from 30% to 45% by weight.
3 Sodium silicate (N Brand) and soda ash are combined in a 3:1 mixture as a deflocculant. They are dissolved in very hot water before being added to the mix. (0.15% sodium silicate by weight and 0.05% soda ash). Darvan No. 7 is used alone as a deflocculant and is added directly to the mixture (0.8% by weight).
4 Power mix the dry ingredients and water together after carefully weighing both materials. The mixture should be thick and almost pasty before the deflocculant is added and it should be very pourable after adding the deflocculant and mixing a few minutes.
5 Never leave slip in an open container. Often slip that is left to stand for any length of time seems almost unpourable upon reopening the container. This phenomena is known as thixotropy (the slip seems to thicken when it is left still). The first reaction to this problem is to add

Fig. 20.3 To accurately determine the specific gravity of a slip, a standard container is used, such as this 250-ml plastic flask. It is weighed carefully to establish a zero point on the balance. The flask is then filled with water up to the top and weighed accurately. The flask is emptied and dried, filled with slip, and weighed again. Dividing the weight of the water into the weight of the slip yields the specific gravity of the slip.

Fig. 20.4 Viscosity is determined by timing carefully how long it takes a specific quantity of slip to pass through the small hole in the tube of the viscometer. The viscosity of successfully deflocculated slips should be established so future batches can be tested and compared to the standard.

water, but this is a mistake. The thing to do in this situation is to power stir the slip a few minutes before any evaluation of the slip is attempted. If the slip is correctly deflocculated, the stirring will restore all the fluidity necessary to cast, and no additional water is necessary.

6 Keep scraps of deflocculated and cast clay separate (cut off spares, etc.). After the scrap is dry, it can be added to new slip batches. However, since the scrap contains deflocculant, the additions of deflocculants to the new batch should be watched carefully, and stopped when the deflocculation arrives at the proper point.

7 If the slip is too thick (not deflocculated properly), but it is useable, the casting will probably be soft because the ratio of water to dry ingredients is too high. If the slip is too thin from over-deflocculation, the casting will work but the piece will be hard and brittle. As the amount of deflocculant is increased, the viscosity goes down until it reaches a maximum of fluidity. After that point, the process reverses itself and results in a flocculated clay body that is very viscous, like a gel.

The material presented in this chapter is certainly not the last word on deflocculation. As was stated earlier, the literature available on the deflocculation process will undoubtedly be of value to anyone interested in obtaining a more thorough understanding of casting slips. Within the literature on various clay body formulas, there are literally hundreds of different clay bodies listed. Each one has undoubtedly been tested and should be easily accessible for developing a successful casting body.

A list of suppliers for a book on mold making is inevitably a very short one. Most standard tools can be purchased from hardware stores or ceramic supply houses. Other tools can be "manufactured" from items such as saw blades or knives. Some special products are discussed below.

PLASTER

The most important material used in mold making is plaster. Two companies manufacture most of the plaster products in this country: United States Gypsum Company and Georgia Pacific. It would be pointless to list all of the plaster products these companies sell; only the products directly related to mold making are listed here.

United States Gypsum Company
101 South Wacker Drive
Chicago, Illinois 60606

1 No. 1 Pottery Plaster. Formulated to provide a strong, long-lasting mold; it is the standard of the industry.
2 Puritan Pottery Plaster. A slightly denser, longer-wearing mold material recommended for jiggering applications in the ceramic industry.
3 Hydrocal A-11, Gypsum-Cement. High-strength gypsum-cement having a very low setting expansion. Adoptable to production on hard, strong, tough models of uniform and stable dimensional accuracy. Used for production of master models and Keller duplicating machines. Rate of stiffening is very rapid after setting action begins. Recommended for slurry-casting technique.
4 Ultracal 30 Gypsum-Cement. Surface hardness and compressive strength are higher and setting expansion is lower than Hydrocal B-11, but it has similar workability and setting characteristics.

Sources of Supplies

Georgia Pacific
Gypsum Division
900 South West 5th Avenue
Portland, Oregon 97202

1 K55 Pottery Plaster. An excellent, general-purpose pottery plaster designed for all types of potteries and sanitary ware plants. Ideally suited for applications where high absorption is required.
2 K59 Pottery Plaster. The industry standard. Designed for both casting and jiggering applications where long wearing properties are required.
3 Densite K-12. A low-expansion, high-strength gypsum-cement designed for block and case mold applications.
4 Densite K-33. The ultimate in low-expansion and high-strength gypsum-cements for block and case mold applications.

Both United States Gypsum and Georgia Pacific have very good publications concerning their products. Each company offers complete specifications for their gypsum products, and this information is available for the asking.

OTHER MOLDING COMPOUNDS AND PRODUCTS

In making the case molds, molding compounds and mold dressings from three companies were used successfully:

Adhesives Products Corporation
1660 Boone Avenue
Bronx, New York 10460

1 7/79/7180 ADRUBRTV molding compound.
2 P Film, a spray film that is used as a sealer and mold dressing compound.

The Perma-Flex Mold Company
1919 East Livingston Avenue
Columbus, Ohio 43209

1 PURE-CMC PL 4042 molding compound.
2 Mold Dressing.

Smooth-On, Inc.
1000 Valley Road
Gillette, New Jersey 07933

1 PMC 724 molding compound.
2 Sonite Seal Release.

All three companies have extensive literature available about their products. The products listed above were used in the preparation of this book; however, each company has other products that may be more suited to a particular molding procedure.

The plastic natches for molds are available from:

Double A plastics
Box 332
Monson, Mass. 01057

The plastic natches come in two sizes and are very useful in a mold that is going to be given hard use.

POWER MIXERS

The Mixing Equipment Company, Inc. (221 Rochester Street, Avon, NY 14414) has a complete line of all types of mixing equipment, as well as regional sales representatives throughout the world.

The Lehman Manufacturing Company (400 Fairground Road, North Kentland, IN 47951) manufactures a wide line of mixing, storing, and pumping equipment for the preparation of slip. They also manufacture the viscometer that was pictured in Chapter 20. Lehman mainly manufactures equipment for the hobby industry; however, their equipment is ideal for small operations where casting slip needs to be made, stored, and poured. Their trade name is "Slip-O-Matic."

TURNING TOOLS

Turning tools are available through:

Leichtung, Inc.
4944 Commence Parkway
Cleveland, Ohio 44128

The Milligan Hardware and Supply Company
320 Smith Street
East Liverpool, Ohio 43920

Milligan has a complete line of potter's supplies, including high-quality, heavy-duty turning tools similar to woodworker's tools. Milligan is also a source of English Crown Soap used as mold dressing.

DEFLOCCULANTS

Sodium ash and sodium silicate (N Brand) can be obtained from most ceramic supply houses.

Darvan No. 7 is manufactured by:

R.T. Vanderbilt Co., Inc.
30 Winfield St.
Norwalk, CT 06855.

MISCELLANEOUS

The Velcro retaining straps were supplied by:

Minnesota Clay
8001 Grand Ave., South
Bloomington, MN 55420

Ohaus weighing equipment, such as the triple beam balance used in Chapter 20, can be obtained from most ceramic supply houses.

Additional or replacement calculators may be obtained by writing to:

Professor Donald E. Frith
University of Illinois at Urbana-Champaign
143 Art and Design Building
408 East Peabody Drive
Champaign, IL 61820

For a list of British Suppliers please see page 228.

Glossary

Alabaster Calcium sulphate; Gypsum ($CaSO_4$ $2H_2O$). The common name for the rock used to manufacture plaster. It is also used as a material for chess pieces and translucent lamp bases.

Batch Any quantity of mixed plaster. "Batch" also refers to a calculated amount of glaze materials or "batch weight."

Bat or Batt As used in this text, a batt is a thin sheet of clay used in pressing. In other contexts, it usually refers to a round disk of plaster or wood used as a base to work on in throwing or hand building. A "drying batt" is a large concave piece of plaster used to dry out moist clay.

Bisque, Bisk Unglazed fired pottery.

Block, Block Mold The first mold taken from a model. It is sometimes used to obtain sample pieces; however, it is usually reserved for case making.

Blunge, Blunger To blunge is to mix clay and water together to form a slip. Blunging is done in a blunger, which is the container holding the mixture.

Calcine To heat a substance to drive off water. Plaster is calcined gypsum. In calcining gypsum, the temperature is carefully controlled to drive off only a portion of the water contained in the rock. A higher temperature would destroy the gypsum for use as plaster.

Case, Case Mold A mold used to reproduce working molds for production.

Casting Slip A mixture of clay and water with a deflocculant added to keep the clay materials in suspension.

Chattering The bouncing or vibrating action of a turning tool when turning plaster. Chattering is avoided in plaster turning by sharpening the turning tool, changing the angle of cut, and/or spraying the surface of plaster with water. Chattering is sometimes used to make a decorative pattern on clay.

Chuck The ring or collar in which a jigger mold is placed. In ceramics, a "chuck" or "chum" is a fired clay ring used to hold pottery for additional trimming.

Cottle A flexible piece of material used to enclose a mold for casting. Roofing paper, aluminum, and linoleum are cottle materials.

Deflocculation The process of adding soluble alkalis to a clay-water mixture to cause the clay to become suspended in the water. Deflocculation enables the mixture to liquefy, yet be very dense, with a high clay content.

Draft A deep draft mold. A term used to describe the ability of the mold to be very deep, yet separate from the model.

Dressing Waterproofing the surface of a mold or model so that plaster poured against it will not stick to it.

Electrolyte A compound that dissociates into ions (electrically charged particles) in solution; a deflocculant.

Fettling The act of trimming excess clay away from a slip-cast piece, usually from the seam on the casting.

Flocculation The opposite of deflocculation. When a clay-water mixture is flocculated, the clay particles agglomerate (form flocs) and rapidly settle out of the water.

Fluidity The ability of a clay-water mixture to flow or pour freely. The term also describes a glaze that becomes a runny glass.

Gypsum *See* Alabaster.

Hump, Hump Mold Any positive form used to press plastic clay on or over. Also "drape mold," "mushroom mold."

Jack A device on which to mount a profile plate to shape moist plaster.

Jolly The turning head of a jigger.

Jigger A machine used to form plates, saucers, cups, and bowls from batts of plastic clay. It uses a spinning mold and a profile attached to a moveable arm to shape or "jigger" the inner and outer surfaces of the item simultaneously.

Keys *See* Natch.

Lute, Luting The process of joining together two pieces of plastic clay. After the two halves of a mold have been pressed separately, the two halves are put together and the pressing is joined by putting a hand or tool inside to "lute" the two pressed halves together.

Mold Soap English Crown Soap is a standard "dressing" used in mold making. It is a fat potash soap that looks and feels like a sticky brown paste. It is diluted with water prior to use.

Natch A locking, or keying, device used on the joining surfaces of a mold to assure correct registry when the mold is put together. "Male" and "female" natches fit together perfectly. The typical shape is a positive and negative hemisphere.

Plaster of Paris A semi-hydrated calcium sulfate; the common name for plaster. The connection of the word "Paris" with the word "Plaster" probably came from the English potter Ralph Daniel, who described a mold-making material found near Paris, France.

Plasticity The characteristic of a material to be worked or deformed with ease; the ability of the material to be formed into a particular shape and retain that shape.

Pressing The act of pressing plastic clay into or onto a mold.

Rail, Rails A pair of rails are the walls that form the outside shape of a case mold.

Rib A flat metal or wood tool used to scrape or press clay or plaster.

Roulette A wheel with a pattern on the rim. By rolling the wheel against plastic clay the pattern is impressed in the clay.

Shrink, Shrink Ruler, Shrink Calculator "Shrink" is the amount that a material shrinks in size as a result of undergoing a process. For example, clay shrinks from the plastic state to the fired state. The amount of shrink is described as a percentage. A shrink calculator enables the mold maker to compensate for any percentage of shrink of a given clay body. This calculator also works to determine the "shrink plus factor" for throwing a specific size object.

Slake, Slaking Allowing dry plaster to combine chemically with water. After adding plaster to water, it must undergo a few minutes' slaking before power mixing begins.

Slip Usually a deflocculated clay-water mixture for casting. In certain contexts "slip" means glaze, and to "slip a piece" means to dip the piece into a glaze.

Slip Ware Describes a decorative surface treatment on pottery. The term has nothing to do with slip casting.

Sodium Carbonate Soda ash (Na_2CO_3). One of the two alkaline ingredients commonly used to deflocculate a clay slip. It is usually used in a ratio of 1 part sodium carbonate to 3 parts sodium silicate. The amount needed to deflocculate a particular clay slip will vary, but a figure of 0.05% by weight sodium carbonate and 0.15% by weight sodium silicate is a starting point.

Sodium Silicate Water glass (Na_2SiO_3). A common deflocculant. *See* Sodium Carbonate.

Spare The extra space at the top of a mold that forms the entryway into the mold for the casting slip. It also provides storage for extra casting slip that is used as the mold withdraws moisture from the slip and consequently reduces the amount of slip in the mold.

Specific Gravity, S.G. A number achieved by dividing the weight of a material by the weight of an equal volume of water.

Sprigg, Sprigging, Sprigg Mold A sprigg is a small clay relief made in a mold, removed from the mold, and applied to the surface of a piece of unfired pottery.

Thixotropy The property of a slip appearing to be a thick, nonpouring gel; yet when it is stirred, it becomes a pourable liquid.

Viscosity Describes the relative stiffness of a casting slip. The higher the viscosity, the less fluid the slip. A viscous glaze is a non-runny glaze.

Waste Mold A mold used as a foundation for pouring the first half of a two-piece mold. It is usually discarded after the first half is cast.

Wedging A process of hand mixing plastic clay to thoroughly blend the ingredients and de-air the clay.

Wreathing A slip casting fault. The surface of a cast piece has a wavy, almost layered, quality. Usually a result of incorrect deflocculation.

Index

See also Glossary, pp. 218–220.
Page numbers in *italics* refer to figures.

Peru,
    mold-made ceramics in, 13–15
    panpipes from, 3
Piccolpasso, Cavaliere Cipriano, *17*, 21, 118
    plaster mold as described by, *17*
    record of plaster molds, 16–17
pipe press, in Old Salem, 124, *124*
Pirotechnia (Beringuccio), 16, 17, 47
Plastelene, 42
plaster,
    avoiding air bubbles in, 153
    coefficient of expansion of, 51
    compared to gypsum-cement, 49–50
    dead, 49
    effect of age of, 55
    effect of pouring new onto old, 55
    expansion and mold separation
        problems, 206–207
    for slip casting molds, 51
    for stamp making, 64
    hand vs power mixing, 53
    methods of making, 47–50
    mixing and quality of, 197
    mixing routine, 53–55
    pouring process, 54, 153
    premarked containers for mixing,
        52–53
    preparation of batch, 51–55, *56–57*
    production process, 48, *50*
    reactions to working with, 47
    relation of weight to volume, 52
    to secure profile sheet and model, 174
    sheets for templates, 65
    sources of supply, 215–216
    stages of setting, 53
    test for moment to pour, 54
    testing expansion of, 207
    tinting, 55
    turning while plastic, 168
    working position for turning, using
        belly stick, 152
plaster batch calculator, 37, 51–52, 151
plaster blank,
    for case mold, 135
    curing, 169
    making for model, 152–153
    for stamp, 64–65
plaster control plates, 164
plaster die,
    removing from clay sheet, 116
    use to form tile, 115, *115*
plaster kiln, woodcut of (1540), 47, *48*
plaster mixing buckets, 41
plaster molds,
    as described by Piccolpasso, 17
    drying time, 95
    first record of use, 16
    historical development, 16–23
    impact on production techniques, 20
    method for making in 1700s, 22
    methods in sixteenth-century Italy,
        16–18
    from Old Salem Restoration, *127*
    physical characteristics of, 50–51
    for slip casting, 149
    vs fired clay molds, 21–22
    wear of, and number of uses, 51
plaster of Paris, 18–19, 20, 21

plaster sculpture tools, 35
plaster shop, 31–32, *32*
plaster wheel, 31, 33
    conversion from Randall kick wheel,
        43–46, *45*
    historical use, 23
    lid mold made on, 186
    mold making on, 172–180, *178*
    role in slip casting mold making, 150
    setting up mold boards on, 175–176
    using for all steps of lid-making
        process, 199
plaster wheel head, 130, *130*, *131*, 135
    casting, 150–152
    fastening model to, 178
    grooves on, *133*, 150, 152, *152*
    restoring after repeated use, 137
    using as base plate, 172, *173*
plastic clay,
    effect on plaster mold, 51
    limits for use in model making,
        92–93
plastic containers, as cottles, 199
plastic natches, 96
    supply sources for, 216
plastic stage, of plaster, 53, 168
"Platter" (Scott Frankenberger), color
    insert 52ff
Plexiglas,
    divider for case molds, 194, *194*
    for jiggering, 139
Pliny, 16
Pope, Rick, "Cast and Thrown
    Teapot," color insert 148ff
porcelain,
    methods of transporting, 104–105,
        105
    rubber molds for, 199
    throwing to thin, 81–82
porcelain bowl, from hump mold, *75*
porcelain factory, pressing department
    of (19th c.), *21*
positive form, 63
positive molds,
    in press mold process, 137
    use with jigger arm, 140
potassium sulphate, as accelerator, 53
potter's caliper, use as divider, 172
*Potter's Dictionary of Materials and
    Techniques* (Frank Hamer), 208
potters ribs, 36
potters wheel, 33
    history, 4
    rotating as Roman practice, 10
"Potters Wheel and How It Goes
    Round in the Nineteenth
    Century," 23
pottery, quality of English, 21
power mixer,
    need for, 53
    for preparing casting slip, 211
    supply sources for, 216
premarked containers, for mixing
    plaster, 52–53
presentation model, defined and uses
    for, 170–171
press molding,
    combined with throwing, 136
    in 18th c. America, 122–128

for production, 129–145
and slip casting, 150
of teapot body, 96, 97
of teapot spout and handle, 98, 100,
    100
for thin clay in Styrofoam mold,
    105–106
press molds,
    bottle from clay, *1*
    for deep relief tiles, 112
    making for teapot, 91–96
    paddle and anvil as, 3
    sculptural forms from, 137
    from Styrofoam, 103–108
    time requirements for piece in, 107
    versatility of, 101–102
    wear of, 73
    wet carving of, 86, 87
    from wood, 109–110
press-molded porcelain jewelry box,
    104
pressed bowl, *11*
"Pressed Tile" (Ron Fondaw), color
    insert 52ff
presserman, 22–23, *23*
presses, automatic, 28–29
pressing knife, 123
production, 129
    case mold for, 136–137
    18th and 20th c. compared, 127–128
    expanded, 145
    by press molding, 129–145
    rail system for, 189, 191
    and slip casting, 150
production quantities, 191–192
profile plate, 139, 140, *142*, 176
profile sheet, 173–174, *173*, *174*
    for coffee pot spout, 181, *183*
    plaster to secure to model, 174
pug mill, 27, 141
    in semiautomatic system, 144
PURE CMC PL 4042, for case mold,
    194
Puritan Pottery Plaster, 59
puzzolana, 16
pyramids, use of gypsum mortar for,
    15

R.T. Vanderbilt, Inc., 209, 210
Racham, Bernard, 3
rail system, need for, 197
rails, 189, 191–192, *191*, *192*
    for rubber case mold, 196, *196*
    shelf for holding, 190
Ram press, 28, 114
    and gutter design in press mold, 126
Ram process, 145
Ram Products, Inc., 28
Randall kick wheel, *44*
    converting to plaster wheel, 43–46
rasps, for model and mold making, 36
rebar clamps, 39, *39*, 94
registry mark, on stamp, 67, 68, *68*
relief-molded piece, combined with
    relief-molded piece, 89
relief molds, procedure for pressing
    clay into, 88–89, *88*
retarders, for setting plaster, 53
ribbing, on teapot, 100

British Suppliers

PLASTER

British Gypsum Ltd
Jerico Works
Bowbridge Road
Newark, Notts. NG24 3BZ
0636-703351

Whitfields Minerals Ltd
Whitfield House
10 Water Street
Newcastle under Lyme, Staffs. ST5 1HP
0782-711155

Cookson Ceramics Ltd
Uttoxeter Road
Meir, Stoke-on-Trent, Staffs. ST3 7XW
0782-599111

OTHER MOULDING COMPOUNDS AND PRODUCTS

J.B. Ratcliffe Engineers Ltd
Rope Works
Rope Street off Shelton New Road
Stoke-on-Trent, Staffs. ST4 6DJ
0782-7173000

Mould making and slip casting equipment

Alec Tiranti
27 Warren Street
London W1P 5DG
071-636-8565
Plaster working tools, releasing agents,
sundries, general sculpture supplies

Kingfisher Ceramics Service Ltd
Bycors Road
Heathcote Works
Burselm, Stoke-on-Trent, Staffs. ST6 4EQ
0782-575254

Natches, releasing agents, mould locks and sundries

Reward-Clayglaze
Kings Yard Pottery
Talbot Road
Rickmansworth, Herts. WD3 1HW
0932-770127

Natches, cottles, mould makers size

Frank W. Joel
Museum Laboratory and Archaeological
Supplies
The Manor House
Wereham, Kings Lynn, Norfolk PE33 9AN

Tools, adhesives, vinyl and sundries

GENERAL POTTERY SUPPLIERS

Potclays Ltd
Brickkiln Lane
Etruria, Stoke-on-Trent, Staffs. ST4 7BP
0782-219816

Potterycrafts Ltd
Campbell Road
Stoke-on-Trent, Staffs. ST4 4ET
0782-745000

Fulham Pottery
8-10 Ingate Place
London SW8 3NS
071-720-0059

Cromartie
Park Hall Road
Longton, Stoke-on-Trent, Staffs. ST3 5AY
0782-313947

228